Get the Job in the Entertainment Industry

D1478879

Online resources to accompany this book are available at:
https://bloomsbury.pub/get-the-job-in-the-entertainment-industry. If you experience any problems,
please contact Bloomsbury at: companionwebsites@bloomsbury.com.

INTRODUCTIONS TO THEATRE

SERIES EDITOR:

JIM VOLZ, CALIFORNIA STATE UNIVERSITY, FULLERTON, USA

This series of textbooks provides a practical introduction to core areas of theatre and performance, and has been designed to support semester teaching plans. Each book offers case studies and international examples of practice, and will equip undergraduate students and emerging theatre professionals with the understanding and skills necessary to succeed—whether in study or in the entertainment industry.

Directing Professionally: A Practical Guide to Developing a Successful Career in Today's Theatre
Kent Thompson
ISBN 9781474288767

Introduction to Arts Management
Jim Volz
ISBN 9781474239783

Introduction to the Art of Stage Management: A Practical Guide to Working in the Theatre and Beyond
Michael Vitale
ISBN 978-1-4742-5720-6

Get the Job in the Entertainment Industry

A Practical Guide for Designers, Technicians, and Stage Managers

Kristina Tollefson

methuen | drama
LONDON • NEW YORK • OXFORD • NEW DELHI • SYDNEY

METHUEN DRAMA
Bloomsbury Publishing Plc
50 Bedford Square, London, WC1B 3DP, UK
1385 Broadway, New York, NY 10018, USA
29 Earlsfort Terrace, Dublin 2, Ireland

BLOOMSBURY, METHUEN DRAMA and the Methuen Drama logo
are trademarks of Bloomsbury Publishing Plc

First published in Great Britain 2022

Cover design by www.ironicitalics.com
Cover image © Haleigh Audet / Haleigh Nicole Photography

A catalogue record for this book is available from the British Library.

A catalog record for this book is available from the Library of Congress.

ISBN: HB: 978-1-3501-0379-5
           PB: 978-1-3501-0378-8
           ePDF: 978-1-3501-0381-8
           eBook: 978-1-3501-0380-1

Series: Introductions to Theatre

Typeset by Integra Software Service Pvt. Ltd.,
Printed and bound in India

To find out more about our authors and books visit www.bloomsbury.com
and sign up for our newsletters.

Contents

Introduction: Owning Your Own Business—Yes, This Does Apply to You 1

1 Where Are You Going and How Will You Get There? 5

2 Creating Your Marketing Materials and Establishing Your Professional Persona 49

7 Talking About Money 201

8 Career Profiles 243

Illustrations

Figures

Plates

Tables

Acknowledgments and Dedication

This book would not have been possible without the hundreds of my current and former Theatre Careers students and all that I have learned from them. My best moments as a teacher are when my students don't need me any more and go out to succeed on their own. Your success is my greatest joy as a teacher.

Sincere thanks to my UCF colleagues, including Michael Wainstein, Bert Scott, Claudia Lynch, Lauren Rausch, Earl Weaver, Megan Friend, and Jessica T. Johnson for making my writing sabbatical possible.

Thank you does not convey the totality of my appreciation for the encouragement and understanding I received daily from Shaina, Marlie, Piper, Mollie, and Misha during the writing of this book. I am humbled to be on this journey with you.

Thanks to my mom, who taught me which fork to use, how to do my taxes, always read the Introduction, and that honesty and integrity always matter.

Thanks to Jason, for all the reasons. This is one of those times when the meditations of my heart will have to suffice. Rutabaga.

A Note on the Text

 This icon is used throughout the book to indicate that further resources are available online at: https://bloomsbury. pub/get-the-job-in-the-entertainment-industry.

Introduction

Owning Your Own Business—Yes, This Does Apply to You

When you envision your future, do you see yourself running your own business? Most people in our industry would reply to this with a resounding "No!", especially when they begin to consider all the things they know they *don't* know about running a business. I've got news for you. Most people working in theatre and the entertainment industry actually do operate their own business at some point in their career, yet some don't even realize it. What many fail to understand is that working as a freelance artist, even once, automatically qualifies you as a business that year in the eyes of the US Internal Revenue Service. So since you are going to be running your own business anyway, it is in your best interest to start making decisions like a business owner from the very beginning.

When you approach your work like a business it means you …

… pursue the education and/or training necessary to propel your career forward

… create marketing materials that represent your brand

… know how to feature examples of your best work in a well-designed portfolio and/or website

… prepare in advance for interviews and networking opportunities

… establish your fees and negotiate for a livable wage, including a profit

… understand the language in your contracts and know when that language needs to change

… establish a system of organization to track your contracts, invoices, receipts, and expenses

… learn how unions can support your career

… understand how taxes work and what records and information you need to keep

… plan for your financial future

… hire professionals to support you when you need them.

Pretty early on, students have a clear idea of the kind of work they want to do and develop a strict definition of success, typically based on limited understanding of the industry. And, often due to familial or peer pressure, they create a "backup plan" just in case. I don't believe in backup plans. I think if you have a backup plan then you are planning to fail. We need to shift our perspective and take off the blinders that allow us only one vision of the path to "success." Having multiple paths by which you can maintain continuous employment isn't a backup plan, it is just sound career planning. Exploring areas of employment outside traditional theatre or entertainment isn't making a backup plan, it's developing a well-crafted, multifaceted strategy for success. Many students come into my classes thinking that if they don't end up doing exactly what they intend or if they end up working outside the entertainment industry that all the naysayers were right about majoring in the arts. I want to emphasize that no matter what you end up doing, from lighting designer to doctor, and anything in between, it will be your theatre training that helped get you there.

Since I started teaching theatre majors how to approach their work like a business in 2004, I have given hundreds of students the tools not only to get their first job, but to continue to build all manner of careers for years to come. More than just a guide, this book (along with the online resources on the companion website) is full of practical advice on how to develop your plan, with examples, worksheets, and exercises to begin applying these ideas to your life right away.

The book opens with discussion and exercises to help you figure out where you want your path to lead. There are a lot of options within the theatre and entertainment industries, and not every path is right for every person. Are you up for a freelance career, or is a staff position going to meet your needs better? What other things can you do with theatre training? How do you find a job, and how do you know how much money you need to make? How are you going to reach your long-term goals? And how can a mentor help you get there?

From this start, the book guides you through creating your marketing materials, from portfolios and business cards to email and social media.

Your unique, unified look will put a polished and professional face on your business, allowing your work to stand out.

I give you specific guidelines and examples of ways to present your experience in resume form to highlight your experience best based on the type of job you are applying for. Writing a cover letter is not just repeating your resume in sentence form; it is an opportunity to address the job description and show your potential employer how your skills match what they are looking for. And there is a strategy to getting letters of recommendation that say exactly what you need them to say.

The detailed chapter on portfolios will set you up for success in digital, physical, and web formats. For many, the most dreaded aspect of getting a job is the interview. Follow the detailed preparation outlined in the book and you will be ready to answer any question they ask, whether in person, by phone, or on video. And if your interview includes a meal, you can use the dining etiquette section to make a great first impression.

Money is such an important subject, and yet very few people are willing to talk about it. In this book I aim to destigmatize the topic as I lay out ways to set your fees and negotiate when an offer doesn't meet your needs. In consultation with financial professionals, I present an introduction to the US tax system as it relates to theatre artists, and to the basics of planning your financial future.

The final chapter shares stories of people who have embraced all that their theatre training has given them. In these you can find inspiration and see proof that the road to success is seldom a straight one. It may be full of curves, forks, detours, and roundabouts. You may be forced, or simply choose, to take a break along the way. You may even end up deciding that your initial destination wasn't correct and choose to go somewhere else entirely. That's not failure, that's just life. Your life.

The Covid-19 pandemic acted as a significant reminder of our vulnerabilities as artists. As we continue to see what long-term impacts the pandemic will have on our industry, it is even more important to remain flexible when considering ways to apply your talents and skills. There may still be many unknowns, but one thing I can tell you with certainty is that strong job search and business skills are even more important now than ever.

I can't wait to see where your path leads!

1

Where Are You Going and How Will You Get There?

Do I Need a College Degree?

The short answer is no. A college degree is not required to pursue a career in theatre design, technology, or stage management unless you are planning to teach. Employers want to hire people who can do the best job for them regardless of their degree status. You can get a basic entry-level job and work your way up through the hierarchy as you learn more. A college degree gives you the knowledge and skills to allow you to start in higher-level positions and work toward supervisory and "decision-making" positions more quickly. College theatre provides you with a laboratory to try lots of different aspects that you may not even know you are interested in or good at. I was an undergraduate on an acting scholarship, and very quickly learned I hated auditioning and there were a lot of people who were better actors than me. I avoided auditioning by always having a technical assignment, and all that time in the costume shop led me to a career as a costume designer—not something I even knew was possible before going to college. Additionally, your peers, faculty, and alumni from your program form a vast network that will help keep you employed and offer advice along the way.

Is Graduate School Right for Me?

Many undergraduate students dismiss the idea of graduate school before learning more about it. For some it can be the right next step; for others it may be necessary to get a few years of professional experience to have the maturity to benefit fully from grad school; and for the rest it just isn't an important step in their career trajectory. Either way, it is a big decision that shouldn't be made lightly, and warrants thought and research to be sure that misconceptions are not the basis of the decision. Graduate school in theatre differs from other disciplines, so when doing your research and getting advice be sure to talk with people who understand these differences.

The biggest misconception students have is that graduate school is the same as undergraduate study—but it is different in many ways. First, the course load is lower. Typically, nine credit hours are considered full time in graduate school. While graduate classes are more rigorous than undergraduate courses, there are fewer courses required in graduate school. Additionally, grad school coursework focuses on the area you are studying and does not include general education classes. A master of arts (MA) degree typically takes two years and a master of fine arts (MFA) degree typically takes three.

Expense is a factor that deters potential students. While it is possible for graduate school to be paid for through scholarships, fellowships, and student loans, assistantships are another and lesser-known funding option. An assistantship means that the department hires you to work part time and in exchange it waives your tuition and gives you a monthly paycheck. Tuition waivers can be full or partial, and some institutions may also waive fees. Ted Ozimek, who attended graduate school on assistantship at Purdue University and now works for ETC (Electronic Theatre Controls), maintains, "A graduate assistantship is the only reasonable way to attend graduate school in theatre. The industry is not lucrative enough to pay graduate school student loans after graduation."[1]

Assistantship packages are typically quarter time or half time, requiring ten or twenty hours of work per week. Assistantship jobs might be working in one of the shops, leadership positions on productions, or teaching classes for undergraduate students. The financial package could fall anywhere between $8,000 and $20,000 or more, so it is very important to get specifics from each school you are interested in as there is a lot of variation from university to university. Some packages come with health insurance. But while much of your tuition will be waived and your basic living expenses may be covered, graduate school can still be a financially challenging period

---

[1]Ted Ozimek, personal communication with the author, December 27, 2019.

of time without additional outside employment, so it is important to budget and plan carefully.

Once you have passed through the misconceptions about attending graduate school, look at the benefits to see if there are any of which you want to take advantage. You have probably heard many times what a small world the theatre and entertainment industries are, and that most people get jobs based on who they know. To increase your employability, you need to know more people. One of the biggest advantages to a graduate education is the growth of your professional network. You already have the faculty members from your undergrad years and all their contacts as part of your network to help you get a job; when you attend graduate school, you add all the faculty and students at your new university and all their contacts as part of your extended network as well.

One distinct benefit of graduate school is experience. As a graduate student you should have the opportunity to work on several fully produced shows under the mentorship of the faculty. Jodi Ozimek received her MFA in Costume Design and points out, "These fully produced shows typically have reasonable budgets and shop support unlike what you would find if just starting out in small community or professional theatres."[2] Your portfolio of work when you leave graduate school will be significantly stronger than the one you started with.

If you decide that graduate school is right for you, your next step is figuring out when to apply. Some programs accept students right out of undergraduate study, while others only accept students who have been working for a few years. Going to graduate school immediately after undergraduate college will build your experience and network early, so you have a longer time to take advantage of the perks. You are already in student mode and will be more prepared to handle the academic load and student lifestyle. If you work professionally for a few years before going to graduate school, you will have a better understanding of what segment of the industry you want to specialize in. Your experience will qualify you for more prestigious graduate schools and financial packages, and you will be better able to take full advantage of what your professors are teaching.

If you plan to go back to grad school after working, be mindful that life may prevent you from doing so. In the time between undergrad studies and applying for graduate school you may take on personal and financial

---

[2]Jodi Ozimek, personal communication with the author, October 12, 2020.

obligations that make working toward an advanced degree more challenging. A successful freelance sound designer, Anthony Narciso, says, "There are days that I would still like to go so teaching could be a future option for me, but I make very consistent income and am booked for the majority of each year. It would be financially difficult to stop what I am doing in order to take classes again."[3]

If your decision is to wait, you must know yourself well enough to know if you will actually go back. Of course, it is always possible that once you get into the job market you decide you don't need to go to graduate school. Pam Knourek headed the costume technology grad/undergrad program at University of North Carolina School of the Arts for twenty years, and says, "You don't have to have a masters to work in this industry. What matters is if you have the skills."[4]

Some people who wait for graduate school end up going for a different area of study. Jeramy Boik began his career as a technical director and eventually went to graduate school to study landscape architecture.[5] And others who had no intention of going to grad school sometimes do after all. Aimee Johnson, costume shop manager at Breneau University, began her career in the costume shop at Busch Gardens: "I had been at the theme park for almost three years and had moved up as far as I could there. I had managed to create more opportunities than a lot of my co-workers, but there were no mobility options."[6] She was looking to expand her skills and build her professional network, and grad school gave her those opportunities.

You should start looking a year or two before you apply. Ask your professors, ask your friends who have recently done their own search, ask people in the industry, solicit advice on social media in one of the many industry-specific groups. The important thing is to find the right fit for you and start grad school at a time that makes sense for your career. Pam Knourek acknowledges that, for some people, she would not be the person to help launch them into a career. She also recommends "talking to current students and recent grads to find out if the school delivered on their promises."[7] Where the person who will be your major professor works professionally is an important consideration. If you want to work in film, you will want to study with someone who has those connections. If you want to work in large

---

[3]Anthony Narciso, personal communication with the author, November 6, 2019.
[4]Pam Knourek, interview with the author, August 28, 2020.
[5]Jeramy Boik, interview with the author, August 12, 2020.
[6]Aimee Johnson, personal communication with the author, November 5, 2019.
[7]Knourek, note 4.

regional theatres or in New York, choose a program and a mentor who will provide you with those networks.[8] As much of grad school is about network connections, you want to make sure you end up with the right ones. Also find out how much your major professor is away on professional work and how often they are on campus. Find out if they typically take their grad students with them as assistants. While all college faculty work professionally, there can be downsides to having a mentor who sees their professional career, and not your success, as their priority.

Many graduate programs from across the US exhibit at the United States Institute for Theatre Technology Annual Conference and Stage Expo. Attending USITT regularly as an undergrad gives you the opportunity to show your portfolio, get feedback, and build relationships, so when you do apply, the programs know you and your work.

The University Resident Theatre Association holds interview events in three US cities every year where prospective graduate students can be interviewed by numerous programs in one day. Aimee Johnson attended an URTA event before choosing grad school at Penn State: "It was much more cost effective than traveling to each school around the country." Research the member schools, and contact any you are interested in ahead of time to request an interview and confirm that it is a recruiting year for them. Even if you don't think there are any URTA schools at the top of your list, participating in the process might reveal a school you hadn't initially considered is a good fit for you. That's what happened to me.

Internships

It is difficult to get most jobs without experience, but how do you gain experience if you can't get a job? In some cases, internships can provide that bridge between school and the profession, and they are encouraged across most college campuses.

Here are a few reasons why internships can be a useful career step:

- Application of education
- Career exploration
- Build experience and increase marketability

---

[8]Ozimek, note 2.

- Networking
- Learn how a professional theatre operates
- Build your resume
- Gain professional feedback
- Figure out what you do and don't like about the job.

All those things can also be said about an entry-level job, which absolutely can be your first step after college, so don't only look for openings labeled as internships.

There are a lot of problems with the internship system in the US and you need to be very careful to evaluate opportunities thoroughly to avoid exploitation. Elizabeth Wislar, a member of Costume Professionals for Wage Equity, a group actively working toward "a more diverse and equitable theatrical arts industry,"[9] says, "I do see value in internships. I do believe that they can be incredibly educational and incredibly beneficial, but the internships need to be ethical. They need to be legal. And they need to be realistic."[10]

The US Department of Labor website outlines the seven factors that must be considered to determine if a position legally qualifies as an unpaid internship. In short, if the employer is the primary beneficiary of the working relationship then the intern is an employee. If the intern is the primary beneficiary, meaning their presence and work is primarily about their education, they can be classified as an intern and not compensated beyond the educational benefit they are receiving from the company. Internships, if done correctly, are more work for the employer because they are providing training and educational experiences for the intern and other employees are taking time from completing their tasks to teach the intern. Employers should not cut costs by calling a job an internship, especially when it requires specialized skills and experience and comes with the job description and duties of an employee. Interns should be coming to the job to learn, not to work. "If analysis of these circumstances reveals that an intern or student is actually an employee, then he or she is entitled to both minimum wage and overtime pay under the FLSA [Fair Labor Standards Act]."[11]

---

[9]"About Us," Costume Professionals for Wage Equity, accessed October 11, 2020, http://cpfwe.org/about-us/.
[10]Elizabeth Wislar, interview with the author, November 4, 2019.
[11]"Fact Sheet #71," US Department of Labor, updated January 2018, accessed October 11, 2020, https://www.dol.gov/agencies/whd/fact-sheets/71-flsa-internships#2.

If you decide to pursue a true internship, determine your learning objectives and be sure to communicate them in your application materials. Are you hoping to work under a specific professional? Do you want to observe specific parts of the production process? Are you looking to shadow people in various positions within the company? Are there specific skills you want to develop? Tell them what your learning objectives are during your interview, and ask them how they would help you reach these goals.

An overwhelming number of unpaid internships posted every year may not even offer you housing—there are actually some places that require you to pay them! All unpaid internships should be given particular scrutiny. These employers contend that they are doing you a favor and boosting your career by letting you come work for them. Watch the language used in the ads. Writing on the Costume Professionals for Wage Equity website, Elizabeth Wisler points out, "The job postings with the lowest wages have the most to say about how good you're going to feel working for them." Watch for phrases like "career-oriented go-getter," "fantastic portfolio builder," "seeking an enthusiastic and experienced intern" who is "passionate," "enthusiastic," and "can handle the stress" of a "fast-paced environment," and references to their company being like a family. All this for no or very little compensation. Elizabeth goes on to say, "The hidden barb under all this emotional language is the implication that you don't care enough if you won't accept their inadequate terms."[12]

Compensation packages can include hourly wage and overtime, stipend, travel, housing, meals, etc. If when totaled up it doesn't equate to *at least* minimum wage you should reconsider this "opportunity." Even if your only experience is academic and you are still growing your skills, your time and training are of value to the employer and you should be compensated. If you are performing a job for them, you deserve to be paid a living wage. Period. It is not uncommon for the places that pay nothing or very little to tout the experience as the remuneration you are receiving for your work, but as Laura Whittenton, a Houston-based cutter/draper, points out in response to an internship posting for no pay that required very specific skills, "If you are seeking skilled labor, you need to pay. Experience is not compensation."[13] Elizabeth Estervig, a tailor in Motion Picture Costumers Local 705, adds,

[12]Elizabeth Wislar, "The Emotional Language of Abusive Job Postings," Costume Professionals for Wage Equity, December 31, 2019, accessed October 11, 2020, http://cpfwe.org/2019/12/31/the-emotional-language-of-abusive-job-postings/.
[13]Laura Whittenton, "Costume People" private Facebook group, May 26, 2017.

"If skills are essential, pay should be too. If you cannot afford to pay your employees, frankly you can't afford to *have* employees."[14] You can't feed your cat or pay your phone bill with experience, so make sure you get paid.

A further argument against unpaid internships is that they are elitist and prevent diversity. If a theatre offers an unpaid internship it is essentially saying "we only want those who already have enough money to live off of for several months" or "we only want people who have families wealthy enough to subsidize our company while their relative is providing us with free labor." What they end up with is a whole group of students from the same socio-economic group with very similar backgrounds and experiences. That is not how you promote diversity within an organization or an industry. Jyarland Daniels MBA, JD, CEO/founder of a racial equity consultancy, wrote in a 2017 article on LinkedIn about how unpaid internships reinforce gender- and race-based inequities. "Free labor disadvantages women and … racial minorities … and students from low-middle families are disadvantaged through their exclusion." She goes on to say, "The consequences of excluding Blacks, Hispanics, and economically disadvantaged students from participation at this initial entry point due to the lack of financial compensation are long-term. For-profit organizations have no justifiable reason for unpaid internships. Non-profits who seek to make the world better in some way should not practice such a moral contradiction to their stated values."[15] Venus Gulbranson, a DC-based lighting designer, put it plainly in a social media post:

> I would like to challenge theatres who pride themselves on diversity to reconsider their internship programs. What's the point of reaching out to low-income communities with your art when your "$5/wk, no housing, 25hrs/day commitment" programs make it impossible for these young artists to ever participate. Don't just pride yourself with your BIPOC/LGBTQ interns and call it a day. Make your programs *economically* diverse.

With this in mind, it becomes incumbent on all of us to refuse to contribute to the lack of diversity within our industry, demand that everyone be paid a living wage, and refuse unpaid jobs labeled as internships. If everyone stopped taking these positions, employers would be forced to pay for the labor they are receiving.

If you feel like you have so few skills that you need to learn a lot more, instead of signing on to an internship consider seeking out volunteer

---

[14]Elizabeth Estervig, "Costume People" private Facebook group, May 26, 2017.
[15]Jyarland Daniels, MBA, JD, "How Unpaid Internships Undermine Diversity & Inclusion Efforts," LinkedIn, June 4, 2017, https://www.LinkedIn. com/.

opportunities in your local area where you can attend on your own schedule and for the amount of time you have available. That can absolutely go on your resume and will help you build your skills, references, and professional network, but will not exploit you because you will be in charge of your time.

Here are some ways you can protect yourself from ending up in a bad internship or first-job situation.

- Avoid unpaid internships. In our industry, you are going to provide the theatre or organization with your labor. You deserve to be fairly compensated for your time and skills.
- Find out the work schedule up front. How many hours a day are you expected to work? When are your days off? Are you paid overtime when you work over forty hours a week? Are these reasonable working conditions? Be sure all dates and hours are communicated up front.
- Make sure you know exactly how much you will be compensated. Be cautious about stipends, and do the math to figure out what that amounts to as an hourly wage. For example, the current (2021) US federal minimum wage is $7.25 an hour. If you were paid this minimum wage for forty hours a week you would receive $290 a week. If an employer is offering you a $500 stipend for a five-week season you are being shorted nearly $1,000, and that's if you only work forty hours a week. What do they pay in travel expenses to move to their town for the season? Do they provide housing or meals? These benefits in addition to pay can offset your out-of-pocket expenses for getting to and from the job location and living there for the duration of the work.
- Know how many people will work in your department and who your supervisor will be. This can help you understand the structure of the organization and how much responsibility you will be taking on. It also allows you the opportunity to research your potential supervisor's experience online and decide if this is a person you want to learn from.
- Understand your specific job duties and the scope of the work. This helps you know if your job would be to get coffee and make copies or if you will be hands on in mounting a production. How many shows are being done, and in how much time? Will you have responsibilities running the shows? How often do changeovers happen, and how much time is allowed for them? Is this a realistic schedule?
- Use your network. Talk to other people who have worked for that theatre in this type of position. These people will typically be very honest about their experiences and whether they recommend it or not.

If anyone tries to tell you that you have to "pay your dues" by working for free, be very cautious of taking their advice. Pam Knourek puts it plainly: "I don't believe in dues. There are no dues. You should get paid for what you do … at least hourly minimum wage. And overtime."[16]

Freelance

We use the word *freelancer* in our industry to mean someone who goes from show to show or gig to gig without a consistent employer. While many stage managers identify as freelancers because they are moving between shows and theatre companies as the run of one show comes to an end and they move into rehearsal for a different show at a different company, they only fit the legal definition of a freelancer if they are non-Equity. If a stage manager is in the union they are always hired as an employee, and are therefore not technically a freelancer by IRS (Internal Revenue Service) definitions. Nonetheless, most union stage managers still operate *like* freelancers because they are not typically hired for long-term contracts and go from gig to gig with the same job insecurity that an actual freelancer has. No one, except the IRS, will deny these stage managers the use of the term freelance.

A true freelancer is self-employed and operates their own business. Freelancers work as independent contractors on a show-by-show or project-by-project basis, with a separate contract for each. They are commonly paid by the project, not by the hour, and they manage their own time and how many hours of work they put into the project. People who enjoy freelancing cite the excitement of getting to work with lots of different production teams and travel around the city, country, or world from job to job. They like setting their own day-to-day schedule, having the power to choose how many and which projects they take on, and deciding who they work with.

Not everyone who freelances experiences these characteristics as freedoms. While a freelancer may have the power to turn down work, the low pay for many freelance jobs in our industry forces some freelancers to take on jobs they don't really want, or more projects than they can really handle, in order to pay their bills. Elizabeth Wislar spent close to twenty years in Chicago as a freelance costume designer and technician, and has a new perspective. "Here's where my narrative has shifted, especially in the past

---

[16]Knourek, note 4.

few years. I used to brag about how much work I did in Chicago. It was my way of protecting myself against the truth." And the truth was, she said: "You should not design and build twenty-five shows a year. I was doing it because it was my only income and it was so paltry. What I was being paid was not enough. Now I'm not allowing myself to find personal value in working like that and I speak out and say, 'that's wrong and we need to fix this.'"[17]

The dream is to get to the point in your freelance career where people are coming to you and you don't have to search out your next contract, but until that happens having to look constantly for your next gig can also wear on people. Shawn Boyle, a lighting and projections designer, remembers, "My first year out of undergrad I responded to 110 job postings. I heard back from five. I was offered one. As a freelancer I had to do something for my career everyday: look to see what jobs were posted, update my resume, follow up on applications. It takes a while to build momentum."[18] Once you have this momentum, you will find that people tend to rehire those with whom they enjoy working. "As a freelancer you must always weigh the choice of not taking every offer you get because every offer you turn down will get picked up by someone else and chances are the person who took the job you passed on will get the first call before you next time," says Chip Perry, director of lighting and television production for World Wrestling Entertainment.[19] Maintaining a healthy network can help to counteract this result. If you have a strong network, you will have multiple people you can call when you are looking for your next gig.

Being a freelancer means running your own business, which also means you will have to spend time on things like scheduling, contract negotiations, managing invoices and income, paying bills, taxes, insurance, and looking for new clients. You are taking on responsibility for everything related to your work life. Freelancing can have a lot of benefits, but it is not for the passive.

Staff Positions

Staff positions at regional or small professional theatres tend to be in technical areas: costume shop managers, stitchers, carpenters, technical directors, master electricians, prop artisans, etc. Designers are not typically hired as

---

[17]Wislar, note 10.
[18]Shawn Boyle, interview with the author, March 2, 2020.
[19]Charles "Chip" Perry, interview with the author, October 7, 2020.

staff members at these theatres unless they are also filling a technical role—for example, a costume shop manager or draper who also designs costumes, or an audio engineer who also designs sound, or a resident designer who is required to build the show as well. This job description for a "Resident Sound Designer" at a professional LORT (League of Resident Theatres)[20] theatre lists the following duties.

1. Design, supervise, and execute the implementation of Mainstage and Youth Theatre sound designs including coordination of projection equipment as needed.
2. Act as Sound Engineer and Front of House Mixer for all Productions.
3. Collaborate with electrics, wardrobe, and running crew.
4. Serve as Master Sound Engineer for all external and internal rental events including: Install speaker systems; Prepare consoles, Maintain and upkeep equipment; Troubleshoot and repair audio equipment, Prepare orchestra "pit" as needed; Install and troubleshoot closed circuit video and intercom systems as needed; and Install and network projection equipment as called for by designs.[21]

In this case there are several jobs being wrapped into one under the title "Resident Sound Designer": sound designer, sound engineer, front of house mixer, event sound engineer, sound technician, and projections/video/intercom technician. Theatres and organizations are trying to find every way possible to save money, and one of the ways is by creating these combination jobs. These types of jobs can easily lead to exploitation if work hours, overtime, and days off are not clearly negotiated and adhered to, but they can be fun and exciting when implemented in a reasonable way.

In staff positions you are an employee, and show up at work during your set hours to do the work you are assigned. You don't get to decide which shows or even which projects you work on, but your paycheck is steady and you likely have health insurance. Staff positions can be full time or part time, year-round or seasonal. It is not uncommon for seasonal employees to work freelance or in another staff position during their off-season months.

Staff positions in corporate entertainment may not have job titles that you recognize, so you will have to do some research to figure out exactly what you are looking for. For example, at Walt Disney World there are

---

[20]LORT is a professional theatre organization that participates in collective bargaining with the unions on behalf of its member theatres.
[21]"Resident Sound Designer Position Profile," Laguna Playhouse, accessed November 5, 2019, https://lagunaplayhouse.com/media/2293/resident-sound-designer-61918.pdf.

many position titles that can translate to "stage manager" though they have different day-to-day responsibilities: entertainment guest experience manager, entertainment manager, entertainment proprietor, and character captain. Technicians have the titles Tech 3 (entry-level position equivalent to run crew), Tech 2 (have passed an interview process/skills test for a specific specialty area), or Tech 1 (crew chiefs, master electricians, audio engineers, etc.). And would you guess that a costume hostess works wardrobe?

Touring

It is a good idea to connect with people who have done the style of touring you are interested in, keeping in mind that everyone's experiences and enjoyment of those experiences may be different. For example, Sherrice Mojgani, a theatrical lighting designer based in Washington, DC, spent a couple years on the road as assistant lighting designer for the out-of-town tryouts of *Come From Away*, and described her tour experience as "seeing the insides of different theatres and local restaurants. And by local, I mean between the theatre and the hotel room."[22] Kelsey Vivian, a freelance stage manager, told me, "I have friends who love touring and cruises and have made a career from it and I have friends who make me promise never to work a tour or cruise."[23] Alexandra McKeown spent two-and-a-half years as a stage manager on tour with Cirque du Soleil in South America: "I'd be lying if I said it wasn't amazing and utterly worth it. For people who want to explore the world, why not get paid to do it? I would never have visited the Iguazu Falls, gotten stuck in the Atacama Desert, or played with monkeys at my Airbnb in Costa Rica if I had never toured."[24] Those seem to be the expectations that many have of touring, though McKeown goes on to say, "It was also a challenging experience. International tours are complex. I remember being incentivized to spend less than 90 days in the US for tax purposes. I personally paid to fly my family to Argentina when I found myself lonely after many months of not seeing them."[25] The dialectic that touring is both a positive and a negative for people seems very common. Christa Arzon was on a national tour of *RENT* for two-and-a-half years

---

[22]Sherrice Mojgani, personal communication with the author, November 5, 2019.
[23]Kelsey Vivian, personal communication with the author, November 6, 2019.
[24]Alexandra McKeon, personal communication with the author, November 6, 2019.
[25]Ibid.

and says, "Touring was the best and worst thing I've ever done … It was extremely lonely at times."[26] Evan Rooney, production manager for multiple touring Broadway shows, says "Touring has been the best and worst days of my life. I've seen more of the world than most, but I've seen far more loading docks and dark theatres than I can count." The tour experience is also influenced by the type of tour. "Rock and roll is tough. The pay is great, but the hours are long and it's very unforgiving," explains Rich Perkin, who toured with Maroon 5 and Smashing Pumpkins. Jeramy Boik, who toured internationally as a technician with Up With People, said:

> I would highly recommend touring to people when they're starting out. It's a great way to get paid to see the world and experience other cultures. I think I was too old to be sleeping on a gym floor the night before we had to get on a plane at three in the morning. I know I would have enjoyed it more if I were younger.

The job you have while on tour will make a big impact on your work hours, opportunities for sightseeing, and down time. As the merchandise manager on a tour, Christa Arzon, who has trained as a stage manager, had more flexibility than most of the others: "I was able to really only work during the show—this meant that during the day I got to explore a lot of the cities we were in. Cast and crew definitely didn't have that luxury. There was always a rehearsal or press event happening." Chip Perry, who toured with Alabama and Kenny Chesney, said he's seen the best parking lots and airports around the world, and points out that tours do not allow you lots of time for being a tourist: "Tours are about making money, remember that. When you are on tour, the client has you on the road to make money for them. You make your money and then go see the world on your own time."[27] Jason Resler toured as head of wardrobe with Disney on Ice, among other shows: "I've done traditional bus and truck tours and those are difficult, especially if you are doing a lot of one-offs. You don't get to see as much on those types of tours. On tours with a week or longer stint in each town you do have more time to see places." He also suggests you have an exit strategy before you go on tour: "Have a plan to leave when you're ready because it's easy to keep accepting tour contracts. The longer you live on tour the harder it becomes to stop."[28]

---

[26]Christa Arzon, personal communication with the author, November 6, 2019.
[27]Perry, note 19.
[28]Jason Resler, personal communication with the author, November 9, 2019.

Cruise Ships

Cruise ships offer another opportunity to work while traveling to different parts of the world. Many of the people I spoke with who worked on cruise ships made comments similar to those who have worked on tour. Caleb Howell, a Broadway dresser, worked on a cruise ship early in his career. He enjoyed the travel and meeting new people, though he cautions that the work hours are intense with "long, long work weeks that average 15- to 18-hour days."[29] Ryan Gravilla, principal lighting designer for Disney Parks Live Entertainment at Walt Disney World, has spent a lot of time working on Disney cruise ships and recommends: "If you are interested in cruise ships, then do it once. After six or eight months you and the cruise line can decide if you come back. If you are good with a very specific routine and working seven days a week because you don't get days off, just hours off, then it might be a rewarding lifestyle."[30]

Just as with tours, your free time is dictated by your role. Working as a designer for a cruise ship is very different than working an extended contract as a technician. When Anthony Narciso, freelance sound designer, designs for cruise ships he is typically on board for only two to four weeks, while technicians are typically on board for six to nine months. He says, "The great thing about being a designer on the ships is that you always have some downtime to explore the places you are visiting. As long as you have your notes done, you can explore the port cities before or after work."[31]

I had the chance to tour backstage on a cruise ship and meet with the designers and crew as they went through the process of updating a show with a new cast and costumes. The onboard technicians did their normal daily schedule of performances and maintenance. Tech rehearsals could only take place when the theatre was otherwise dark, which sometimes happened during daylight hours and sometimes after the last show of the night. When seas were rough and it wasn't safe for performers to be on stage, these rehearsals were cancelled and crammed into another already full day. That's a good reminder that if you get seasick, cruise ships are not the best choice for you. Tiffany N. Thetard Roby, who worked on tour and on cruise ships as a stage manager, said that her time on the ship "taught me a lot

---

[29]Caleb Howell, personal communication with the author, November 6, 2019.
[30]Ryan Gravilla, interview with the author, October 2, 2020.
[31]Narciso, note 3.

about who I was and where I saw myself moving forward. The cruise ship is a confined space where you live and work with your cast and crew. There are a lot of great friendships that are built and lots of great memories, but I was ready to be on dry land after eight months."[32]

Jobs in Academia: Faculty or Staff, Tenure, and Promotion

Wary of the uncertainty of freelancing and because educational theatre is most familiar, it makes sense that many students say they plan to teach at some point in their careers. It is important to think hard about this as an option. Don't decide to teach as a consolation prize for a lackluster career. Teachers must be a balance of great educators and talented working professionals.

While academia can add a greater level of stability than many jobs in the industry, if you talk to university professors you find that most of them have taught at more than one school—some of them many more. Politics and the tenure and promotion process can be a big challenge to job stability. By taking an academic position you also give up a lot of freedom, flexibility, and quite possibly money. You forfeit the ability to set your own schedule and select your own projects in exchange for a regular paycheck.

If you are planning to teach at the high school level, find out the requirements to get teaching certification in your state. Typically these will include an undergraduate degree and some level of training in education.

While the precise requirements can vary, to get a long-term teaching position at a US university you will need to have a master's degree at minimum. But while an MA can allow you to teach undergraduate students as an adjunct (temporary, course-to-course employment) or possibly as an instructor (typically full-time annual contracts), it will not usually lead to a tenure-track position. With few exceptions, you will need a terminal degree to land a full-time tenure-track teaching position ("terminal" means it is the highest level of academic degree available in that discipline). The MFA is the terminal degree for most areas in theatre, including design, technology, and management, while theatre history and other theatre studies areas have a

---

[32]Tiffany N. Thetard Roby, personal communication with the author, November 17, 2019.

PhD as the terminal degree. An MFA typically takes three years to complete beyond a bachelor's degree; a PhD typically involves first getting an MA (two years) and then a PhD (three years).

Tenure is the process by which faculty are evaluated on their qualifications to receive a permanent teaching position. "Tenure track" means you are hired into a position that will eventually be evaluated to receive tenure. The tenure and promotion process will vary from university to university and even department to department. There should be tenure and promotion guidelines you can review before accepting a tenure-track position, so you are clear on what the expectations will be from the beginning. The requirements typically include publishing or completing professional creative activities that lead to a national or international reputation. This means that to keep your job in a tenure-track position you will need to undertake a large number of professional gigs in addition to your regular university job (many places don't count the shows you do at school and also don't give you time off to do outside work), and/or present your original ideas at conferences around the country or internationally, and/or write and publish journal articles or books. The university sees these things as evidence that you know what you are talking about and confirmation that you are an expert in the field.

The tenure process typically includes an annual review and evaluation of the faculty member's productivity (number, quality, and location of shows/articles/conference presentations/workshops, etc.), quality of teaching, and level of service to the department, university, community, and discipline. In a tenure-track position the faculty member is usually hired as an assistant professor, the lowest academic rank for someone on the tenure track. Typically, the faculty member formally applies for tenure in the sixth year. Their work is evaluated by "outside reviewers," who are academics in the same discipline at other institutions. They review the criteria of the department and the evidence provided by the faculty member, and write a letter saying if, in their opinion, the faculty member has met the requirements to receive tenure based on the criteria. The letter and evidence then go through a series of committees and administrators, depending on the process at the institution, and eventually the faculty member is told whether or not they will receive tenure and be promoted to associate professor. If denied tenure, the faculty member is typically given a one-year terminal contract so they can look for a new job and the department can look for a replacement.

Being promoted to full professor, the highest academic rank, is a similar process but with even higher expectations of outside production work, publishing, and/or conference presentations. Because the faculty member has tenure at that point, if they are denied promotion they are not required to find a new job and can continue at their previous rank. Faculty members who are promoted to associate or full professor typically receive a raise.

It is also possible to be hired in non-tenure-track faculty positions. Lecturer and instructor posts are non-tenured positions that typically have a larger teaching load and lower salary, and do not require continual professional work outside the university. There are also temporary visiting faculty positions, typically with contract lengths ranging from one to four years, and it is understood from the beginning that the faculty member needs to look for a new job at the end of the contract.

Those in technical or management areas may find there are not as many faculty positions as there are in design areas. This doesn't mean, however, that you can't make a career in educational theatre. Staff positions still give you the opportunity to work with students, and in some cases can even provide you with teaching opportunities. They do not come with the demands of outside professional work and, in fact, can be so time-consuming as to preclude the staff member from pursuing any outside employment. Staff positions at universities can either be for the nine-month academic year or twelve-month contracts. Shorter contracts allow time for other professional employment during the summer months to supplement your income.

What Else Can You Do with a Theatre Degree?

Each student who comes into my class has visions of working in a specific area of theatre on fairly traditional productions, either in theatre or entertainment (theme parks, circus, arena shows, concerts, etc.). They want to be electricians, or stage managers, or pyrotechnic operators, or drapers, or sound designers, or any one of a long list of traditional theatrical jobs. Those students also come with stories of family members or roommates who warn the student to have a "backup plan." The idea of a "backup plan" really irritates me. It assumes that the student is likely to fail in their chosen career. Instead of a "backup plan" I encourage students to engage in comprehensive career planning and always look for opportunities where they can apply their skills. A good career plan will provide you with multiple options for revenue streams, so if one path is slowing down you can activate other options. Part of your education should be to learn about all the possibilities that abound with the skills you have acquired. Theatre skills are absolutely transferable, and theatre training can prepare you for vast numbers of wide-ranging employment opportunities when you look beyond the bounds of traditional theatrical job descriptions. Kate Murphy, a costume designer and technician with thirty years' experience in Chicago theatres, points out that theatre training prepares you for any position that is "high pressure, detail-oriented, requiring creative solutions, dealing with difficult personalities, and short deadlines."[33] Jenny Sargent received her BFA (bachelor of fine arts) in Stage Management from Rutgers, and after working in opera for over a decade made a transition to banquet management and is training to become an assistant general manager.

> As a stage manager I learned how to deal with people and different personalities, how to be a good communicator, to get people on the same page, to keep them on task, time management, to create calm under pressure. Those are things that definitely have transitioned with me from the live theater world. Working with a bride on their wedding day is just like opening night of an opera.[34]

Acknowledging these opportunities and considering them as a component of your career plan can help you weather difficult economic storms. The entertainment industry is vast. Susan Nicholson, a lighting designer/programmer/production electrician for live events and theatre, points out, "You don't just have to be a designer. I think so many other areas of the industry get forgotten. You can go into sales, manufacturing, rentals, journalism. There are other things out there than being a designer or teacher."[35]

Consider these fields, and how they all need people who know how to do what we do.

Banquets	Cruise ships	High school teaching
Blogs	Dance	Ice shows
Cartoons	Dinner theatre	Magic shows
Circus	Fairs and carnivals	Movies
Concerts	Fashion shows	Museums
Conventions	Festivals	News

---

[33]Kate Murphy, personal communication with the author, October 30, 2019.
[34]Jenny Sargent, interview with the author, March 11, 2020.
[35]Susan Nicholson, interview with the author, February 13, 2020.

Nightclubs
Opera
Parades
Podcasts
Private parties

Publishing
Radio
Special events
Sports entertainment
Television

Theme parks
Themed restaurants
Trade shows
Video games
Web design

Additionally, here is a list of over fifty other types of jobs and employment fields beyond traditional design, tech, and stage management for which theatre would be a good training ground (advanced training or licensing may be required for some of them). Many of these are jobs pursued by people I know with backgrounds in theatre design, technology, or stage management.

A/V installer
Agent
Architectural lighting
Architecture
Arts administration
Audience relations
Booking agent
Box office manager
Bridal industry
Catering manager
Child guardian
College professor
Communications
    specialist
Company manager
Computer animation
Construction
    management
Corporate production
Cosmetics rep
Cosplay
Custom closets
Development director
Digital artist
Digital sculptor
Entertainment lawyer

Entertainment
    manager
Entertainment sales
Entrepreneur
Escape room designer
Etsy shop owner
Event designer
Event planner
Executive assistant
Executive director
Fabric librarian
Facility manager
Fashion shows
Festival manager
Finish carpenter
Floral designer
Furniture maker
General manager
Graphic designer
Graphic novelist
Hair or wig stylist
High school teacher
House manager
Illustrator
Interior designer
Landscape architect

Makerspace manager
Managing director
Marketing assistant
Muralist
Museum exhibition
Television news design
Patron services
Personal assistant
Photographer
Project management
Real estate
Restaurant designer
Social media manager
Stylist
Teaching artist
Textile designer
Theatre librarian
Union management
Wardrobe manager
Website designer
Wedding planner
Welder
Window display
    designer

If you do a web search and read any articles about what employers are looking for, you will get a long list of what are called "soft skills." Soft skills are not about what you can do, but how you do it. I challenge you to find one of these soft skills that you have not had to use and practice in the course of your theatre training and production work.

- **Effective and timely communication**
  - design meetings, production meetings, rehearsal reports, email communication, design presentations, meeting scheduling, giving notes, explaining to collaborators, etc.

- **Problem solving**
  - items out of stock and need for immediate alternative solutions, rehearsal conflicts, impacts of natural disasters, actor or crew member injury, unforeseen delays, too-small budgets, limited labor, meeting the needs of the script, limited equipment, etc.

- **Critical thinking**
  - script analysis, design decisions, construction decisions, electrics and audio troubleshooting, quick change planning, etc.

- **Work ethic**
  - daily work calls, commitment to finishing projects on time, weekend calls, 10 out of 12s, repetition in tech rehearsals, etc.

- **Teamwork and collaboration**
  - the entire process of producing a show is a giant collaborative group project—group projects are our specialty!

- **Planning**
  - rehearsal schedules, build schedules, project planning, budgeting, etc.

- **Task prioritization**
  - planning steps of a build, deciding which notes need to be completed first, prepping projects for others before doing your own notes, etc.

- **Comfort in positions of leadership**
  - serving as a crew chief, stage manager, master electrician, draper, technical director, shop manager, run crew, etc.

- **Adaptability and resilience**
  - a change in plans or the discovery of a major problem won't derail a theatre person. Every day, every moment in theatre is all about adapting to changes and pressures in the workplace. That's what we do. We anticipate and identify problems, and then solve them together.

People with theatre training know how to take initiative, and understand how we fit into the successful completion of the project. We are trained to give and receive feedback respectfully with peers and superiors, and incorporate that feedback into our process and product. We learn from our mistakes as well as our successes. With theatre training comes an ability to work under pressure and a respect for rules, the chain of command, and above all else, deadlines. What employer wouldn't want an employee with all those characteristics? When applying for a job outside the theatre, make a connection between your experience and the characteristics needed in the job you are applying for.

Finding Job Openings

There are formal and informal ways to find out about job openings. By far you will find most of your jobs by word of mouth. There is a saying used in pretty much every industry: "Who you know will get you the job, what you know will let you keep it." The bigger your network of people who like to work with you, the better. Networking is one of the most important things you can do to keep yourself working. Don't miss that section at the end of this chapter.

For those just starting out who don't have a network to lean on, there are several free options to search out potential employment. OffStageJobs.com is a very popular website among both employers and job seekers.[36] Employers post open positions which, using detailed search features, can be filtered by location, job type, and several other characteristics. All job listings "are required to include the numeric pay rate, starting pay rate, or potential pay rate range of the job, or state that there is no pay."[37] Patrick Hudson,

---

[36]Figure 53 (the maker of QLab, Go Button, and other products) is the exclusive sponsor of OffStageJobs.com and presumably what makes the system free for all users.

[37]Additional information regarding pay rate posting for union jobs can be found at www. OffStageJobs.com.

the creator of OffStageJobs.com, explains that he wants to make sure that employers are not adjusting pay rates based on biases, and the "post-the-pay" rule allows people to know if they can even afford to apply for the job.[38]

Social media networking groups abound in every aspect of theatre production, and jobs are often posted in these groups.[39] Professional organizations like USITT, the Stage Managers Association, and the Costume Society of America all maintain jobs pages, so be sure to join those most relevant to your area. With the exception of upper-level corporate entertainment and non-profit executives, the industry professionals I have interviewed indicate that LinkedIn has not yielded any significant job opportunities. If there is a specific company you want to work for, regularly check its website and follow its specific social media accounts for updates and leads.

Figuring Out What You Need and What You Want

The first step in figuring out what you need and if you can afford what you want is analyzing how much it costs to maintain your current lifestyle. This is something people tend to avoid, because we all know we are spending money on a lot of things that we want but don't necessarily need. Coming to terms with this fact is uncomfortable. Using money and resources effectively requires discipline. That discipline becomes much easier when you have clear and specific goals, and incentives for meeting them. You can download worksheets from the companion website that will help you lay out and compile the information you need to gather next.

Go through your bank accounts, credit card statements, and receipts to review your spending over the last several months or year. Include expenses that may be paid by someone else at this time but for which you are going to have to take responsibility in the future, so you have a clear picture of what it

---

[38]Patrick Hudson, "A new option for our 'Post-the-Pay' rule," January 5, 2019, http://topofshow.com/.

[39]Examples of some of these specialty groups as of 2019 include Costume People (6K members), Lighting Designers (34K members), Everything Stage Lighting (55K members), Scenic Artists, Fabricators, Set Designers (6K members), and Stage Managers (6K members).

will cost to support yourself on your own. At a minimum, find the monthly average for the following expenses that apply to you:

- suitable housing in appropriate location (including home or renters' insurance)
- commuting and transportation (car payments, insurance, gasoline, parking, ride-shares, taxis, and/or public transit costs)
- groceries
- dining out/convenience food
- communication (including cell phone, internet, etc.)
- utilities (gas, water, electricity, etc.)
- business expenses (office space, office supplies, travel/transportation related to business, research, etc.)
- health insurance, prescriptions, and medical bills
- savings (emergency fund and retirement)
- clothing
- student loan repayment
- credit card or other debt payment not already accounted for, etc.
- city/state/federal taxes
- other lifestyle expenses like pets, charitable donations, entertainment, coffee, gifts, travel, gym membership, sporting events, etc.—these will be specific to you and your priorities.

Remember to divide annual expenses by twelve to get the monthly expense. For example, not many people buy clothing every month, so it makes sense to figure out how much you spend annually and then divide it by twelve months.

Once you have your totals you should probably add 10–15 percent contingency for all the things you forgot to calculate and any unexpected expenditures. That will give you a better idea of what it costs to support yourself each month if you want to continue your current lifestyle. That doesn't mean this total is your goal; this is your survival budget. And if you are working freelance, remember that you may not have work every week and you have to plan for downtime, so you need to make even more during the weeks you are working.

When you are considering a move to another city you should repeat this exercise. Because you don't know what it will cost to live in the new city you need to do research online to figure it out. You can find cost-of-living calculators which give you an idea, but it won't be as detailed as completing the full checklist shown above specifically to your needs. If you know someone who lives in the area, they can be a great resource for you. This is an exercise you need to do *before* accepting a job; in fact, it would be good for you to do it before being offered a job. That way when you go into negotiations you know what is a living wage and what isn't.

Relocating to a new city is more than just an economic or career decision, it is also a lifestyle choice. I recommend creating a "what I want" spreadsheet to help you organize information important to you and your ideal location. Once completed, you'll have a simple chart where you can fill in the details and characteristics of the city you are considering so you can evaluate how closely the location matches your ideal. You aren't going to find a place that checks all your boxes, but this helps you decide what your priorities are. You can find a worksheet on the companion website to help you organize this information:

- small, medium, or large city
- transportation options
- airport hub proximity
- demographics
- local culture and activities
- proximity to family and friends
- political climate locally and statewide
- weather
- social activities
- apartment living versus house
- renting versus owning
- theatre and arts scene
- shopping options and convenience
- your personal and professional networks
- vibe of the city or neighborhood
- school quality
- sports teams
- religious community
- healthcare needs
- childcare options
- outdoor activities
- other lifestyle characteristics that are important to you.

You should complete both the financial needs chart and this lifestyle audit for every city you are considering moving to, especially if you are anticipating that the move will be long term. This will allow you to prioritize your needs and wants and help you make informed decisions as you plan and prepare.

Don't overlook how expensive moving can be. Not preparing for these expenses could start you off with a lot more debt than you have planned. There is a planning worksheet on the companion website to guide you in compiling all the potential expenses, including:

- moving truck (including extra equipment like dolly or car trailer, gas, tolls, etc.)
- packing materials: boxes, tape, padding
- hotel during move (if drive is more than one day)
- food during move and early set-up
- furniture (even secondhand furniture comes with a cost)
- utility hook-up fees: electricity, gas, water, internet
- cleaning old and/or new place
- first/last month's rent and/or security deposit on new home
- food and drinks for any friends helping you
- start-up groceries—it is expensive stocking a kitchen from scratch
- start-up household supplies (laundry soap, lightbulbs, cleaning supplies, toilet paper, etc.)
- setting up/decorating new place (shower curtain, blinds, towels, lamps, etc.)
- money spent settling in (unexpected expenses that just have to happen)
- contingency for other unexpected expenses.

Once you have completed the moving expenses worksheet, you may discover that the high cost means you need to make some different decisions regarding your upcoming move. And that's OK. Perhaps you schedule your move so you can do your own cleaning as you leave the old location and arrive at the new one, so you can avoid the expense of hiring someone. Perhaps you decide to pack food for your trip rather than stopping for fast food along the way. There are lots of compromises you can make if you take the time to plan ahead.

Gathering this information is a big task; one that I see people dreading and avoiding. However, I also observe that having this information gathered and done helps reduce anxiety for those who were overwhelmed by it. If you can get over the hurdle of starting, you will find these documents very helpful as you make financial and lifestyle decisions for yourself. You will no longer be operating in the realm of the unknown, and will feel empowered to make decisions that once felt impossible.

Long-Term Planning

"How am I supposed to make a five-year plan when I don't even know what job I'm going to be doing next month?" This is a reasonable question that I'm often asked when I talk about the benefits of a five-year plan. Thinking about where you are going to be in five or ten years is intimidating, and yet this critical planning exercise can help you make the decisions that will propel you toward what you want most. Having and using a five-year plan to make decisions keeps your priorities in the front of your mind and guides you to more strategic decision-making.

I advocate a systematic approach if you are to create a holistic plan that isn't just about a single aspect of your life. Start by imagining what you want for yourself. If you have a partner, you will need to discuss your mutual goals as well. This should be a "blue-sky" exercise. Blue-sky thinking doesn't set limits based on practicality or reality; it demands that you don't discount any idea just because it doesn't seem possible. Also take time to think about and note what makes you feel most accomplished and motivated. As you review these notes, think about ways you could represent these goals and feelings visually.

Researchers have shown that visualizing the hard work required to achieve a goal can lead to positive outcomes. Don't just visualize the completed goal; the effort is key. For example, in one study with students preparing for an exam, those who visualized themselves acing their exam didn't study as much and therefore didn't perform as well as those who visualized their process of studying. Those who envisioned themselves studying as a means of success actually studied more and received higher grades on their exam.[40]

An easy and effective way to keep your goals in front of you is to create a visual reminder—a vision board—and place it where you will see it regularly. If implemented correctly, this can help keep you on track toward achieving your goals. Keeping your literal sights on your goals and envisioning yourself making the decisions you need to accomplish them makes you more likely to take the steps that will help you to reach those goals. It is about action and decision-making, not wishing and dreaming.

---

[40]L. B. Pham and S. E. Taylor, "From Thought to Action: Effects of Process-Versus Outcome-Based Mental Simulations on Performance," *Personality and Social Psychology Bulletin*, 25(2) (1999), 250–60, https://doi.org/10. 1177/0146167299025002010.

While the focus of this book is your career, when making a plan like this you need to be holistic. Our industry has an extreme problem with work–life balance and the expectation that we will devote our entire lives "to the show." Balance is not static. There will be busy periods when you may lean into work, but balance means that you also have times when you lean over to your non-work side to refresh and refuel. If you just plan for your career and not for your entire life, you are much more likely to end up looking back on your path with regret.

There's no one way to make your vision board. It can be digital or paper, "artsy" or straightforward. Your vision board is not an inspiration board. It is not about making yourself feel good. It is a tool to remind you every day to make decisions and take actions that will move you closer to the outcomes you want. Some sort of organization is important: if you have multiple travel destinations, group those together; if you have items related to finances and your career, group those together; and group things related to friends and family together as well. Avoid the urge to include inspirational sayings, labels, or other written elements that will clutter up your board. The images or objects you select should be enough for you to recognize what they represent. Examples can be seen in Plates 1–3, and you can view them in more detail on the companion website.

It's also important to recognize that your goals may change, and you can change the images you have gathered on your board at any time if they no longer represent what you are working toward. If and when you do, be sure to follow through the rest of the process of planning for that goal as well.

Once you've laid out your vision for yourself, you need to set measurable goals, establish an action plan, and give yourself a timeline. Each vision you have for your future will be achieved by accomplishing a bunch of smaller goals. If you don't identify the steps you need to take to reach your goal, then what you really have is just a dream. On the companion website you will find a goals and actions planning sheet to help you get started on this process. This worksheet has space for you to identify each goal at the top and then list the action items you need to accomplish along the way, with a place to give yourself a deadline. Think of it as a to-do list. The things on the list should be things you literally have to do. For example, if you have a five-year goal of making and maintaining swimming as a major component of your exercise plan and you don't yet know how to swim, your goals and actions may look something like those shown in Table 1.

Table 1 Example of effective planning to meet five-year health goal

Five-year health goal: Make and maintain swimming as a major component of my weekly physical activity

Actions steps to achieve goal		Complete by
1.	Mentally commit to learning to swim	May 15, 2022
2.	Buy a swimsuit and other needed items	June 1, 2022
3.	Research where I can take swimming lessons and swim regularly	June 1, 2022
4.	Find a swim instructor and calculate cost	June 15, 2022
5.	Figure out plan to earn extra money or save money to pay swim instructor	July 1, 2022
6.	Schedule a once-a-week swim lesson and don't cancel!	August 1, 2022
7.	Finish swim lessons!	January 1, 2023
8.	Add one additional day of swimming per week every month up to five days a week after completion of swim lessons, and maintain five day a week swim schedule into the future	July 1, 2023

The most difficult aspect for many people seems to be breaking their visions down into specific, attainable goals and listing the actual step-by-step process necessary for meeting each goal. Look at the difference between the examples in Tables 2 and 3 below.

Even though the second plan doesn't quite reach the goal at the five-year mark as written out, which of these plans do you think is going to be more effective? Financial stability might be the overarching goal illustrated on your vision board, but to achieve it you will probably need several simultaneous, specific, actionable goals. In addition to saving, you may also have a goal to earn more money and a step-by-step plan to make that happen. You may have a goal to learn about investing, with a completely separate action plan. As you accomplish those goals, you get closer and closer to your vision board goal of financial stability. Each time you review and revise your five-year plan and accomplish some of your goals, you can adjust your targets higher and higher.

Make sure your goal is specific and attainable, and make sure your action steps create a step-by-step to-do list. Tables 4 and 5 illustrate another goal that I often see on planning sheets, and ineffective and more effective ways to accomplish it.

Table 2 Example of ineffective planning to meet five-year financial goal

Five-year financial goal: Financial stability	
Actions steps to achieve goal	Complete by
1. Get a good job	February 2021
2. Save up money	Ongoing
3. Invest money	When I have enough
4. Get a raise	Ongoing

Table 3 Example of effective planning to meet five-year financial goal

Five-year financial goal: To have an emergency fund of at least $7,500[41]	
Actions steps to achieve goal	Complete by
1. Open savings account with $1,000 from graduation gifts	May 2020
2. Set up an automatic transfer of $20 a week, and then pretend all the money in this account doesn't exist	June 2020
3. Balance of $2,140 Increase transfer to $25 a week Deposit additional $100 of freelance money	June 2021
4. Balance of at least $3,340 Deposit additional $100 of freelance money	June 2022
5. Balance of at least $4,740 Deposit additional $100 of freelance money	June 2023
6. Balance of at least $6,040 Deposit additional $100 of freelance money	June 2024
7. Balance of at least $7,340 Deposit additional $100 of freelance money	June 2025

[41] Adapted from Johan Gallardo's action plan, April 2019.

Table 4 Example of ineffective planning to meet five-year personal goal

Five-year personal goal: Find someone to marry	
Actions steps to achieve goal	Complete by
1. Think about the kind of person I am interested in.	Now
2. Make time to go places.	Ongoing
3. Hang out at fun places.	Ongoing
4. Go on a bunch of dates.	Ongoing
5. Do fun things.	Ongoing

Table 5 Example of effective planning to meet five-year personal goal

Five-year personal goal: Find someone to marry	
Actions steps to achieve goal	Complete by
1. Talk with friends about the type of person I'm looking for and ask if they know anyone.	Three months from now: March 2022
2. Go on dates with anyone my friends set me up with. If I click with someone, continue to date them. If not, go to step 3.	Three months from now: March 2022
3. Look at the various dating websites, decide which one to join first, and join additional sites as needed.	Join first one by June 2022
4. Go on at least three dates a month for the next year (unless I find the one).	June 2023
5. Research meetup groups, book clubs, etc. and go to at least two activities a month. Continue to go on dates from online dating as applicable.	June 2023
6. Hope and pray that I've met someone by this time!	June 2024
7. Continue to date and hope they are the marrying kind.	June 2027

If your steps are not actually action items, you can't put them on your to-do list in any meaningful way. You also can't cross them off if it is unclear whether you have accomplished them or not. Table 6 shows how you could express an overall professional goal on a vision board, and how you think you might achieve it.

This might be OK as your first draft, moving from an image on your vision board into a written plan, but there are no details here that will help you make your vision a reality. Each of the items in Table 6 should have its own list of action items, as shown in Tables 7–10.

Table 6 Vision board goal

Be an ASM on Broadway	
Actions steps to achieve goal	Complete by
1. Get a job that will count as my internship.	Now
2. Graduate.	Next year
3. Move to NYC.	As soon as I graduate
4. Network intensely to start getting jobs so I can move up to PA and eventually ASM.	Ongoing

Table 7 Get internship: action items

Short-term goal: get job for internship requirement	
Actions steps to achieve goal	Complete by
1. Refine resume and be sure it is completely up to date.	February 1, 2022
2. Draft basic cover letter.	February 1, 2022
3. Spend at least an hour a week looking for job openings online.	April 15, 2022
4. When I find jobs to apply for, customize resume and cover letter for each application.	Weekly by Sunday
5. Try to apply for at least three jobs a week.	Weekly by Sunday
6. Update answers to possible interview questions.	April 15, 2022
7. Make list of questions to ask interviewers.	April 15, 2022
8. Do interviews as scheduled.	
9. When offered a job, negotiate	Must have job by May 15, 2022 for it to count as internship

Table 8 Graduate: action items

Short-term goal: graduate	
Actions steps to achieve goal	Complete by
1. Complete internship.	August 15, 2022
2. Stage manage the large musical at school.	November 22, 2022
3. Do independent study in calling from a score.	End of fall semester
4. Submit application to graduate.	End of fall semester
5. Get tickets for graduation.	End of fall semester
6. Pass all my classes.	End of spring semester

Table 9 Move to New York: action items

Short-term goal: move to NYC	
Actions steps to achieve goal	Complete by
1. Do needs chart for NYC to estimate my budget.	December 1, 2021
2. Calculate moving expenses.	February 1, 2022
3. Research neighborhoods—talk to friends who are already in the city.	March 1, 2022
4. Figure out how to look for a sublet and decide which one to take.	May 1, 2022
5. Buy my plane ticket and arrange ground transportation.	May 1, 2022
6. Sell my car by listing it online and putting up flyers at school.	May 15, 2022
7. Pack my bag and leave!	June 4, 2022

It will take multiple short-term goals to achieve the vision of your future and the long-term goals you set for yourself in your five-year plan. For each short-term goal, you should be able to answer the who, what, when, why, and how, and in addition know how often, with whom, and how long it is going to take you.

Table 10 Professional networking: action items

Short-term goal: professional networking to become PA/ASM	
Actions steps to achieve goal	Complete by
1. Begin to reach out to all the NYC alums from my program on social media and set up meetings with as many as possible to network and get advice.	Post by March 30, 2022 Complete by May 1, 2022
2. Ask for contacts and leads, and follow up all these the day after receiving them.	Daily
3. Post in alumni group to ask if it is possible to shadow contacts in their jobs.	April 15, 2022
4. Get advice on a survival job while I'm looking for a theatre job.	May 1, 2022
5. Search for, apply for, and find a survival job (note: this should have a to-do list all its own).	June 1, 2022 if possible. Might have to wait until I get to NYC
6. Continue to follow up with alums, friends, and those they referred me to as contacts.	Weekly
7. Keep in touch with anyone I work with to let them know when I am available.	Biweekly or monthly depending on the person

Once you have your goals for the basics—career, finances, personal goals, and location/relocation—you can begin to populate these into your larger five-year plan and put deadlines on each of the steps. You can have more than one goal for any area and can add any other categories that are important to you, like leisure, personal development, lifestyle, health/wellness, social/ relationships, pet ownership, travel, etc.

I have provided a five-year plan layout on the companion website, or you can find dozens online if this one doesn't work for you. The two things I think are important are a layout that gives you enough space to put in your action steps and not just your higher-level goals, and a spot to include your "what if" plan. This is where you put options when you reach a fork in the road. What if, despite your best effort, you don't get that job, or meet that person? You should consider what your best alternative to the perfect scenario might be, and have a plan for that as well.

This process deserves the time it takes to do it well. It will end up being a lengthy document. Also understand that these are your goals and plans now, but you may not follow the plan you've laid out exactly. At any point you could decide that you have a different plan, or life could change drastically and require your plan to change, potentially forever. Don't let the unknowns of the future prevent you from envisioning your future now.

Once you have your plan laid out, start to schedule things into your calendar to make the plan even more real. You should revisit your vision board, planning worksheets, and five-year plan whenever necessary, but at least every year. Upon review you can revise your goals and action steps and extend the plan for another year. You may find that some goals you had thought would take multiple years have been completed more quickly, and it is time to shift your target higher or to something else. This is a living document that allows you both to dream and to plan.

Networking and Mentors

Every person I've interviewed confirms that most of the job opportunities they get in their established careers come from people they know and word of mouth. Kelsey Vivian, an AEA (Actors' Equity Asociation) stage manager, reflects, "I'd wager more than 75 percent of the jobs I've had were by word of mouth. In the past six years I only applied to two of the jobs I worked. I still had to interview for most of the shows I ended up working, even if recommended."[42] Allison Dillard, a freelance costume designer based in Los Angeles, echoes this sentiment: "Mostly word of mouth. I don't send resumes out very often now, but I did right after school for about a year. Then people began to recommend me and now I turn down lots of jobs each year because I'm booked up."[43]

You have probably heard the adage "It's not *what* you know, it's *who* you know that matters." The updated version is "It's not who you know that matters, it's who knows you." There are many ways to maintain your network to ensure that people continue to know you and what you are up to. Having dedicated social media pages is one way to tell people about your latest work. I have a few former colleagues who send out email updates once or twice a year. A website is another great way to keep people up to date with your work, but it only works if people are going to your website regularly, so you have to put in some effort to remind people it is there.

---

[42]Vivian, note 23.
[43]Allison Dillard, personal communication with the author, November 8, 2019.

Cultivating a network takes time and effort. You want people you've worked with and who support your work to be thinking about you. "Stay in touch with your friends. Tell everyone you are looking for work and what kind" is the advice offered by Roger Rosvold, who has worked as a technical director and IATSE[44] stagehand and is currently a house technician/carpenter, as a means of maintaining your network.[45]

To be done well, networking of some sort should be built into your daily or weekly schedule, whether it is updating your website, sending a text message to someone you worked with a while ago to see what they are up to, sending an email update to former teachers and co-workers, or reaching out to the artistic director at a theatre you work at regularly to ask if they have any openings or contacts you could approach for work. As faculty members we often get asked if there is an alum we could recommend for a gig. I've had literally thousands of students in my twenty-year-plus teaching career, but if I have recently received a communication from you updating me on what you are doing and your availability, chances are you will be the one I think of first.

When someone in your network does something nice for you, whether it is giving you advice, recommending you for a job, or reviewing your resume, be sure to thank them and follow up to let them know how what they did impacted you. If it was a gig they got you, thank them right away. When you finish the gig that's another great opportunity to thank them again and tell them about your experience. Give them credit for the experience, the new connections, or the positive feedback you are getting because of their advice or recommendation. Offer to return the favor, and let them know if your schedule is open again in case they come across anything else that might be good for you. As much as possible you also want to share opportunities with those in your network, and you will find they are more likely to do the same for you.

It is best to develop your contacts before you need them. While you have work you should be making connections, so the only time people hear from you isn't when you are looking for a job.

Lily Novak is a props assistant working at Tyler Perry Studios in Atlanta. When she is between gigs she reaches out to her network—prop masters and

---

[44]The International Alliance of Theatrical Stage Employees, Moving Picture Technicians, Artists and Allied Crafts of the United States, Its Territories and Canada is a labor union representing technicians, artisans, and craftpersons in the entertainment industry.

[45]Roger Rosvold, personal communication with the author, March 6, 2020.

assistant prop masters she has worked for in the past—to let them know she is available, and she usually ends up working a day on this production and another day on a different one until her next full-time gig starts up. "I have never had to call people I didn't know, but I have been contacted for work by people I didn't know because other prop people recommended me. If I get contacted for work but am already busy on a show, I decline but pass on another prop person's contact information."[46]

The practice of passing on jobs to other people you know is one of the most powerful ways to strengthen the value of your network. While it might seem counterintuitive to give jobs away to your "competitors," someone needs to do the work if you aren't available, and if you pass along other people's names they will know and be more likely to do the same for you. Keep in mind that they will only recommend you if they are confident in the quality of your work and your work ethic, because how you do on that gig will reflect directly on them and their reputation, so one of the ways you keep your network strong is to always do your job well.

People you go to school with are going to be people helping you get work later. Be mindful of how you treat people. How you communicate, how you handle stress, and how you fix your screw-ups are all important ways to maintain positive professional contacts. No one expects perfection, but you should accept responsibility for your mistakes and make sure you don't make the same mistake twice. Nurturing a network that grew naturally from fellow students and faculty members at school, along with the production teams you work with as you are developing your career, is important. Sabrina Wertman has worked in many facets of the entertainment industry as a lighting technician, and says her network is healthy and vast because she follows this advice: "Be friendly to everyone, work hard, check in with folks from time to time, and visit people if you're traveling in their location."[47]

Strategically and intentionally grow your network in the direction that you want your career to go.

As Lily Novak was going through school she always said her dream job was to work on props for *The Walking Dead*. Prior to graduating she contacted the head of the show's props department for an informational

---

[46]Lily Novak, personal communication with the author, December 10, 2019.
[47]Sabrina Wertman, personal communication with the author, November 4, 2019.

interview, to find out what it would take for her to get a job on the show, and get general advice about breaking into the industry. Next thing she knew, she was on set shadowing the props department, and upon graduation she was hired as a props department production assistant on *The Walking Dead*. Even if her networking had not led directly to a job, she still would have gained valuable insights about the industry and a terrific network connection that she could continue to check back in with as she developed her career.

Lily engaged in intentional network building by requesting an informational interview. Most people like to talk about themselves and how they got where they are, and if you hit it off they often end up willing to remain in touch and continue to offer you advice throughout your career. Obviously emailing someone out of the blue whom you don't know and who doesn't know you is not a very likely way to get a job, but it is a good way to get information and make a connection that can lead to great things down the road.

Grace Trimble is a freelance stitcher and Broadway dresser in New York City. The summer after she completed her MFA she worked at the Santa Fe Opera. She wasn't very clear what her plan was beyond that, so when her former roommate suggested they move to New York together she decided to give it a try. She shared her new plan with her co-workers at the Opera, and they promised to keep their ears open for any jobs that might come up. She completed her contract and got on a plane to New York City not knowing what she was going to do once she arrived. When her plane landed she had a voice mail from someone she didn't know offering her her first professional gig in New York. One of those connections in Santa Fe followed through and recommended her for a job that started the next day![48] Never underestimate the power of your network.

Another way to engage in intentional network building is by attending professional meetings, conferences, and trade shows.[49] "Go to conferences," says Chip Perry, director of lighting and television production at World Wrestling Entertainment. "You can maintain a relationship pretty well

---

[48]Grace Trimble, personal communication with the author, November 6, 2019.
[49]Some of the better-known and larger conferences in the US include IAAPA (International Association of Amusement Parks and Attractions), LDI (Live Design International), LightFair (architectural and commercial lighting), Info COMM (Audiovisual and Integrated Experience), USITT (United States Institute for Theatre Technology), and SETC (South Eastern Theatre Conference), among many others.

virtually and with phone calls, but it is next to impossible to start a professional relationship virtually."[50] Whether you want to meet one of the keynote speakers or are looking to connect with other people in your specialty, these are great places to expand your network. In between talks, at receptions, and on the show floor are all effective places to introduce yourself to people. If the thought of walking up to someone, introducing yourself, and striking up a conversation sounds awful to you, then a conference or trade show is the perfect place for you to practice. One of my favorite ideas comes from Margaret Peot, a costume painter and dyer for Broadway at Parsons-Meares, Ltd. She suggests that you turn networking at conferences into a game, especially if you have a friend you can play with.[51] Have a contest for who can get the most business cards, and the loser takes the winner out to dinner. Even though it is a game, remain professional and have legitimate conversations with all your contacts, and your ulterior motive just might give you the confidence you thought you were lacking or, even better, get you a job.

These events often have a show floor where exhibitors of all kinds display new equipment and products. The people at the booths are specifically there to talk to visitors, and are certainly people you can welcome into your network, but the real value is in practicing your networking skills. Get comfortable with the approach and introduction, and fine-tune your "elevator pitch."

An elevator pitch is a short introduction about who you are and what you do. It gets its name because it should be short enough to give the key information in the amount of time it takes to ride an elevator a few floors. Your pitch will necessarily vary slightly depending on the exact situation, but in general an elevator pitch should go like this.

1. Introduce yourself.
2. Tell them what you do.
3. Mention your goals or aspirations.

Here are some examples.

My name is Darius. I'm going to work in New York as a sound designer, mixer, and technician after I graduate with my BFA next year.

---

[50]Perry, note 19.
[51]Margaret Peot, *The Successful Artist's Career Guide: Finding Your Way in the Business of Art* (Cincinnati, OH: North Light Books, 2012), 127.

I'm Rosibel, a costume technician working to transition from theatre into dance costuming, specifically ballet. Ultimately I plan to be a draper, and will likely go back to grad school for that.[52]

Hi! I'm Jazlynne. I'm a stage manager who remains open to all possibilities, which has led me to work on cruise ships, for the circus, and on large-scale private events. If it needs a stage manager, I'm ready to call the show![53]

I'm Joanie, a costumer for film and television. Maybe you saw my work in *Godzilla: King of Monsters*, *Spiderman: Homecoming*, or HBO's *Watchmen*. I'm currently working as a stitcher on an untitled feature film.[54]

My name is Enid, and I'm developing my career as a designer for the themed entertainment industry. I'm finishing up an internship with a local theme park right now, and it's time to figure out what my next step is going to be.[55]

I'm Alexis and I work in digital marketing, though my background is as a theatrical scenic artist. Whether I'm employed in theatre or marketing, my work is always about visual storytelling. I enjoy freelancing and love to hear about new projects.[56]

Creating your elevator pitch will help you feel more self-assured as you venture into networking situations like conferences and receptions. Use your elevator pitch to introduce yourself to others and strike up a conversation. Don't stick with one person for the whole event: remember that your goal is to meet as many people as possible. Keep your business cards in an easily accessible place and offer one as you are closing, with an invitation or request to keep in touch.

To build your network locally, attend industry events and, suggests Chicago-based freelance scenic designer Ryan Emens, go see shows and let the people whose work you admired know that you genuinely enjoyed it.[57] Seek out networking organizations and events in your area, and invite your friends to come along. "Invite co-workers to coffee. Ask friends to introduce you to people in the industry and do the same for them. Go to opening night parties."[58] These are some of the tips that Kelsey Vivian, New York-based AEA stage manager, offers to keep you permanently in the mindset of

---

[52] Adapted from Rosibel Hernandez's elevator pitch, January 30, 2019.
[53] Adapted from Jazlynne Williams's elevator pitch, January 30, 2019.
[54] Joanie Ming, personal communication with the author, August 17, 2020.
[55] Adapted from Enid Montalvo's elevator pitch, January 30, 2019.
[56] Alexis Castellanos (adapted), personal communication with the author, November 6, 2019.
[57] Ryan Emens, personal communication with the author, November 5, 2019.
[58] Vivian, note 23.

networking. If you have contacts out of town, always be sure that you take the opportunity to reconnect if you are visiting their city. Even if you aren't able to meet in person, just reaching out helps to strengthen the connection.

If you are a student and have a guest speaker in one of your classes, you have a prime opportunity to add this person to your network. Try to introduce yourself before they leave and be sure to send a follow-up thank you note; mention what you especially appreciated learning from their presentation. The trick is continuing to follow up or check in periodically. Perhaps you ask for advice, or wonder if they might review your resume and give you feedback. Contacts don't become part of your network until you establish them as relationships, so find opportunities for meaningful connection. Caleb Howell, a full-time dresser on Broadway and a member of Lynne Mackey's millinery studio, credits the connections he began making while in college with getting him to this point in his career: "I never would be where I am without having made the connections I did. I worked every day on networking when I was in school and I continue to do so now."[59]

If you are lucky, someone who becomes part of your network will become a mentor. A mentor is like a guide or a coach. They are typically someone with more experience than you who has a positive reputation in the field. Your mentor should be sincerely interested in, and not feel threatened by, your success. Brad Berridge, director of sound operations for Feld Entertainment, reflects on his mentors: "I have had a few experiences with mentors who were kind and willing to help me when they had nothing to gain. Not only did they help me through the specific professional issue I was having, but they were also great role models."[60] Greg Williams is a regional rigging manager for PSAV, and says, "The best mentors are the ones who can relate to you where you are and then show you the path to get better."[61] A mentor can help you in a variety of ways—with goal setting, developing your five-year plan, offering you the benefit of their experience, passing along best practices, and helping you avoid the mistakes they made. A good mentor should challenge you to move out of your comfort zone, offer ideas on how you can get where you want to go, and provide you with opportunities either by connecting you with members of their own network or by forwarding you job opportunities as they arise. "I had a mentor who would yell at me to leave the tech table during breaks," AEA stage manager Kelsey Vivian recalled.

---

[59]Howell, note 29.
[60]Brad Berridge, personal communication with the author, October 30, 2019.
[61]Greg Williams, personal communication with the author, November 6, 2019.

"While I didn't appreciate it at the time, he eventually got me to see that it was necessary to take a break and leave the room. That was an important lesson."[62] Jodi Ozimek, a high school family and consumer sciences teacher with degrees in theatre costuming, recalls, "I can't imagine my career and especially my first teaching job without my mentor Gretel Geist. She created so many opportunities for me and really set me up for success."[63]

As a mentee you must be ready to receive honest feedback. A good mentor isn't just going to tell you what you want to hear, they are going to tell you the truth. So the person who becomes your mentor needs to be someone you trust completely. You have asked this person for their opinion, so for the relationship to continue to be productive you have to be open to giving it a try.

Mentoring relationships are generally long term and can evolve naturally as unspoken relationships, as may happen with a favored professor or supervisor, or they can be intentionally formed. If you decide that you want to ask someone formally I suggest you start with an informational interview. By coming prepared and asking intelligent questions, you will present yourself to the potential mentor as serious about your career. After the interview, follow up. If you think it went well and can see yourself benefiting from additional meetings, ask if you can meet again sometime in a few weeks. If you meet again and decide to ask formally if they will be a mentor, be sure you are clear yourself about exactly what it is you are asking of the person. How often are you hoping to communicate? Are you looking for general advice, or do you need help with something specific? Your request could go something like this.

> I have really appreciated your advice at our last couple of meetings, and I wonder if you would be willing to mentor me as I …
> … work through this upcoming job transition.
> … figure out where I fit in this industry.
> … apply for my first jobs.
> … figure out how to build my network.
> … make a career change.

Don't be disheartened if the person says no. On parting you can ask if you can send the person updates every once in a while, and then be sure to do so.

---

[62]Vivian, note 23.
[63]Ozimek, note 2.

Perhaps this isn't the right moment, but over time a mentoring relationship may develop. Kristi Ross-Clausen wears many hats, including vice president of IATSE Local 470, for which she manages apprentice training and coordinates ongoing educational opportunities. She says, "There are a lot of people in the industry who are eager to talk about what we do and encourage others."[64] So go on seeking out others, formally or informally, as you continue to find your way.

---

[64]Kristi Ross-Clausen, personal communication with the author, November 2, 2019.

2

Creating Your Marketing Materials and Establishing Your Professional Persona

Thinking like a business and presenting yourself like a business means creating marketing materials to represent your brand, including a professional email account, resume, letterhead, website, business cards, etc. You work in an artistic field, so everything you present demonstrates your aesthetic and attention to detail.

Professional Email

If you are still using a school email address or an account you created when you were a teenager, it is likely time for a new email address that represents you as a professional. In an ideal world you will have an email account ending in a personal domain name that follows the general conventions outlined below. Mine, for example, is kristina@tollefsondesigns.com. It matches my website, which is www.tollefsondesigns.com. While this sort of alignment is professional and ideal, you may not be able to make that move yet, and that's OK. Using one of the free email options available to you, like Gmail, Outlook, iCloud, or dozens of others, is just fine. These services typically have a paid business version that allows you to personalize your domain name, so when you are ready to take that step you could do so and still use a platform with which you are familiar.

Your professional email address should include your name. Be very thoughtful about what you choose, because once you establish it, it is best to stick with it long term. Depending on how common your name is, it may take a bit of effort if you are using one of the free email platforms, but with some creative thinking you can find an address that will work for you even on the most popular services. If you struggle to find an available address with your name, or you simply prefer to have something additional as a signifier, you can add a word related to your line of work, though don't make your address too long. Some options include SM, LD, TD, Creates, Lighting, Lights, Sound, Design, Designs, Costumes, Tech, Theatre (though keep in mind the necessity of always having to clarify the spelling in considering whether "theatre" is your best choice), Scenery, etc. So a sound designer named Susan Haney could consider various permutations in creating a professional email address: SHaney@, SusanH@, SusanHaney@, HaneyS@, HaneySusan@, SoundSusan@, SusanSound@, HaneySound@, SHaneySound@, HaneySounds@, HaneyAudio@, AudioSusan@, SHSound@, SHAudio@, HaneyDesign@, SHaneyDesign@, HaneyCreates@, ContactHaney@, SusanContact@ etc. The options are nearly endless when you consider nicknames or middle initials as well. Do not resort to adding a number just to find something that works. Remember you are setting up your professional persona, and SHaney1987@ just doesn't look professional. You may have to try many versions, but I promise there is one out there that will be perfect for you without adding a random number.

Don't choose something so specific that it can't serve you for years into the future. You may think your career will go in a certain direction only to decide later to shift focus (for example, one of my former stage manager students is now a costume technician, and a theatrical scenic designer now does props in film), or you may end up working in several aspects of theatre. For example, if you work as a technical director and as a scenic designer, SHaneyDesigns@ may be too specific and SHaneyScenery@ provides more flexibility.

Choosing a Typeface and Fonts

After your email address, your marketing materials (resume, cover letter, website, business cards, etc.) are what give a first impression of you to hiring officials, so it is very important that they communicate the message you want them to. Choosing the right typeface and fonts (hereafter just referred to as fonts for simplicity, though technically the terms are not interchangeable) can take some time, so be patient in your search. Consider consulting people who know you professionally with the options you come up with to get their feedback. Fonts have moods and personalities and, like the design aspects of a show, they use the elements of design to send a message to the viewer. Start by identifying a couple of guide words that you want your materials to communicate about you as a professional. Don't be seduced into selecting more than two words, or your search will become muddy. Here are some ideas to get you started.[1]

Analytical	Enthusiastic	Rebellious
Approachable	Formal	Reliable
Casual	Friendly	Sensitive
Confident	Kind	Sophisticated
Dependable	Lighthearted	Thoughtful
Direct	Organized	Traditional
Dramatic	Playful	Upbeat
Eclectic	Precise	

Do not constrain yourself to the fonts that came as a default on your computer—there are innumerable web pages of fonts to explore and download. Confirm that the fonts you choose are either rights-free, including commercial rights, or can be licensed for commercial use, since you will be using them for your business.

I suggest that you use two different fonts on your materials, with each font having its own job. You can also think about your fonts as Derek Halpern describes them.[2] He divides fonts into two categories: fancy and simple. The first category, often referred to as a *display font*, can have a bit more personality. Display fonts are typically intended to be set above 14-point size to grab the reader's attention, and you will use one for your name and possibly your job title/category. In some cases this font can also be used for section headings on your resume. A second font, the body font, should be more neutral and clearly legible when used at 14-point size and below (though you may choose to set it larger than that). This font will be used for most of the text. Some

---

[1] If you need additional inspiration, do a web search for "positive personality adjectives."
[2] Derek Halpern, https://socialtriggers.com/best-font-website/.

people have a third font for subheadings, but use this option wisely because too many font varieties can make your materials look muddy.

Take care that the two fonts you choose complement each other without matching. You want some contrast, but not so much that they conflict. Using one "fancy" font and one "simple" font helps you establish the right balance. Two "fancy" fonts will lead to visual confusion and lack of legibility; two "simple" fonts will make your materials bland and boring. Remember that most fonts have several weights (like thin, script, light, regular, medium, bold, heavy, and/or black) and several styles (like narrow, extended, oblique, and/or small caps), and those variations can be helpful in establishing contrasting font weights. You can search the web for "typeface classifications" if you would like to understand better how fonts are categorized, as there are several different categories.

The most important characteristic to pay attention to is serif versus sans-serif styles. Serif fonts have a little extra embellishment stroke at the end of the major strokes of most letters. Times New Roman is probably the most well-known serif font. Sans-serif fonts do not have this additional flourish. Arial is probably the most recognized sans-serif font. While you may receive the advice to combine a serif font and a sans-serif font, I find this often leads to disharmony and I recommend avoiding it. Douglass Bonneville has written an article giving additional help in understanding how fonts do or do not go together; it is more geared toward web design and publishing than marketing collateral, but the visual examples really give life to the concepts. You can see some examples of combinations, both good and bad, in Plate 21.

In addition to having the right emotional and artistic impact, make sure your fonts are legible at the point size you are using. Sometimes you find a great font, but the combination or order of letters in your name make it look odd or affects the kerning[3] in a way that makes the text hard to read. Because of variations in fonts and font sizes, there is no formula for what point size each item of your materials should be, and what you are creating will influence point size as well. Text on business cards will likely be smaller than that of your resume. My students tend toward fonts and point sizes that are way too small, especially for contact information. When establishing your designs, different point sizes help differentiate the job each font is doing. Your name should be the largest thing on the page, no matter if we are talking about your business card, resume, letterhead,

---

[3]Kerning is the space between letters in a font. It can be adjusted to create more attractive and/or readable text.

or website. Your job title should be next largest, with any headings slightly smaller than that—though adding in styles (for example, bold) can also help with this differentiation. Your contact information should not be any smaller than the point size you are using for the body of your document.

When you tire of looking at list after list of fonts and are starting to figure out what you like, I suggest you create a document with your name repeated down the page and then some sample body text repeated down the page. Then you can, on the same page, change each of your names to a different "fancy" font and evaluate them with the words you selected as your guiding concepts, then do the same for the body fonts you think you like. Eliminate fonts from these groups until you narrow them down to those you like best.

Marek Marquez

Marek Marquez

Marek Marquez

Marek Marquez

Marek Marquez

Marek Marquez

Marek Marquez

If you can't narrow it down to the two perfect fonts right away, that's OK. It can be a good idea for you to choose two or three display fonts and two or three body fonts, then evaluate these after placing them in your materials. Sometimes fonts seem perfect until you start to use them, and then you realize they aren't working the way you had hoped.

Choosing a Color Palette

Using color in your marketing materials helps with readability, as it guides your reader to the key information, looks nicer than plain black text, works to communicate personality and aesthetic, and helps your materials to be recognizable. A person who selects a bright blue is communicating something about themselves that is very different to what is communicated by someone who chooses a deep red. You may encounter people who do not like color on resumes, but you will find many, many more who appreciate it.

I see trends moving more and more towards color being not only accepted but expected. Having a signature color palette as part of your aesthetic carried through all your materials strengthens your overall package.

Many people use their favorite color as a starting point and explore from there. It is not a bad idea to do some research on the psychology of colors and what messages the color you choose may send. You can find lots of websites to help you create good color pairings through a quick internet search, but there are three sites I recommend. There are four great tools at canva.com/colors: a color palette generator that uses your uploaded photos, pre-made color palette ideas, an interactive color wheel, and a tool that provides color meanings and suggested combinations. If you want to explore options and see lots of different color palettes that you can customize and save, I have found nothing easier than coolors.co. Go through the fifteen-second tutorial and you will be ready to use the site. And finally, if you are looking for something fully customizable and very detailed, you will enjoy using paletton.com. I suggest starting by selecting adjacent, triad, or tetrad from the color scheme options just above the color wheel, and then adjusting the location of the dots in the color wheel until you stumble on something that works. There are many options for adjusting things in this tool if you click around. You can find links to all these tools on the companion website.

Your color palette should consist of a minimum of two colors: one for your display font and one for your body font. Most people use black for their body font, likely as a default, but you can explore using an alternative dark color like navy, brown, burgundy, teal, etc. Remember that the colors you use also need to go along with those professional persona keywords you decided on when we were discussing fonts in the previous section. And you need to focus on readability, so colors like baby pink and nearly every shade of yellow don't work well for any text. Some people choose to have a third accent color: this should be used sparingly, but can help draw attention to components of your marketing materials—perhaps contact information and/or headings. If a signature color for your display font and black for the body text is what works best, then use that. You should feel no pressure to make your palette more complex.

Logos

Your specific font choice and color palette will create a recognizable aesthetic all on their own, and the addition of a logo could just make things overly complex. However, some people do feel very drawn to incorporating a logo or some other type of artwork into their materials. Be judicious in doing so. It is important that it is original and not taken off someone's website. If it is not a royalty-free image it would be stealing just to take it and use it; also, if you found it and liked it, someone else could do the same. You are creating materials that are unique to you and represent you as an artist. Originality is important. If you do decide to create a logo, it should not be overly complicated or distracting, it should be small, and it should be a high-quality image so that it prints without pixelating and is scalable for multiple uses. Make sure it is relevant. Sierra Labrousse, a props designer and set decorator, explains: "I love flowers and was a florist by trade. But I am not going to use a flower logo on my props business cards. They have nothing to do with each other."[4]

Do not create your logo in your word processing program; instead, use graphics creation and editing software like Photoshop, GIMP, Procreate, or one of the many others. Be sure to incorporate your color palette, and that it matches the aesthetic you are working to establish. Stay away from cliché images for our industry, like comedy/tragedy masks, lighting instruments, headsets, needle and thread, etc.

Letterheads

While traditional letter writing has given way to email and texting, letter writing does still exist in business and you need something to go at the top of your resume. You must have a professional letterhead that coordinates with your entire marketing package. The letterhead is the easiest place to start sorting out your layout and proportions. Remember that the design you create will be on all your materials: letterhead, business card, website, resume, postcards, portfolio, thank-you cards—anything you create to represent you and your business. Here are some guidelines to get you started. Keep in mind that all of this should fit into about a 1.5–2-inch vertical space.

1. Your name (the one you want to be called) should be the biggest thing on the page. If you use your middle name or go by a nickname and would prefer people to call you by this, use that name on your

---

[4]Sierra Labrousse, USITT Women in Theatre Network Facebook group, September 4, 2019.

materials. It is best if this is the name you are already known by, so that when called for reference checks your references will know who they are talking about. You have no obligation to use your legal name on your job search materials—you can give your legal name for the official paperwork once you are hired. If you are in the middle of a name transition then be sure to let your references know, to avoid confusion.

2. What you do should be the next largest thing on the page. Deciding what to put here may take strategizing. I've worked with many students who see themselves heading into careers as scenic designers, technical directors, stage managers, etc., and want to claim that title on their materials. A glance at their resume shows they have never actually held those positions yet, or have only done so once or twice. You must make sure that your title matches not only your aspirations but also your experience. If you fall into this group, you might go with a job category instead of a job title. If you plan to work as both a designer and technician, using the category may also work for you. So instead of scenic designer you might use "scenery"; instead of "stage manager" you might use "stage management." Other categories could include lighting, costumes, technician, etc. You may eventually grow into the full title—the title you use now isn't necessarily the title you will use forever. And, in fact, you may use a different title depending on the job you are applying for. We discuss that more in the chapters on resumes and cover letters.

3. You should include your city and state, phone number, professional email address, and the URL to your website portfolio in a font size that does not draw attention but is large enough so no one will misread it or have to squint to see it. Keep in mind that not everyone will be able to read small print as easily as you do. Traditionally a letterhead would also include your snail mail address, but that is no longer required—current city and state will suffice.

4. Incorporate color to help you further your aesthetic.

5. Double and triple check to be sure that all information is accurate and correctly formatted.

   a. Phone numbers can have parentheses around the area code or a dash after the area code, but not both: (407) 555-5555 or 407-555-5555, *not* (407)-555-5555. It is also acceptable to use dots or periods: 407·555·5555 or 407.555.5555.

b. It is no longer necessary to include the "www." in front of your website URL. It isn't wrong to do so, but it is unnecessary since everyone will recognize mywebsite.com as your web address and name@myemail.com as your email address. Including the www adds visual clutter to URLs.

c. It is not necessary to indicate what your bits of contact information are by placing Cell:, Email:, or Web: in front of them. The only time this becomes necessary is if you are including more than one option (for example, including a work number in addition to your cell phone number). In that case you would want to specify the purpose of the additional contact information; otherwise, you are just adding visual clutter and slowing down the reader's ability to find the information they are looking for.

d. Your city name should be capitalized with a comma following it, and the caps two-letter state abbreviation with no additional punctuation, as if you were addressing a letter. For example: Brookings, SD.

Beyond those basic guidelines you have some flexibility. If you have no idea where to start, a quick internet search for "letterhead examples" will reveal an endless stream of inspiration. But be careful. You do not want to copy anyone else's letterhead, and you don't want to use a template you find online or in your word processing program. You want your materials to be original. I have been on the hiring side of things when two people turned in aesthetically identical materials they had gotten from a template. It reflected poorly on them, and made it more difficult to differentiate them.

There are innumerable layout options. The two most common layouts are your name over your job title left justified to the left margin and your contact information on several lines right justified to the right margin, or vice versa. The third most common layout is to have most if not all the information centered, or your name and job centered with some contact information left justified and some right justified on either side of the page. Contact information could also go at the bottom of the page. If you choose this option you need to be sure that it doesn't get lost and your reader can easily find it through font choice, font style, or color. While you are not limited to one of these three common options, I suggest you do a few of these layouts as part of your first few drafts before you try unconventional options. Create several draft possibilities so you can incorporate the fonts from the shortlist you narrowed down, different colors, and different layouts to figure out just which combination is right for you. It is wise to do each of these drafts on a full-size piece of paper rather than doing several on one page. You want to see how the proportions of your fonts and margins all work together, and you can't evaluate this if you try to cram several on one page.

After creating your drafts, this is a good time to consult with a mentor and other professionals in your field who know you well and whose aesthetics you trust. You need to know how other people will interpret what you are creating, and you want to make sure it is communicating what you think it is. Don't forget to keep your key traits in mind as you evaluate your options. It is unlikely that one of these first designs will be the one you go with exactly as is; it is likely that you will tweak colors, font sizes, margins, etc. several times before you settle on a design. Examples can be found on the sample resumes and cover letters shown in Plates 13–20, with additional examples on the companion website.

You can use these questions to evaluate your letterhead (in fact, you can use them to evaluate all the materials you create for your personal marketing).

1. Is the text an ideal size for the space, and is it legible?
2. Do the font styles capture my ideal persona?
3. Is the use of fonts consistent and appropriate?
4. Is the layout balanced, and does it lead the eye to the important information?
5. Are the spacing and margins appropriate and balanced?
6. Is the quality of both the print and the graphic elements crystal clear?
7. Have I checked for and corrected any spelling, punctuation, or grammatical errors?
8. Does the color choice enhance the appearance?
9. Is color appropriately and effectively incorporated?
10. Once you have developed more of your materials (resume, website, etc.), you should also ask yourself if these are clearly aesthetically connected to your other personalized marketing materials.

When you can answer yes to all of these questions, you likely have a strong letterhead design that will help guide you in the creation of the rest of your materials.

Business Cards

Business cards have standard sizes and layouts. Horizontal (known as "landscape") cards measuring 3.5 inches × 2 inches are expected by people in the US. It makes it easier for the receiver to use and store a card, and for those very simple reasons I encourage you to follow the standard. Some of the non-standard things I discourage include vertical layouts (known as "portrait") and different dimensions like credit card size (3.375 inches × 2.125 inches), square (2.5 inches × 2.5 inches), or UK size (85 mm × 55 mm). Oddly sized or shaped cards may grab attention, but they also have a higher likelihood of being thrown away because they don't fit into wallets and can't be easily carried together with other business cards.

Your business card must have the same aesthetics and information as your letterhead. Remember you are establishing your visual brand with a consistent look across all your materials, so that when a person sees something of yours they know it is connected to you. Sierra Labrousse explains, "A business card is like an art composition. You have to think about weight and fonts and how it's aligned."[5]

Take what you learned from putting together your letterhead, and apply these things to your business card. Even though all the same information is typically used on your business card, it doesn't work just to shrink down your letterhead because of different aspect ratios, although you might be able to keep the same general justification or centering. You can arrange things differently as long as you are using the same fonts, the same proportions in your font sizes, the same colors, etc. Your mailing address is not necessary on your business card unless you have a specific need to include it. The rest of your contact info is unlikely to change even if you move, so without a mailing address your business cards will be usable longer.

Just as with letterheads, I recommend developing several options for your business card with different layout combinations. By this time hopefully you have settled on a color palette and font plan, and it is just about moving the required elements around. Keep in mind that you can always search the internet and find endless examples of business card layouts to use as inspiration, but don't simply copy any of them.

There are more and more people trying to take advantage of both sides (front and back) of the business card by including a production photo or

---

[5]Ibid.

additional graphic element as part of their design. However, remember that you need to have white space on the card for people to write notes—an extremely common practice that helps people remember who you are or follow up the contact. If you choose to use a logo, perhaps it goes on the back of the card. Other ideas include a mini-bio or a list of skills, specialties, or expertise, or, if you use social media as part of your business, you could use the back of the card for your online names since this would be too much information to fit on to the front of the card. If you are not active on these sites or only use them for personal contacts, this is not a good idea. I've seen some cards use the back to encourage notes by including the prompts of "how we met," "date," "place," and "follow up," with lined space for the answers. A QR code that links directly to your digital portfolio, thus making it easier for someone to see your work, is another option.

The one thing I do not recommend is having your name on one side and your contact information on the other. Keep your name, title, and contact information all on one side of the card. If you really like vertical layouts, perhaps you use a vertical layout on one side of the card and a horizontal layout on the other. This way you appeal to traditionalists as well as the mavericks. It is also perfectly acceptable to leave the back of your card blank, keeping in mind that blank does not necessarily have to mean white (though plain white is most common). Do not make the back black or another very dark color which makes it impossible for anyone to write legible notes on it. Examples are shown in Plates 14, 16, 18 and 20, with additional examples on the companion website.

Once you have settled on a design and obtained feedback from mentors and colleagues, run your design through the list of ten questions in the section on letterheads to see if you have met your objective for your business card.

Writing Your Bio

Most bios are boring, minimally informative, and often don't get read all the way through. Typical bios tend to be lists of plays that most readers will have no connection to if they didn't see the productions or have never heard of the plays you cite. But there is a way to write a descriptive bio that will help people who visit your website (or read the playbill) get to know you and how you work.

Don't approach your bio as a reduced version of your resume where you try to cram in as many show titles as possible. Start with where you see yourself going and your future plans. Include a variety of shows that demonstrate a range of styles and genres. Then think about what you contributed to each show that you can highlight. Tell people about the places you have worked, as there is greater chance they have heard of these than individual shows. Tell people about your education, if applicable. Here are some sample descriptive bios to give you an idea how to make yours interesting.

Aiesha Carrillo looks forward to a career on Broadway. She has stage managed large-scale musicals and Shakespearian productions, including *Spring Awakening* and *A Midsummer Night's Dream*, as well as more intimate shows like *Ada and the Engine* and *School Girls; or, the African Mean Girls Play*. Her attention to detail was put to good use tracking script changes as stage manager for the world premiere of *Showtime for Shakespeare*. As an assistant stage manager for shows including *The Ballad of Emmett Till* and *He Brought Her Heart Back in a Box*, she helped facilitate communication between rehearsal and the production team, allowing her organizational and people skills to shine.

Lachlan Novak is an entertainment industry carpenter. Their work with Show Support Scenic Group includes installs at Universal Studios Wizarding World of Harry Potter and Halloween Horror Nights. In addition to regular work with Show Support, Lachlan also does freelance and over-hire work in the Central Florida area at theatres including Orlando Shakes, The Rep, Winter Park Playhouse, and an upcoming gig at Theatre Downtown.

Upon completion of his BFA in Theatre Design and Technology, Alexandre Brennan plans to pursue a career in the themed entertainment industry as a hard-goods specialist in props and costumes. His eye for detail can be seen in his work as a commissioned artist, which includes suits of armor, full body costumes, and smaller props and costume pieces based on a wide variety of movies, video games, and comic books.

Kamile Haley is a theatrical technical director. She gained experience collaborating with all departments as a production management intern for the Williamstown Theatre Festival. As master carpenter for a production of *Skeleton Crew*, her metalworking skills were showcased in her builds of two helical metal staircases. Kamile's combined experience in the scene shop and production office has given her the organizational and people skills to ensure that day-to-day operations run smoothly.

Reegan Tanner is looking forward to working with large regional entertainment and touring companies as a lighting technician. Reegan has experience in various theatrical styles, including dinner theatre, fringe festivals, Shakespeare, and educational theatre. As master electrician for *Edith Can Shoot Things and Hit Them* and assistant master electrician for *Passing Strange*, Reegan's quick problem-solving abilities enabled the shows to proceed when there were last-minute electrics failures. Reegan has a BFA in Theatre Design and Technology from Southern University, with a minor in Music.

Kenneth Mills is making his career in live sound reinforcement and broadcast audio. As an associate sound designer for large-scale musicals, his system knowledge and adaptability prove crucial to mitigating issues, resulting in uninterrupted performances. Last summer he was the mixer/electrician for the Illinois Shakespeare Festival, and he has locally engineered touring productions of *Something Rotten*, *Sesame Street Live!*, and *Wicked*'s second national tour.

Headshots

While you don't need a headshot in the same way that an actor does (it will never be a part of your application materials for a job), you should have one to include on your website, and at some point you will be asked to provide a photo to accompany your bio in a playbill or for inclusion on a feature on some project you've worked on. Whatever the reason, you want the photograph to represent your professional persona. While you don't necessarily need to hire a professional photographer, it should be taken with care and purpose. Avoid group photos or action shots of you driving a forklift. Dress as if you were meeting a potential employer for an interview, not about to head to the shop, choose a neutral backdrop, and have a friend or family member take a portrait-oriented shoulders-up photo of you. Smiles are encouraged.

Artist Statement

In addition to the professional bio, there is a movement among theatre artists to create a statement of values to draw connections between their core values and their work. This statement can be used to communicate how your point of view informs your work, discuss your expectations for collaboration and communication, and outline the kinds of projects you prioritize. Your artist statement can be used on your website, on social media, and to inform your long-term planning. The statement need not be long—some are only a few sentences, though they can be as long as you would like. You can learn more about incorporating a statement of values into your website and your work from Wingspace, "an organization of theatre artists that fosters conversations on design, strengthens our community, and furthers activism in the field" and offers regular opportunities for roundtables and workshops centering on topics related to their values.[6] Another source of inspiration is Beehive Dramaturgy Studio, which demonstrates incorporation of values into its web presence and work.[7] There are also many individual artists who incorporate their personal values in their professional websites and the projects on which they choose to work.[8]

Managing Your Online Persona

We are living in a mix of generations, including people who didn't grow up with the internet and those who did. As I interact with college students today, I find the vast majority have received a good education about the dangers and permanence of the internet and may see the topics below as common sense. Nevertheless, it is still good to review these guidelines, so that even if you are social media savvy you can be sure you have taken care of your online persona as you embark on your professional career. Most people don't post on their social media with the thought that their future employer is going to see it, but it is a good idea to keep this in mind. As a theatre professor, Kerri Packard always told her students to be careful about what they put on social media, but she didn't take her own advice:

> I was working on a production that is remounted every year and vented on social media about the number of hours I had put in on a single day. Nine months later the producer contacted me and wanted to know if I was even

---

[6]See Wingspace, www.wingspace.com.
[7]See Beehive Dramaturgy Studio, www.beehivedramaturgy.com.
[8]Examples include www.katherinefreer.com and www.elizabethmak.com.

interested in working on the production again because they saw the post. I was able to repair the situation, but my venting could have cost me the job.[9]

Yes, you can vent, have a social life, and have fun, but you should be judicious in deciding what to share publicly. As the social media *de rigeur* changes frequently, the platforms I discuss here may be things of the past when you are reading this, but the lessons can be carried forward to whatever platforms you are using.

You should expect that anyone thinking of hiring you will do a web search for your name, so your first step should be to do this same search yourself, with a plan to repeat it every couple of months to find anything new. I have set up a Google alert which sends me notifications any time it finds new content about me on the web. If you have a common name, you might be hard to find. If that is the case it is good to know who does come up with a search of your name, in case that becomes useful information in the future. If you don't find anything about yourself, try adding theatre, or stage manager, or whatever your industry or field is. In addition to your own social media accounts and personal website, you will likely discover content and photos of you posted by others. If you find things you didn't post and don't want online, you will have to go through the process of requesting those things be taken down by contacting the person or site that posted the information. If you end up needing to contact a company to get your copyrighted information removed, be sure to review and reference the US Digital Millennium Copyright Act (Section 512(c)), which requires that copyrighted materials be removed as soon as notification is received regarding the copyright infringement. If things you posted online are showing up as public and you want them to be private, go to those individual sites and update your privacy settings or remove the content altogether.

Before you can start using social media to your advantage, you need to do an inventory of your active and inactive media sites to look for things that potential employers may see as "red flags." A 2018 survey revealed that "70 percent of employers use social media to screen candidates before hiring,"[10] and that number is likely even higher today. These employers are hoping to get a glimpse of the candidate's personality and fit for the company. Among the top things employers reported finding that left a bad impression were

---

[9]Kerri Packard, personal communication with the author, November 7, 2019.
[10]CareerBuilder, "More Than Half of Employers Have Found Content on Social Media That Caused Them Not to Hire a Candidate According to Recent CareerBuilder Survey," press release, August 9, 2018, http://press.careerbuilder.com/.

provocative content, drinking or drug use, discriminatory comments, unprofessional screen names, and criminal behavior. Keep in mind that even if you have a dormant account, people can still find you there. Those pictures you posted on Facebook in middle school? Yep, still there. Some people reading this may even still have a Myspace page from the early 2000s that now serves as some sort of time capsule. It seems that daily we hear in the news about a public figure who tweeted something regrettable ten years ago, and their professional lives are negatively impacted today even if that tweet no longer represents them. This underscores the importance of going back through everything you have posted in every account you have to be sure it represents who you are today, and taking steps to delete or keep private anything that is not part of your professional persona. Even if you have things "locked down," remember that you have still put it out into the world and there is a chance someone may gain access to it. If you don't want it to become public, remove it (or even better, don't post it in the first place). It is good to keep things public or even highlight aspects that will help people looking for you know that it is you. For example, keeping your employment and educational information public helps to differentiate you from other people with similar names.

I have helped people review their social media pages to point out potential red flags they may want to reconsider. Among the first things I check is personal information that should be kept private due to identity-theft concerns, like birth date. "Familiar fraud" is the act of a friend or family member stealing your identity for financial gain. Think of the things you need to prove your identity when you forget a password or want to gain access to a bank account. If those things are public information, you have compromised your own accounts. Additionally, if you have your birth date posted and post photos of yourself engaging in things which you are not of legal age to do, potential employers may notice. I suggest you would want to remove both your birth date and the photos.

Photos that may raise questions with an employer are an important point for review: early-morning pictures of you in bed in a state of undress, that pudding-wrestling party from college, and things others could consider compromising are worth a second thought. If you have shared, liked, responded to, or posted off-color, racist, homophobic, or discriminatory jokes or memes, those can be problematic as well, no matter how long ago they were. You may choose not to remove them—that is, of course, completely up to you—but there is value in the exercise of deciding if these represent who you are and if they should stay. Be aware of the people you are connected to on social media. If their profiles can be accessed from your page, what they post can reflect on you.

Once you have done an inventory and made decisions about what should stay and what should go, take the next step to consider ways you can use the platform to your advantage. Post about your latest projects or shows, use the appropriate hashtags, and tag the people involved so that your work gets shared with a wider audience. Post about the shows you are seeing, and compliment your peers and colleagues on their work. Find an interesting industry-related article? Post that as well. Make sure that these types of posts are made public, so anyone looking you up for a potential networking or job opportunity will not only see your work but also see you being a gracious artist and collaborator. You may consider making a separate professional page or account that has all your public-facing information, and keeping your personal interactions separate.

Either keep up with your social media accounts or deactivate them. I worked with someone who had created video content for their YouTube channel, and this content came to the attention of a large corporation that wanted to discuss the person creating viral marketing videos. The corporation attempted to contact the person via their LinkedIn account. Unfortunately, the person had never logged back into LinkedIn after creating the account. They didn't discover this potentially life-changing message for several months. By the time they replied, the corporation had moved on and the offer was no longer available. I was guilty of this as well. I signed up for LinkedIn many years ago and then did absolutely nothing with it for the next few years. In fact, as I was writing this I realized that it had been a few months since I last logged in, and I was chagrined to discover an overdue message from a colleague I worked with fifteen years ago looking to reconnect for possible work opportunities. If you don't check all your accounts with some regularity, there is a chance you may be missing out on a networking or employment opportunity. Perhaps a biweekly or monthly calendar reminder can help you (and me) keep up to date. If you really don't want to use that platform any more, look into archiving your account. Do you have a Facebook account but don't use it much because you've mostly moved on to Instagram or Snapchat? Did you sign up for WhatsApp and never really use it? If so, it's time for a social media inventory.

The most popular social media sites evolve, as do their uses. From my informal polls of professionals in our industry, in 2021 Facebook and Instagram are by far the sites that people find most useful for networking and making potential job connections. While LinkedIn might be a great resource in some fields, people in our industry (with the exception of upper-level corporate entertainment and non-profit executives) indicate to me that it has not been useful for them for networking or job seeking (though employers may be looking them up on there). Even so, many of the people who say it isn't helpful still have a LinkedIn account. As social media evolves daily, perhaps it will become more useful in the future. Whichever social media you decide to use (Facebook, Instagram, LinkedIn, WhatsApp, Pinterest, Twitter, etc.), you can always find lots of websites that give advice on the best ways to use each of them for professional purposes. I encourage you to research and implement those strategies, but don't try to maximize all the sites at once. Pick the one that makes the most sense for you, and do that one site really well before moving on to another. Trying to master all the social media sites all at once will just end in haphazard coverage, or will become so overwhelming that you will stop altogether.

As you are working with social media, don't neglect the "social" aspect of it and think of it as a networking event. Follow people you admire and want to work with. Interact with their posts in a positive manner. Add to the collective conversation in the industry in a way that reflects your skills and expertise. The most important thing to remember is that everything you do and say online could become public.

3

Resumes and Curriculum Vitae

Most books and websites about writing resumes don't address the specific needs of theatre artists. There are special requirements and considerations for resumes in our field, and an MS Word template or table is not a good option. Despite the multitude of templates online that might work well for other industries, you will be better served by creating your document from scratch. Once you have your resume created and have gone through the revision and tweaking process, you will be all set up to maintain and update your resume regularly. It is much simpler to add things to your resume as you go along than to scramble when you get an email from a producer who wants a copy of your resume for a job starting next week.

Your resume and cover letter create an important first impression with potential employers. While there is no "right" way to put together your resume, there are several things you want to avoid and some standards you will want to meet. A resume is not merely a list of the things you have done: a lot of thought needs to go into what you list, how you sort it, and what it looks like. Presentation—how your materials are visually planned and organized—is of utmost importance, and demonstrates respect for the people reading your materials. The assumption is that you will put as much energy and quality into these materials as you can, so employers will assume that the quality of your application is the highest level of quality they could expect from you once you are hired. That is why it is so important to be sure there are no spelling errors, layout oversights, or other mistakes on your resume and other application materials. Those types of errors could be what lands you in the "no" pile.

The Differences Between a Resume and a CV

The terms *resume* and *CV*, or *curriculum vitae*, have different meanings in different countries; here I discuss the US definitions and uses. Be sure to investigate the expectations in the country where you are applying.

In the US, a resume is used for nearly every type of job application. It is a one-page outline of your applicable education, experience, work history, and accomplishments. A CV is significantly longer and has additional information not necessary on a resume, including academic appointments, teaching experience, research you have conducted, your publications (journal articles, book chapters, books, and book reviews), grants you have received, awards, exhibitions, gallery shows, symposia, adjudications, mentorship, consulting, graduate student supervision, student or mentee success such as presentations, publications, and awards, workshops and lectures you have presented, conference presentations, professional development, service activities to the profession, community, and university, professional memberships, and any other relevant accomplishments or activities. After having been in academia for over twenty years, my current CV is twenty-five pages long and includes everything I have ever done related to my work as a costume designer, costume technician, educator, and theatre professional since about 1997. In the US, CVs are only used for academic, scientific, and medical fields, so unless you are applying for a position at a university it is unlikely you will ever need to compile a CV. However, if you think that one day you may go into teaching at the college level, it is advisable to keep a running list of items that will go on your CV some day, as it is very difficult to compile after the fact. I won't go into more detail on CVs here, but many of the formatting and layout topics we cover in the section on resumes should also be applied to CVs.

People are usually surprised to hear that a potential employer will spend less than twenty seconds reading a resume, but many sources agree it is more like six seconds. If the employer can't find what they are looking for right away, they move on to the next application rather than spend more time trying to uncover the information they want. This means that the weaker a resume is, the less time an employer will spend reviewing it. Your goal is to create an easy-to-read/skim document that offers up the most important information in the simplest, cleanest way possible. It is advisable to follow customary formatting and layout for our industry, as well as characteristics that make skimming easier, so that potential employers will immediately be able to find the details they need.

First, they want to know what you do and/or what kind of job you are looking for, to confirm your resume has ended up in the correct pile. Next they want to know if they have any connections to people you have worked with, so they look for names and places they recognize. Then they see if you have the kind of experience that will make you a good fit for their opening. And if they can't find all of that information *fast*, they move on to the next resume.

What Resume Style Is Best for My Purposes?

Resumes fall into one of two main styles: chronological or functional. The chronological resume is the style most employers expect in our industry, and is the one I recommend. In fact, I cannot think of a time when I would recommend a strictly functional resume, though I have worked with a few people for whom a cross between the two, a style I call a descriptive chronological resume, worked best. You can see examples of the various styles described in this chapter in Plates 13, 15, 17, and 19, with additional examples on the companion website.

Let's start with the basic chronological resume, which a lot of people refer to as a "theatre resume" and is the most common style in our industry. The key feature to this style is a list of production and work history in reverse chronological order: the shows or other work you have done most recently are at the top of the list, and it moves backward through time so the work you did longest ago is toward the bottom.

For people who are changing industries, who have only a few projects or jobs to list, or who want to provide more details, a descriptive chronological resume can be a good alternative. This type of resume fills a lot more space on the page for each job than a strictly chronological resume, because in addition to the jobs you list two or three concise bullet points under each. Bullet points could include accomplishments, responsibilities, awards, reviews, noteworthy challenges you solved, scope and scale, etc. So, for example, a makeup artist might list a haunted house they worked for. Their bullet points could be the number of makeups they did and in what time frame, the specific types of applications or materials used, and the number of assistants they had to train for the applications. If you use the descriptive chronological style because you do not yet have enough experience to fill the page using the straight chronological format, at some point you will likely have more credits than will fit on one page and will need to switch to a more compact chronological style or decide which things to take off of your resume.

The descriptive chronological resume allows people changing direction in their career to frame experience in one area and its connection to the new area. For example, consider someone whose previous work was as a stage manager (SM) who wants to transition into box office management. An employer hiring a box office manager won't be interested in a listing of every show the applicant has stage managed, but they need to know how that SM experience would translate into a box office setting. While this should also be discussed in the cover letter, the applicant could choose to list shows or events with specific details that help the employer see how their skills would transfer. Attributes such as computer competence, working as a team, strong organizational skills, a high level of professionalism, and excellent communication skills can all apply in the new environment. The SM can select what to include based on the shows/events where they best demonstrated those skills. As you transition into the new field and gain more experience in it, you will have the option to transition to the chronological style as your work history becomes more specific to your current field.

How Many Resumes Do I Need?

Some people can manage with one resume with one job title. I have one resume now, as the work I seek has narrowed into one area, but at the beginning of my career I had multiple resumes depending on the job I was applying for. For example, when applying for costume design jobs I used a resume with that title and placed my design work most prominently, followed by a mention of my technology skills. When applying for a costume technology position I used that title and made my costume construction work most prominent, with my design work as a side note. When applying for jobs that were a combination of design and construction, I used a resume with the title of costume design and technology and prominently included details about both aspects of my work. Why the need for all three? You should customize your application materials to the job you are applying for. If I apply for a costume shop manager position but give myself the title of costume designer, the employer will think that I actually want to be a designer and don't really want a job as a costume shop manager; it is unlikely I would be interviewed for the position. Employers are looking for people who will be a good fit—not only good at the job, but also happy working in that position, especially if it is a long-term contract and not just a single show or seasonal gig. If they think the job being offered is not really what you want to do, they will be hesitant to hire you for fear that the moment you find something more in line with your actual ambitions you will leave, forcing them to repeat the recruitment process all over again. This not only costs them time and money, but could also derail their season if you leave before it's over.

People just starting out in the industry often don't have the experience to back up the title to which they aspire. For example, consider a student who has a professional goal of being a lighting designer but has only worked as an assistant designer and master electrician, with maybe one lighting design in their college credits. They don't yet have the experience to claim the title of lighting designer, but the student does not want to market themselves as a technician and wants work that will bring them closer to being a designer. This student could use the generic title of "lighting" and list their design-related work first (this might be a good opportunity to use the descriptive chronological resume style discussed earlier), and then make mention, perhaps with less detail, of their work as a technician. This resume could be used to apply for lighting design jobs or assistant positions. The student may also still sometimes work as a technician, and would likely also need to have a resume for those applications which could either use the title of "lighting" or a master electrician or lighting tech title, highlighting work related to the job being applied for. As they gain more experience in the area and are growing their career, the student will be able to claim the title of lighting designer and organize their resume accordingly.

What Should I Include on My Resume?

There are different categories that can and should appear on your resume. How you label each section is important, depending on your experience level and job titles. You must also remember what it is that employers need to find quickly on your resume: what you do, if you worked with anyone they know, and if your experience matches what they are looking for. Here is the key information you must include.

Your name. This should be the largest thing on the page. It should be the name you want to be called and the name by which all your referees will recognize you. If you always go by your middle name or a nickname, or if your legal name is Max but you are now Jackie, you should use Jackie and not your legal name. Your resume is not a legal document. There will be times when you have to use your legal name, like for filling out tax documents, but your application materials can be in the name by which you want to be known. If you are transitioning to a new name during this time, be sure to tell your referees and colleagues so that if they get a call about you they will recognize your name.

Your pronouns. Including your pronouns (e.g., she/her, he/his, they/theirs) promotes an inclusive environment for all. They need not be as large as your name.

Your title. What do you do? This should be the next-largest thing on your resume. Choosing the right title is important: it should directly connect to the job you are applying for. The phrasing can be important as well. Consider the difference between the titles "Scenic Designer," "Scenic Design," and "Scenery." "Scenic Designer" communicates that you are specifically looking for work as the person who designs the scenery. However, if you use the title "Scenic Design" you could be applying to design the scenery, but you could also be applying as an assistant or associate scenic designer or a design intern. The title "Scenery" could be used for any of the above positions, but also for a variety of other scenery-based jobs. Perhaps this title is one to use when you are applying for more than one position at the same theatre. If you are applying for assistant technical director and master carpenter positions, you would not want to put just one of those titles on your resume as it would exclude the other. The more generic title of "Scenery" gives you flexibility. You should always choose the most detailed title possible based on the job you are applying for and your relevant experience, but be sure you have the experience to back up the title you use.

Contact information. At a minimum you need to include your phone number, professional email address, and the URL for your professional website. It is no longer necessary or recommended to include your mailing address, though it is a good idea to indicate the city and state where you are based. Your task as an applicant is to make hiring you as easy as possible. It tells employers your most likely time zone, so they can keep that in mind when contacting you. It also tells them if you are local or will have to travel to take the job. Some argue that this is a reason not to reveal what part of the country you are in, because someone may pass you over for a job due to your location before even contacting you. I say always err on the side of providing information that will make the hiring process easier for the employer and save them time. If they have decided in advance that they must hire someone local, why waste their time (and yours) in contacting you only to find out you don't meet their needs, thus leaving a bad impression? Best for them to know up front. You can always indicate your willingness to travel or relocate in your cover letter.

Education. This section will differ depending on where you are in your education. Professional resumes do not include high school education unless you are still in high school (in which case it isn't really a professional resume), have recently graduated and are applying for an undergraduate college program, or do not have a college degree and are applying for a job that says it requires a high school diploma. I have had people assert that they should keep their high school on their professional resume because they went to a performing arts school or had some other special circumstance. While this could be helpful when applying to college, once you've gone beyond that high school doesn't belong on your resume.

You should list any higher education program currently in progress or your most recently completed higher education degree first, then work backward in reverse chronological order. So, if you are in a graduate program, put that first along with your area of study, then bachelor's program next (listing majors and minors), then an associate's degree if you have one, and any certificates or other special training. If you completed a study-abroad program you can list that here or it can fit into another section. List only the year the degree was completed, not the date range of attendance or months for any of your degrees or education.

When listing a degree you have not yet completed, you should not list the year you plan to graduate without indicating that it is a projected graduation date. If you began a college program but didn't complete it, or transferred to another school, do not list that part of your educational background. You should only list degrees earned (or in progress). If you don't have a completed degree after high school but do have upper-level advanced coursework from a college program you did not complete, you can list a few of your relevant advanced courses in a section titled "Relevant Coursework" instead of an "Education" section, but if you do have completed degrees it is not necessary or even recommended to include coursework on your resume. You can mention any significant coursework in your cover letter if you deem it necessary.

Other titles you could use for this section, depending on your specific circumstances and the information you include, are "Education and Training," "Academic Training," "Significant Coursework," or "Education and Certifications" (more about certifications in the "Skills" subsection below).

Experience. This section needs to list what you did, the show or event name, producing organization, supervisor or director, and year. Employers glean most of the information they need from this section, so it is important that the details are complete and easy to read. This is the main section the employer uses to determine if they have any people or places in common with you, so it is your opportunity to name-drop in a way that is not considered obnoxious. Don't forget the names. Different ways to lay this section out in much more detail are given in the section on organization later in this chapter. For now, make a list of your experience with all the pertinent information you'll need on the resume worksheet found on the companion website.

Skills. I see a lot of resumes where people use the heading "Special Skills," and I always ask them "What is special about these skills?" Invariably they have no reply. Unless you really are listing skills unique to you or are in some other way exceptional, I recommend you leave the qualifier out of it and just stick with "Skills."

If you have certifications, you could include them here under a "Skills and Certifications" heading if you decided not to list them with your education. Or you could put your certifications in their own section, especially if the ones you hold are specifically required for the job for which you are applying and you want to be sure the potential employer does not miss the fact that you have them, or if you want to bring special attention to them because you believe they will set you apart from other applicants.

I find that people who have difficulty figuring out what to include in a skills section think that everything they can do seems obvious. They end up not leveraging their skills to their advantage.

Below is a non-exhaustive list from which you can draw, and which may spark other ideas. You do not have to list all the skills you have: if they aren't applicable, don't list them. For example, I can program a light board and read music, but I don't ever expect those things to advantage me when applying to be a costume designer so they are not on my resume. We discuss how to organize your list of skills in the Layout section; For now, just compile your list on the resume worksheet that can be found on the companion website.

Skills

3D printing
Adobe suite
AutoCAD
Calling from a score
Carpentry
Child coordination
CNC router
Crafts
Dance or choreography
Draping
Drawing
Dyeing and distressing
Electrical wiring
Embroidery
Facial casting
Final Draft
Flat patterning
Fly-rail loading/ operating
Foam carving
Front-of-house experience
Internet shopping for specialty items
Jewelry making

Knowledge of AEA rule books
Languages (include proficiency level)
Laser cutting
Laundry and stain removal
Leatherwork
Lettering
LED fixtures
Leko/Source4 fixtures
Light-board programming (specify which boards)
Light hang and focus
Lightwright
Mac and/or PC
Makeup
Microsoft Office (or list individually if not all programs)
Millinery
Model making

Moving light troubleshooting and repair (list fixtures)
Musical instruments (list those you play)
Networking (net, hippo, media servers, etc.)
Painting
Photography
Photoshop
Puppeteering
Projectionist (focus/ keying)
QLab
Reading music
Reading ground plans
Reading light plots
Run follow spot
Scene painting
Sculpting (foam, clay, etc.)
Serger threading
Sewing (hand or machine, industrial or domestic)

Sight-read music	Virtual callboard	Wig styling and/or
Sketchup	Visualization software	maintenance
Soldering	(specify)	Wiring LED tape
Tailoring	Wardrobe	Wonderflex/Fosshape
Vectorworks 2D/3D/	Web design	Working with children
spotlight	Welding (MIG, TIG,	
Ventilating	stick, materials)	

Certifications[1]

OSHA lift	ETCP certified arena	OSHA30
certified	rigger	Varilite certified
CPR/AED	ETCP certified theatre	Forklift certified
certified	rigger	Aerial lift certified
Valid passport	ETCP certified	First aid certified
Valid driver's	electrician	Welding certified
license	ETCP certified PPDT	CDL license
Belay certified	IATSE (list local)	Mediation
SCUBA certified	OSHA10	

You may have other hobbies or skills that don't seem immediately related to what you do in the entertainment industry. Technical director Sam Miller pointed out that she likes to see people who have sailing or rock climbing listed on their resumes because they will have experience tying knots, understand the importance of safety, and likely have body awareness that will benefit them in the scene-shop setting.[2] If you aren't sure if hobbies or skills are germane to your career goals, ask a mentor who can help you evaluate those activities.

Awards. Include awards received for related activities or that communicate something about your work ethic. As always, it needs to be relevant to the

---

[1]OSHA = Occupational Safety and Health Administration; CPR/AED = cardiopulmonary resuscitation/automated external defibrillator; SCUBA = self-contained underwater breathing apparatus; ETCP = Entertainment Technician Certification Program; PPDT = portable power distribution technician; IATSE = International Alliance of Theatrical Stage Employees, Moving; Picture Technicians, Artists and Allied Crafts of the United States, Its Territories and Canada; CDL = commercial driver's license
[2]Sam Miller, personal communication with the author, November 15, 2019.

position for which you are applying. For example, winning a blue ribbon at the state fair for your baking or growing the largest sunflower does not belong on your professional resume; but if you won a blue ribbon for embroidery or carpentry, that may apply. Other things to list in addition to actual awards might include scholarships, Dean's List, Eagle Scout, etc. If you served as an officer of a theatre student organization or were inducted into a theatre fraternity like Alpha Psi Omega and want to include that, you could make this section "Awards and Activities" or "Awards and Honors." You could list study abroad here if you chose not to include it in your "Education" section. If you don't have any awards but do engage in activities which may be beneficial to highlight, you can have a "Related Activities" section to list those items. If you don't have any awards or activities to list, that's OK too! People won't even notice if it isn't on your resume, so there's no need to feel self-conscious. And definitely, no matter what, *do not* make up awards that you did not receive or exaggerate those you have.

Other options. Every person and every resume are different, so there may be categories you have on your resume that other people don't. You may have a version of your resume for a specific job where you include a category that you don't use on any other resumes you send out. For example, I once worked with a stage manager who applied for a job in event management for a children's charity. On that resume they listed non-theatre-related volunteer work they had done for other organizations to help emphasize that they already had a connection to charitable work and the mission of the organization, even though it was with different organizations. Because it was non-theatre work it wasn't included on any of their other resumes, but it was an important factor that helped them get that job.

References. You should always include references at the bottom of your resume. Information should include the person's name, job title, professional affiliation (theatre they work for, freelance, university, etc.), phone number, and email address. The standard number to include is three, but some choose to use four for reasons such as added diversity in people, places, positions, etc. For example, I typically include four references. One is a scenic designer with whom I have often collaborated and I feel can discuss what it is like to work with me on a design team; the other three are directors/artistic directors I've worked with at different types of theatres— my university, a local regional theatre, and an out-of-state professional theatre. They each have slightly different perspectives about working with me and can address different aspects of my work. These are not the only people I have on my list of potential references and, depending on the job, I will swap in different people. For example, if I'm applying for a job designing at a theatre for young audiences, I would swap in my reference who knows that aspect of my work. If applying for a primarily technical job, I'll include references who can best speak to my work as a technician. If looking for a teaching job, I want to make sure I include references who appreciate my skill as a teacher.

This is exactly the kind of strategy you need to use when selecting your references. You should have a list of people who know about different aspects of your expertise. You want these references to represent a variety of past employers and experiences that can speak to your abilities for the specific job for which you are applying. Don't include three references from the same theatre or school. By the time you graduate from college you should be able to include someone from outside work you have done. If you have worked in several places and only include references from one place, it can send the message that nowhere else you worked has anything good to say about you. At the same time, be sure you have at least one reference from your current or most recent job or school. While there may be legitimate reasons for not doing this, such as not revealing your job search to your current employer, I always find it suspicious when I review a resume and there are no current references. Whatever your reason, if you do this you may want to include some sort of explanation in your cover letter to eliminate the possible red flag.

Providing references is not just a matter of writing people's names and contact info at the bottom of your resume; there is important preparation and communication you need to do first. You can download a reference worksheet from the companion website to organize this process. Make a list of at least five people who represent a variety of your experiences and would be able to talk knowledgeably about you and your work. Only consider people whom you believe would have positive things to say about you. Though you will likely only use three at a time, having a longer list of potential references will better prepare you for a variety of job-search scenarios, like tailoring your references to a specific job or providing a last-minute replacement because someone is out of town or in tech and not available to take a call. On your worksheet, make notes next to each person's name about where you worked with them and on what projects or shows, and one or two things you think they can say about you. Your next step is to contact each of them individually and ask their permission to use them as a reference. You can use whatever method you typically employ to contact this person. Your message could go something like this:

Dear Cherry Payvar,

I am putting together my materials to apply for _____. Because we worked together on _____ I think you could speak to my _____ [fill in whatever it is that you think this person would know about you]. Would it be OK if I list you as a reference on my resume and, if contacted, would you be able to give me a positive reference? If so, what email and phone number would be best to list? If you have a specific job title you would prefer I use, let me know that too. I have attached a copy of my resume so you can see what I've been working on lately, and will forward the job descriptions of the jobs I apply for.

Thank you for your consideration.

You will want to personalize this for your circumstances and for each potential reference. You could also consider adding in a sentence to the effect of "If you can't provide me with a positive reference, I would appreciate the chance to learn from you what areas I can improve." Of course, only include that if you really are open to hearing what they think. It could be a very difficult, albeit very valuable, conversation.

Once you've compiled a list of references from whom you have received positive responses, be sure to send them a list of places to which you are applying and, even better, include the job descriptions so they can consider how they will speak to your qualifications. If it has been some time since you first asked to be able to list them as a reference and you are sending out applications again, be sure to touch base and give them an update on what you have been doing lately, so you are fresh in their mind if they do get a call about you. This is also a good time to re-evaluate your references and see if any should come off the list because you haven't worked with them in a long time and they've become stale, or if there are any new people you should add to the list from your more recent work. You will continually make updates to your list of references as you progress through your career.

What Not to Include

Just as important as the things you must include on your resume are the things you should not include.

Lies, half truths, or exaggerations. The most important thing is never to put anything on your resume that is not 100 percent true. I once reviewed the resume of a designer who had listed a show on their resume that I knew had been designed by someone else. I asked them why they listed themselves as the designer when they were the assistant designer, and they explained that the original designer left the production after submitting their designs and they had been left to see the show through the shop, and therefore felt that they deserved the title. I pointed out that while that may be true, it was the original designer's design on the stage and the company did not credit them as the designer. This was a situation where they should list themselves with their official title of assistant scenic designer, and then possibly discuss in their cover letter how they were able to take on the additional responsibility in that role.

Things you hate. If there is a job or skill you would hate to be asked to do again, you should never list it on your resume. I helped a technical director with their resume and noticed they listed their scene design credits. I knew this person hated every aspect of designing and never wanted to design anything ever again, so I asked them why they listed it on their resume. They were confused by this question and responded, "Because I did it." Just because you've done something doesn't mean it has to be on your resume. By telling people they had design experience they were opening themselves up for people expecting that they would be willing to do more of it. I suggested instead that they mention how having had design experience made them a better technical director and what they learned from it in their cover letter, but to not highlight that activity on their resume.

Unrelated personal info. Actors put personal information like height, weight, and eye or hair color on their resumes, but that is not expected or appropriate for design, tech, and stage management resumes. Nor should you include a photograph of yourself.

High school experience. If you are still in high school then it is OK to include high school experience or awards on your resume; but once you have experience beyond that, all your high school information should be removed. There will come a time when your college work should be deleted from your professional resume as well.

Soft skills. Flexibility, organization, positive attitude, self-starter, and such are buzzwords that lots of people use, but they don't really mean much unless backed up with examples. These things are best discussed in your cover letter or at the interview itself.

Unrelated work experience. The fact that you worked bagging groceries on weekends is probably not germane to your professional theatrical resume. This goes back to the idea of tailoring your resume to the job you are applying for. Don't take this to mean that non-theatrical jobs never have a place on your resume. If you are a stage manager hoping to use your management skills in a front-of-house role, bagging groceries might be something to work into your materials in some way in a section for "Customer Service," or simply include it in your cover letter and emphasize what that work taught you about customer service and interacting with patrons.

Unrelated hobbies. You should not include hobbies on your resume unless there is a way that they could tie into the kind of work you do. I worked with a technician whom I knew to be an avid scuba diver, and noticed they did not include this on their resume. I pointed out that there are theatre jobs, especially shows in Las Vegas, that require scuba certification. They added it to their resume and ended up getting a job working for one of those shows right out of college. Hobbies that can apply to your theatre work should be included in your skills.

Outdated skills. If you haven't done it in years, aren't up on the latest developments, or aren't really able do it any more, you probably shouldn't include it. For example, I used to develop black-and-white film in a darkroom. While I am confident that if I had the equipment and space I could pick it back up again quickly, I haven't done it in more than twenty years so it is not listed as one of my skills (not to mention that it isn't germane to my area).

"References available on request." It is very frustrating to receive resumes that include this phrase. Remember, you want to make it as easy as possible for the employer to hire you, and that means including all the information they are potentially going to need up front so they don't have to do any extra work to get it. The main arguments people make for using this phrase in lieu of listing references include space, the privacy of your references, and wanting to know if you have made the first cut by forcing hirers to contact you to ask for your references. None of these is a good reason.

As to the issue of space, remember that one of the main things potential employers in our industry want to know is if you have worked with anyone they know. Your references are a prime opportunity to include additional names that may not appear in other places on your resume. Including references is space very well used.

As for the privacy of your references, if you asked them properly to be a reference they will have given you the email address and phone number they want you to use, and it is all likely the same contact information they have listed publicly on their own website. That being said, you may have a high-profile reference at some point whose contact information should be protected. In that case, you can provide contact information for their agent or manager, or list their name and position and put "available on request" in place of their specific contact information while including complete information for all your other references.

Lastly, restricting references so you know if you made the first cut is a move that could absolutely backfire. If there are two candidates with resumes that the employer views as equal, and one lists references while the other doesn't, the potential employer will be more likely to check references on the candidate who provided them, and that person now has a distinct advantage. Keep in mind that your references should be people who are looking out for you and hoping you get a job. If they get a call from a potential employer they are likely going to let you know anyway, so you will know if you are in consideration for the job as soon as they contact one of your references.

Grade point average. This isn't a strict "don't," but it really isn't necessary. If you have a good GPA you will likely have made the Dean's List or graduated with a Latin honor like *cum laude* and can list that elsewhere on your resume, so including the actual number is adding needless clutter. On the other hand, if you have a particularly low GPA you have even more reason not to include it on your resume. (If you do have a low GPA and you are asked to provide it in an application or at a job interview, for example, it is worth working out in advance what your GPA was in your major rather than your overall GPA, as that number will likely be more favorable and indicative of abilities related to the job you are applying for.) Either way, just leave it off.

Objective or summary statement. Although the objective or summary statement has been ubiquitous in the business world for more than a decade, you don't need to include one on your resume, especially for traditional theatrical jobs. They take up valuable space, and most I've seen make one want to roll one's eyes. Isn't your objective to get the job you just applied to? The only time you might consider including an objective is if you are applying to work with a large corporate entertainment company such as PSAV, Universal, Disney, etc. In my work with hiring managers and recruiters at those companies, the corporate culture is to accept an objective or summary statement, but only if it really needs to be there and adds something that can't be covered another way. As Sheri Croft, who has thirty years' experience as a leader in entertainment at the Walt Disney Company, put it, "As a hiring leader I'm not taking your word for what your professional strengths are, so don't waste space on your resume with that. That's what your references are for."[3]

If you do choose to include an objective anyway, a typical formula is to highlight your most valuable traits or relevant skills, list the position you are applying for at the specific company you are applying to, and connect how you would be able to help them accomplish their goals. You need to find a balance between what you want and what you can do for them. Here is an example of an objective:

> Experienced and efficient theatrical audio technician seeking to make magical guest experiences as an A1 or A2 with Walt Disney Entertainment.

How is a summary statement different? It may have some similarities to an objective, but it focuses on your strengths and skills and not a specific job. A summary statement for the same person may read:

> Experienced and efficient theatrical audio technician specializes in live performance and is especially skilled in system setup, live mixing, and troubleshooting

If you are applying for jobs where you believe an objective will give you an advantage in the hiring process, remember that you must write a new objective for each job you apply for. You might even be able to pull keywords from the job description for which you are applying. Does the job description say they are looking for someone to work in a "fast-paced environment" or that the successful candidate will be a demonstrated multitasker? If so, including that language will tie you more closely to the criteria. All that being said, I advise you to avoid objective or summary statements altogether.

How Long Should My Resume Be?

Resumes, especially those used early in your career, are expected to be one page, including references. (There is typically no limit to how long your academic CV can be—in fact, there is a joke that the person with the longest

---

[3]Sheri Croft, "Theatre Careers for Production," guest lecture, University of Central Florida, February 18, 2020.

CV will get the job.) Remember that potential employers will review your resume in about six seconds. If you run things on to a second page, they are unlikely even to get to it before making an initial decision about whether to move you forward or not.

As you gain more experience, keeping it to one page can become more challenging. So if you have too much to fit on one page, what do you do? If you are just slightly on to two pages, adjust formatting like margins, line spacing, or font sizes. If you are more than a little bit over, or formatting adjustments still don't allow you to fit everything on one page, you need to consider other options. Perhaps the easiest is to remove some items from your resume. Do you list some related experience that isn't directly tied to the type of job you are applying for? If you are applying for a scenic design position but have also done lighting design and don't have space to include it, put lighting design in your skills section instead of listing the individual credits. You can also mention it in your cover letter. Maybe as a scene designer you think it is important to leave the lighting design work in as additional examples of design experience, so you could instead remove your technical roles like carpenter or run crew.

If neither of these methods succeeds in shortening your resume sufficiently, your only remaining option is to begin removing individual credits from your list of experience. When doing so, you should add the modifier "Selected" to the heading of that section, so the reader knows it is not a comprehensive list. There are two schools of thought when it comes to choosing which credits to remove: either remove all shows before a certain year and add a small note that reads "credits prior to 20XX available on my website," or cherry-pick individual shows throughout the list. If you have a significant credit you don't want to delete, cherry-picking can allow the impressive item to stay on your resume.

What if you have the opposite problem? What if, even after adding all the relevant information you have, there's lots of empty white space on the page? You can start with the same techniques used when working with a too-long resume, and see if there are formatting adjustments you can make in the margins, line spacing, or font sizes to allow the information you do have to fill the available space better. This technique will work only if you have just a small amount of space to fill or balance out; large adjustments can quickly begin to look comical, or as if you are *trying* to fill the space. If you have a significant amount of space to fill on the page, a better option is to use the descriptive chronological resume format mentioned earlier. This allows you to include additional relevant details that will provide more information yet not feel like padding. Let's look at an example of how this can work: the resume of a developing technician applying for a lighting position. Even with a skills section, education, and references, their experience doesn't fill the rest of the page:

Lighting Experience—Gadsden State University

Assistant Lighting Designer	*The Bubbly Black Girl ...*	Esmee Estes	2022
Master Electrician	*The Amen Corner*	Jermaine Robbins	2021
Assistant Master Electrician	*Before It Hits Home*	Kerri Sisselman	2021
Programmer	*Fires in the Mirror*	Merilee Barrera	2020
Electrics Crew	*The Colored Museum*	Myra Katzker	2020
Spot Op	*Fetch Clay, Make Man*	Willis Chico	2020

By switching to the descriptive chronological format it's possible to add detail and length in a way that still feels professional.

Lighting Experience—Gadsden State University

Assistant Lighting Designer   *The Bubbly Black Girl ...*   Esmee Estes   2022
- Visual research related to variety of moods in play
- Drafted light plot based on designer's notes and instructions (157 instruments)
- Created/maintained paperwork: instrument schedule, magic sheets, cue lists (392 cues)
- Took notes during meetings and techs to support designer

Master Electrician   *The Amen Corner*   Jermaine Robbins   2021
- Managed team of four electricians during hang, focus, work calls
- 176 instruments
- Ordering and prepping show expendables (gel, gobos, etc.)
- Created custom hand-held electric lanterns

Assistant Master Electrician   *Before It Hits Home*   Kerri Sisselman   2021
- Cut and prep of color and templates for hang and focus
- Tracked work notes during technical rehearsals

Programmer   *Fires in the Mirror*   Merilee Barrera   2020
- 168 conventional fixtures, 22 automated
- Creation of focus palettes to aid designer during cue creation

Electrics Crew   *The Colored Museum*   Myra Katzker   2020
- Operation of scissor-lift AWP during hang and focus

Spot Op   *Fetch Clay, Make Man*   Willis Chico   2020

In the example above, we take the concept of providing additional details from the functional resume style and apply it to the job responsibilities and accomplishments in the chronological style, creating the descriptive chronological style.

Jobs with more responsibility tend to have more details you can use. Include things unique to each show or project, since most people reviewing your resume will know the basic job descriptions and it could come across as padding if all you list are the basics.

Organization

Now that you've gathered all the information you plan to include in your resume, you need to decide exactly how it all goes together on the page. Regardless of how you ultimately choose to organize your resume, your name, title, and contact information should be at the top of the page so they are easy to find.

Of all the sections of a resume, the one that engenders the most debate about placement is "Education." Does it go at the top or the bottom? The answer is … it depends. As with most things, there are strategies to consider. Are you a recent graduate or still in school? Put it at the top so that your experience is reviewed in the proper context. Did you graduate from a strong or prominent program? At the top, so this is highlighted for networking purposes. Are you applying for a job in academia or one that requires a certain degree? At the top, so there is no mistaking that you meet the minimum requirements.

If you have professional experience you want to make prominent, especially if the job description requires a certain kind or amount of prior experience, then put your education at the bottom. If you have been out of school for a long time and you don't see your education as having a big impact on your qualifications for a job, put it at the bottom. You decide if "Education" goes at the top or the bottom based on what matters most for you and the specific job for which you are applying.

Experience is next. The strategies you should consider when organizing this section will depend on the job you are applying for and your experience. You may opt to use a different organizational plan for every application to ensure you are highlighting your key features for that specific job. Don't get stuck on always doing it the same way just because that is how you have always done it before. Let's explore some of the most common methods.

Organization by Job Title

Job title is the most common organizational plan, with the job titles serving as headings: stage manager, assistant stage manager, production assistant; technical director, master carpenter, carpenter, run crew; lighting designer, associate lighting designer, assistant lighting designer, programmer, master electrician, etc. You get the idea. This system only works well if you have at least a couple of shows to list under each heading you want to use. It can serve to highlight your progress into jobs with more responsibility or to feature the positions you've held that are most applicable to the job to which you are applying. A typical layout using this system might look something like this:

Cutter/Draper			
Pass Over	Theatre South	Gabriel Santos	2024
The Bluest Eye	Union Theatre	Jaidon Simmons	2023
First Hand			
Trouble in Mind	Dragon Productions	Freja Sullivan	2023
An Octoroon	Mojo Theatre	Liberty Hassan	2022
Kill Move Paradise	Mojo Theatre	Liberty Hassan	2022
Stitcher			
Fires in the Mirror	Theatre South	Gabriel Santos	2022
Dutchman	Theatre South	Gabriel Santos	2022
Topdog/Underdog	Mojo Theatre	Liberty Hassan	2021
Wardrobe			
Blues for Mr. Charlie	Lifeline Theatre	Esme Wallis	2021
Fairview	Lifeline Theatre	Esme Wallis	2021

Or like this:

Master Electrician			
Theatre South	*Force Continuum*	Payton Lyon	2024
Kimball Theatre	*Blood at the Root*	Kaylan Sandoval	2023
Board Operator			
Theatre Jacksonville	*Sweat*	Payton Lyon	2023
Theatre Jacksonville	*Hurt Village*	McKenzie Carpenter	2023
Follow Spot			
Black Ensemble Theatre	*Black Nativity*	Lisa D. Cook	2023

Electrician

Onstage Atlanta	*Bootycandy*	Korey Yang	2022
Onstage Atlanta	*Jar the Floor*	Korey Yang	2022
Kimball Theatre	*The Mountaintop*	Felix Pitt	2021
Theatre South	*White Noise*	Taryn Washington	2021
Black Ensemble Theatre	*Jitney*	Amara Jackson	2021

When just starting out as a student or recent graduate, it is fine to list your other theatrical/entertainment-related experience even if it isn't directly related to the job being applied for. Once you've been working professionally for a while, those things will be viewed as superfluous and will need to be removed from your resume. For example, I was a lighting designer in college as well as a costume designer. While in college and shortly thereafter, I listed that experience on my resume to show a diversity of skills and an understanding of the entire process; but on my resume I set this below all my costuming work because I was not marketing myself as a lighting designer and it deserved a less prominent location. Once I established myself as a costume designer, I took the lighting design credits off my resume and have not listed them in years. Most people I work with have no idea!

Organization by Employer

If you are in a situation where you want to emphasize the places you have worked over the types of jobs you have done, organization by employer makes sense. Perhaps you've primarily worked in staff positions or for corporate entertainment companies. Is the job to which you are applying a staff post where you may be asked to fill a variety of roles, so you don't know what job category to list first? In these cases, emphasizing who you've worked for may be better than highlighting what specific jobs you've held. If you are a freelancer looking to move into a more traditional job and are listing your work by employer, you can still put freelance work as a separate section, positioning it either above or below the staff jobs depending on the type of work you want to emphasize. I knew one student who did an internship with an international corporate entertainment company while in college. When they were about to graduate and looked for a full-time position, they planned to apply to that same company. If their resume had been organized according to job title, the work they had done for this company would get buried somewhere in the middle. I encouraged them instead to reorganize their resume, sorting by employer, with that employer at the top of the list. This was a situation where only having one entry under a heading was acceptable because they were making this choice for a very specific reason—to ensure that the company they were applying to knew that they had completed an internship there. While it is impossible to know if it was this strategy that helped them get the job (which they did, by the way), we certainly know it made the hiring department's job easier because that very important information was not buried among other credits. Here is an example of what it looks like to organize by employer.

Stray Dog Theatre			
Scenic Artist			
No Place to Be Somebody		Brandy Clements	2023
Fisk University			
Scenic Charge Artist			
And Jesus Moonwalks the Mississippi		LJ Williams	2023
What to Send Up When It Goes Down		Desiderio Roybal	2022
Scenic Artist			
Fabulation, or the Re-Education of Undine		Joel Ebarb	2022
Zooman and the Sign		Reji Woods	2021

When organizing your resume by employer, you can use the descriptive chronological format if your official job title may not communicate to anyone outside the company what your responsibilities actually were. Here is an example.

Walt Disney Entertainment 2004–2018

Production Planner

- Planning and implementing technical aspects of entertainment offerings, including lighting, sound, staging, and graphics for numerous events.
  - **Special events**: Super Soap Weekends, ESPN The Weekends, Tom Joyner family reunions.
  - **Major conventions:** Outback Steakhouse, One Mighty Party, Kawasaki, Grainger, and Pampered Chef among many, many others.
  - **Private parties:** Joey Fatone, Paris Hilton, David Hasselhoff.

Tech 2

- Offline preprogramming editor; working with LD and ME on system control assignments and data management; onsite console programming and operation
  - **Special events:** American Idol press event, Night of Joy, New Year's Eves, Finding Nemo press event.

Organization by Level of Experience

Some job advertisements indicate that you must have a certain amount of professional experience. That might be a reason to sort your experience by level to make sure the potential employer sees you meet that minimum qualification without having to read through your resume to get this information. Your headings could look something like this.

Professional Experience [or Professional Lighting Experience if it is all lighting]

Lighting Designer	Lifeline Theatre	*Choir Boy*	Jazmyn Murphy	2024
Programmer	Annex Theatre	*Jitney*	Kingston Williams	2024
Lighting Designer	Teatro Dallas	*The Invaders*	Katia Porro	2023
Board Op	Annex Theatre	*Paradise Blue*	Kingston Williams	2022
Master Electrician	Annex Theatre	*The Sirens*	Brogan Rosario	2021

University Experience

Assistant Lighting Designer	Florida A&M	*Day of Absence*	Seren Grace	2021
Master Electrician	Florida A&M	*The Piano Lesson*	Amy Davis	2021
Assistant Master Electrician	Florida A&M	*The Amen Corner*	Reji Woods	2020

Notice the repetition of "Florida A&M" above. This type of repetition causes an unwanted focal point; in these situations, move the repetitive information into the heading and eliminate the column so the heading and section look like this.

University Experience—Florida A&M

Assistant Lighting Designer	*Day of Absence*	Seren Grace	2021
Master Electrician	*The Piano Lesson*	Amy Davis	2021
Assistant Master Electrician	*The Amen Corner*	Reji Woods	2020

In the "Professional Experience" section above, notice how when listed in reverse chronological order the job titles are all mixed up and it is hard to see how often the person has worked in each job. You could further subdivide this by place or by job, and then remove the column that is named in the heading.

This layout emphasizes that you have professional experience, separating it from your collegiate experience, and highlights the names of the places you've worked. This style can really help to show how often you've been hired again at each theatre, and remember that this is just like a recommendation because it means they liked you enough to hire you again. Each entry remains in reverse chronological order within each section.

Professional Experience

    Lifeline Theatre

Lighting Designer	*Choir Boy*	Jazmyn Murphy	2024

    Teatro Dallas

Lighting Designer	*The Invaders*	Katia Porro	2023

    Annex Theatre

Programmer	*Jitney*	Kingston Williams	2024
Board Op	*Paradise Blue*	Kingston Williams	2022
Master Electrician	*The Sirens*	Brogan Rosario	2021

An alternative to the example above, which subdivides by place, is to subdivide your levels of experience by job title instead, like this:

Professional Experience

    Lighting Designer

Lifeline Theatre	*Choir Boy*	Jazmyn Murphy	2024
Teatro Dallas	*The Invaders*	Katia Porro	2023

    Programmer

Annex Theatre	*Jitney*	Kingston Williams	2024

    Master Electrician

Annex Theatre	*The Sirens*	Brogan Rosario	2021

    Board Op

Annex Theatre	*Paradise Blue*	Kingston Williams	2022

This organization emphasizes the level of work you have attained and the jobs you have done at that level. The job title isn't needed on each line because it is covered in the subheadings.

It is also possible to organize by job without giving up so much space to subtitles by putting a small space between the different jobs instead. This format helps to emphasize how many times you have worked in each position.

Professional Experience

Lighting Designer	Lifeline Theatre	*Choir Boy*	Jazmyn Murphy	2024
Lighting Designer	Teatro Dallas	*The Invaders*	Katia Porro	2023
Programmer	Annex Theatre	*Jitney*	Kingston Williams	2024
Master Electrician	Annex Theatre	*The Sirens*	Brogan Rosario	2021
Board Op	Annex Theatre	*Paradise Blue*	Kingston Williams	2022

Choosing one of these layouts over another will depend on what you want to emphasize for each job application. I suggest starting with organization by job title to see how that works for you, and consider the other organizational schemes if one or another supports the nature of your experience or there is a specific job for which it would make sense.

Formatting and Layout

When laying out and and formatting your resume, you want to focus on making it both reader-friendly and skimmable for potential employers and easily scalable and editable for you. Let's start with some basic readability tips.

Prioritization

The average potential employer may only make it halfway through your resume before moving on to the next applicant. You want to make sure they see the most important information first, so they are enticed to move you into the "maybe" pile. This means the most important information for that application goes at the top and down the left-hand side. Think of your resume like an outline. Things specific to you are most important, so what you did on a show should be given more priority than the name of the show.

Headings and Subheadings

Clear labels help guide the potential employer to what you and they want to see, so the formatting of your headings and subheadings is important. Incorporate your color palette into your headings and subheadings—this helps you create a visually unified and appealing document and also guides the person reading it to the information they are looking for.

No Centering

Centered text is more difficult and slower to read. You want a potential employer to take in as much of your resume as possible, so speed of reading is critical. Avoid centered text in general and stick with left-aligned text for everything except columns on the far right, which can be right aligned.

Avoid Long Descriptive Sentences

- Sentences take longer to read.
- Employers want facts—quickly.
- Lists are easier and faster.
- Don't overuse bullets—they become visual clutter.

Be Consistent

People's brains are set up to recognize patterns quickly and react positively to them. Consistency in font styles, formatting, and layout help the reader find what they need as quickly as possible. Consistency in how you word things is also important. Stick with the same parts of speech for headings and other labels. For example, when listing your work experience choose either the job category (Sound Design, Audio Engineering, Scene Design, Carpentry, etc.) or the job title (Sound Designer, Audio Engineer, Scene Designer, Carpenter, etc.). Don't mix the two together. Pick one and stick with it.

Spacing

Once you have decided on your headings and know what information you need to include for each, it is time to start putting it all together. The information and exact spacing on every resume will, of course, be unique depending on what you need to include, but generally you can start with the layout shown in Figure 1 for a standard 8.5 inch × 11 inch page.

If you need to add additional sections, "Awards and Honors" for example, then you must shorten one or more of the other sections to make space, but do not remove any. The sections shown in Figure 1 are the bare minimum for a complete resume.

Most resumes have half-inch margins on all sides, so set your margins there to begin with. They can always be adjusted as you go, but don't make the margins any smaller than half an inch. The eye needs some white space to rest.

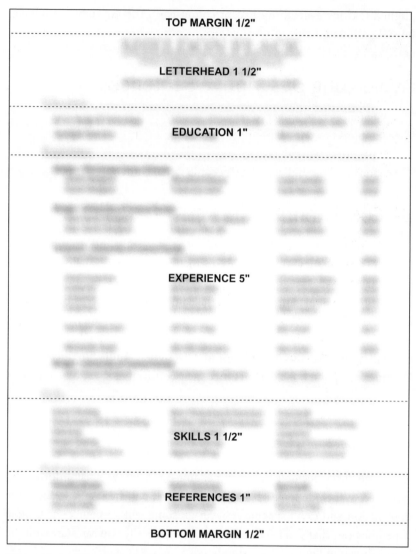

Figure 1 Resume spacing

Setting Tab Stops Instead of Templates or Tables

It is very tempting to open up your word processing program, find a template that is attractive, and just plop all your information into it. Don't do it. There are two major problems with using a template for your resume. The most practical of them is that resumes in theatre and the entertainment industry don't look like resumes in the rest of the world. You could do an internet search for "theatre resume template" and find a couple of options that aren't just for actors, but they are not particularly well done and may not fit your specific experience details. You also don't want to submit your resume to a job and have it look exactly like another applicant's resume. You can create a much more effective and attractive design from a blank document using a well-planned layout and custom tab stops.

The system I recommend for laying out the horizontal look of your resume is using tab stops. People who've tried to use inserted tables in their Word document almost all eventually run into some sort of layout problem they couldn't overcome. Also, since applicant tracking systems (computer programs that scan and read resumes at larger companies) often struggle with tables, there is no compelling reason to use them and more reasons to avoid them.

Your word processing program has default tab stops set every half inch, but you can adjust and customize these tab stops to be anywhere you want along the top ruler. Be sure you understand what the symbols mean and what they do, so you can maximize their usefulness. Under no circumstance should you resort to adding in individual spaces here or there, or at the beginning of a line to nudge it over a bit; use a tab stop so you know for sure that everything will be lined up. Spend some time on the web viewing tutorials about how to set tab stops before you begin to format your resume, paying special attention to your ability to adjust all the tab stops in a section by highlighting the section and adjusting your stop locations; this allows you to adjust whole sections very easily.

Placing Your Content

In Chapter 2 you created your letterhead and that is a good place to start your resume, as it has all the information you need to include: name, job title, email, phone number, website address, city, state. Some people change the layout of their letterhead for the top of their resume, using the same fonts and colors so it is still clearly their personal brand, but arranging it slightly differently.

The information you have for each of your sections will determine how many tab stops you need in each section. It is not necessary that each section has the exact same number of tab stops or stop locations. English is read from left to right, so you want the most important information (your headings) on the left to guide your reader to what they want to see. Information below the headings should be organized in columns using custom tab stops. Our eyes can spot very slight indentations, so you don't have to use the standard half-inch tab space; even a tab stop a few spaces over will organize the information visually. If you make your tab stops too wide, you may not be able to fit all your columns into the available space.

Education Layout

Under your heading, the degree you earned goes to the far left, including the major because that is the most important part of your degree. If you had a minor that can go next, or below your major. Then comes the school from which you received the degree, and finally the year you completed the degree or anticipate completing it goes to the far right. You can use "anticipated," "projected completion," "projected," "Completion in month/year," etc. to communicate that you have not yet graduated. Just including the year if you have not yet graduated, even if the year is in the future, can easily be misread.

EDUCATION

BFA Design & Technology	Central State University	Anticipated 2025
Minor in Studio Art		
Associate of Arts: General Studies	Bishop State Community College	2022

Skills Layout

Your goal in laying out your skills section is to group the information in a logical way and evenly spaced across the page so there is no large, odd blank space. Here are a couple of layout options.

Skills

Sewing: Industrial machine stitching, embroidery machine, serger threading, millinery

Crafts: Dyeing, distressing, clay sculpting, leatherwork, Fosshape, Wonderflex

Computer: 3D printing, Photoshop, Microsoft Office, FileMaker Pro, Mac and PC

Other: Basic carpentry, wiring, and soldering, valid passport and driver's license

Skills

Industrial machines	Leatherwork	Microsoft Office
Embroidery	Fosshape	FileMaker Pro
Serger threading	Wonderflex	Mac and PC
Millinery	3D printing	Basic wiring
Dyeing	Basic carpentry	Valid passport
Distressing	Soldering	Valid driver's license
Sculpting	Photoshop	

References Layout

Each of your references should include the name, position or job title, where they work, email, and phone number. Horizontal layout takes less space.

References

Morgan Burhoe, Event Designer, Metropolis Productions, morgan@metpro.com, (555) 122-1212

Kyra McNeil, Shop Foreperson, Dillard University, kmcneil@dillardU.edu, (975) 323-6532

Tasha Mohr, Scenic Designer, Timeline Theatre, tasham@timeline.org, (243) 645-9856

However, I find horizontal reference layout difficult to read, and advocate vertical layout using tab stops to place each reference. It is easier to find the information fast because we are used to looking at this format when reading addresses. Right justifying the third reference keeps a clean edge down the right side of the page.

References

Morgan Burhoe	**Kyra McNeil**	**Tasha Mohr**
Event Designer	Shop Foreperson	Scenic Designer
Metropolis Productions	Dillard University	Timeline Theatre
morgan@metpro.com	kmcneil@dillard.edu	tasham@timeline.org
(555) 122-1212	(975) 323-6532	(243) 645-9856

Sending Your Resume

When it comes to printing your resume, be sure to use a high print quality paper. The paper does not necessarily have to be marketed as "resume paper": it should be nicer and a slightly heavier weight than the paper you print on every day, but do not use cardstock or other very thick papers—these make your resume stand out, but not in a good way. You want your resume to be elevated above the everyday printing you do. If you want to use colored paper, remember that the color you choose needs to fit within the color palette you have selected, and you need to plan for that additional color from the beginning as you will also need to incorporate it into your business cards, cover letter, website, portfolio, etc. Do not use dark colors or papers with textures or patterns, as this will make your resume more difficult to read.

When providing your resume electronically, it is important that you never email a Word document of your materials or paste the resume into the body of an email. Always convert documents you are sending to PDF, so you don't lose the fonts and formatting you have spent so much time perfecting. When naming your files, "[Last Name] Resume" is most appropriate. Leave out other words like *final, latest, new, updated*, etc. As a potential employer it is very frustrating to download resumes during a search process and discover fifteen files all named "resume" on your desktop!

You can find examples of full-color resumes in Plates 13, 15, 17, and 19, and on the companion website.

4

Cover Letters and Other Correspondence

While people don't write many letters in day-to-day life any more, letter writing is still an important business skill. Unless the advertisement specifically says not to send one, a cover letter remains a standard expectation for job applications. Some people are of the opinion that no one ever reads your cover letter, but while that may be true in some situations, cover letters can also be a very important tool in getting you into the "yes" pile or helping the potential employer decide between you and another applicant with commensurate experience. One thing's for certain: your application will never be discarded because you included a cover letter, but you may be overlooked for the job if you don't.

Your cover letter is your first, and possibly only, chance to demonstrate to the potential employer that you are a good fit for this specific position by addressing the job requirements in the advertisement and relating them to work listed on your resume. You can use your cover letter to highlight any particularly strong experience you have, and it can be used to provide context for anything that may not be clear from your resume (career change, gaps in your production history or employment, etc.). Cover letters also demonstrate your written communications skills and your attention to detail—skills that are needed for any job. A well-formatted letter will catch the employer's eye. You can find examples of cover letters in Plates 14, 16, 18, and 20, and can view them in larger size along with additional examples on the companion website.

Formatting Your Formal Cover Letter

Formal letter writing, also called business writing, is not emphasized any more, and I find many young professionals have no idea how to format a letter or even that there are "rules" to formatting letters. Maybe you were taught formatting for business letters years ago but haven't used it in so long you don't remember what to do. Either way, it is important for you to follow the conventions of formal letter writing for job applications and business purposes. You typically write a formal business letter to someone you do not know asking them to do something. Formal letters communicate important information, and are often a matter of record.

There are three different styles of formal letters, but the one that is most common and expected is called full block. The "modified block" and "semi-block" are not recommended for business writing, so I will not cover them here. "Full block" style aligns everything to the left and does not use indents at the beginning of each paragraph. Full block is all single spaced, with double spaces to separate different parts of the letter. That spacing is specific and important. The full content of your letter should be centered in the available top-to-bottom space on the page (see Figure 2). That means there is no set amount of space down from the top of the page before the letter begins. The size of letterheads will vary as well.

The first item on the page, a couple of lines below your letterhead, is your return address (assuming it is not included already as part of your letterhead). If your address is included in your letterhead there is no need to repeat it in the body of the letter. If your letter is only being emailed, you can forgo the snail mail address. After your address, hit enter/return twice to leave one blank line and then type the date, being sure to spell out the month; for example, October 24, 2010 or 24 October 2010.

After the date, hit enter/return twice to leave another blank line, then type the name and address of the person to whom you are sending the letter, using the US Post Office standard format. This is called the inside address. After the inside address hit enter/return twice to leave another blank line, then type your salutation, such as Dear M. Cohen:, Dear DeAndre Harris:, Dear Dr. Bird Bear:. Be very careful about using a title that specifies gender if you do not know what gender signifier you should use. If you are at all concerned, simply use the first name or first initial and last name. Do your best to find out to whom you should address your letter, but if that information

Figure 2 Cover letter spacing

is not available you can use something like "Dear Hiring Committee" or "Dear Hiring Team." Do not ever use "To Whom It May Concern" or "Dear Sir or Madam." They are too impersonal and show a lack of thought. I once received a cover letter addressed to "Dear Sirs" sent to an all-woman search committee; that person did not make a good first impression. A colon (:) should follow your salutation in business letters; commas after the salutation are for informal letter writing.

After your salutation, hit enter/return twice to leave another blank line, then begin your first paragraph without indenting the first line so that everything stays aligned with your left margin. Leave a single blank line after each paragraph. After the body of your letter (letter content is covered in the next section) hit the enter/return key twice to leave another single blank line and then type your closing, followed by a comma. Hit the enter/return key four times, then type your name. This leaves three blank lines and provides space for your signature. If sending the letter electronically you have the option of printing the letter, signing it by hand, and then scanning it back into the computer, or an easier method is to scan a clean, high-resolution (300 ppi or greater) copy of your signature and insert the image of your signature and position/size it as needed to fit in the signature space.

Cover letters always come with at least one enclosure, your resume. After your name, hit the enter/return key twice to leave a single blank line and type "Enclosure." You can, if you like, detail exactly what is enclosed, like this: "Enclosure: Resume."

Once you have composed your whole letter you should check if your content is centered in the available space. Adjust the spacing above your address as necessary to move your letter up or down. Do not adjust any of the other spacing in the letter, as the internal spacing is specific for formal business letters. You can make slight adjustments to your margins either to help fill the page or to fit more on the page. Your cover letter, like your resume, should never be more than one page and should not be so full that it looks cramped. If it does, it is likely that most of it will not be read. If you cannot fit the text on to one page, you need to go back and revise the letter until you can.

What Goes in My Cover Letter?

A cover letter shouldn't be a repackaging of your resume, but should provide additional detail that can't be gleaned from your resume and should specifically address the job description for which you are applying. That being said, the body of cover letters follows a pretty standard pattern.

Opening Paragraph

The opening paragraph is typically only a few sentences in length. It should clearly state the purpose of your letter, beginning with an opening sentence stating the job for which you are applying. Do not make your recipient read past the first sentence wondering why they are reading the letter. Tell them where you learned of the opening, and share any connections you have to the company. Do you know someone who currently or formerly worked there who suggested you apply or told you great things about the company? Did you work at the company in previous years and are interested in coming back? Are you a frequent patron and go to lots of their shows? Did you meet a recruiter at a conference? If so, tell them. Then give a one-sentence taste of what is to come in your letter. Below are some examples of opening paragraphs—but it is not wise to copy any of these examples as written, because yours may not be the only letter with the same opening.

> Please accept this letter and the accompanying materials as my application for the Milliner position which I found advertised on OffStageJobs.com. My friend Johan Gallardo was a stitcher with your company last season, and spoke highly of the experience and your great production values. I think my millinery training and experience would align well with what Johan has shared with me.

> I am writing to you to apply for a Milliner position with your company. I met with Janet Arnold at USITT in March and she suggested I apply. It was very exciting to hear about the kinds of materials you work with and the high level of craftsmanship and artistry that is expected from everyone in the costume shop. I would love the opportunity to make a contribution to your team.

> I found your job announcement in *ArtSearch* seeking a Milliner, and after researching your company online I knew this was a job I needed to apply for. Your mission of creating an ensemble of theatre professionals who develop long-term collaborative relationships sounds like an ideal environment in which to produce the outstanding work demonstrated in your wonderful production photos and reviews.

Details

The next paragraph or two should provide details of your skills and experience, with examples from your past work to demonstrate what you mean. Pay particular attention to any language in the job description regarding the job requirements, and be sure to address those points in your cover letter. Let's say you're applying for an assistant stage manager position and the job description lists these responsibilities:

- act as the hub of communication between artistic and technical areas
- ensure safety measures are always followed
- oversee rehearsals
- maintain the show's paperwork and daily records
- manage backstage areas during the run of the show
- experience on large-scale productions a must
- must be fluent in English; other languages appreciated.

These are all things you can try to address in your cover letter. Give examples. Don't just list them and say "I can do all these things," but actually talk about a time when you have done them. Avoid cliché phrases like "goal oriented," "passionate," and "hone my skills." Use details and specific words that describe you and your work. For example:

As I complete my BFA degree in Stage Management at the University of Central Florida, I am grateful for my hands-on experience on so many productions. As an assistant stage manager for *Oklahoma!* performed in the Disney Theatre (capacity 2,500) at the Dr. Phillips Performing Arts Center in downtown Orlando, I had to adjust our production almost daily to accommodate an understudy put in. I updated all the necessary paperwork, was in constant communication with artistic leadership, my crew, and front of house to be sure everyone had the correct information, and I collaborated with my team to be sure all the performers had everything they needed for a safe, quality performance. My quick thinking, organization, strong instincts, and people skills aided me in this situation.

I am currently working as the stage manager for *Writes of Spring*, a new play workshop program produced by the Orlando Rep. I am sure to track all the script changes accurately and communicate the daily script changes to everyone on the team, so I can ensure that everyone is literally on the same page. Prior to this position, I was the assistant stage manager for Theatre Downtown's production of *She Kills Monsters*, where I oversaw weapon safety and stage combat in addition to choreographing backstage traffic patterns, weapon handoffs, and frequent costume changes. These experiences have uniquely prepared me as a strong leader and communicator ready for a fast-paced environment like yours.

These paragraphs addressed communication, safety, rehearsals, paperwork, backstage management, and large-scale productions—almost all the requirements of the job.

Wrap Up

After you discuss how you fit the job description, you need to close your letter and indicate the next step. Reiterate your qualifications and how you can meet the company's needs. Here are some examples.

> I would love the chance to uphold the creative and high-quality production values for which the Orlando Shakes is known. I will follow up in a week to see if there is anything else I can provide.

> I am very excited to learn more about working at Orlando Shakes and show you how my experience will allow me to meet your expectations for this position. I'm especially interested in learning more about your new play festival and how I could help contribute to its success. I hope we can talk soon.

> I would love the chance to show you why the directors I work with consider me an essential part of their team. Please feel free to call my references or anyone I've worked with. I will check in next week to be sure you received my materials.

There are some things you do not want to say in your closing (or anywhere in your letter, actually). Do not tell them you are the perfect person for the job, as you don't know who else has applied. They will decide who is perfect for the job, and it might not be you. Express enthusiasm but don't tell them how much you want the job. Focus on how you can contribute, not how much you would get out of the job. Do not tell them you will call to schedule an interview. Checking on your materials arriving is one thing, but scheduling an interview is up to them. Don't be overconfident or arrogant.

Closing Salutation

"Sincerely" is a perfectly acceptable closing salutation. Other options include "Thank you," "Best regards," "Respectfully," or a variation thereof. You don't want to use a closing salutation that is too informal, like "Take care," "Best wishes," "Faithfully," "Peace and Love," or "Fondly."

Professional Emails

A well-written formal cover letter does not eliminate the need also to be able to write an appropriate professional email. You will often be asked to submit your application materials via email, attaching your resume and cover letter. In this case simply write a brief email message to indicate your interest and direct them to your attached materials. Do not include your cover letter or resume in the body of the email. While email is a less formal form of communication, you are not writing to one of your friends. You are writing to a professional and hoping they will hire you to represent them or their company in some way, so it is important that you demonstrate your professional communication skills here. An application email might go something like this.

SUBJECT: Scenic Artist Application: Sadiyah Bridges

Dear Wanda Raimundi-Ortiz:

Please accept this email and the attached cover letter and resume as my application for the Scenic Artist position at the City of Maples Repertory Theatre. I hope we can talk soon.

Thank you,
Sadiyah Bridges
Scenic Artist
www.sadiyahbridges.com

Remember these points of email etiquette whenever using email for professional correspondence.

- Always send professional emails from your professional email address.
- Always include a subject line specific to your message that is clear and concise. A poor subject line is a quick way to annoy the person to whom you are writing or for your email to get lost.
- Until given permission to use a more casual greeting, keep it professional. Include a non-gendered greeting like "Dear S. Hwang:" Remember that titles are important, and use them if the person has one. For example, if the person has a PhD, they have earned the title Dr. and will notice if you leave it off. Only stray from a formal greeting if they ask you to. If they say "call me Sooyoung" then you are free to change your greeting to "Dear Sooyoung:"
- Use the To, CC, and BCC fields correctly. The To field indicates the person or persons for whom your message is specifically intended. Those whom you also wish to receive a copy of your email are placed in the CC field. To help you remember, CC actually stands for "carbon copy," though that term is outdated and "courtesy copy" is a more contemporary definition. When you send a CC an identical copy of the message is sent to the email addresses in this field and

everyone who receives the email will see that it was also sent to them. Think of BCC as "blocked courtesy copy."[1] When using the BCC field, those listed in the field get an identical copy of your message, but no one else receiving the email will know about the BCC recipients (unless they reply all) and they will not receive any further replies to the thread. Be careful using this field; its secrecy has a negative connotation. However, if you are sending an email to a large group of people and want to make sure a "reply all" fiasco is avoided, BCC is a good tool to use. If you put yourself in the To field and place all the recipients in the BCC field, the only person they can reply to is the sender.

- Write in complete sentences. This is not a text message, group chat, or email to your sister. Do not use abbreviations or text language in your professional emails.

- If you use an automatic signature block that goes below your name, keep it simple. First and last names, pronouns, email address, phone number, and website URL are sufficient. Other things you may want to add if applicable are title, company name, and links to your professional social media accounts. Avoid cliché quotes and clip art.

- Avoid exclamation points and emojis.

- Do not put the intended recipient's email address into the To field until you have completed and proofread your email, to avoid accidentally sending it too soon. You may even consider drafting messages in a word processing program and then copying and pasting into an email once complete.

- Reply promptly.

- Check your spam or junk-mail folder regularly in case a professional inquiry has been placed there by mistake.

Thank-You Notes

Thank-you notes are especially important following a job interview, but there is never a bad time to thank someone. Trends seem to be shifting to view email thank-you notes as acceptable. They are timely, and likely mimic the

---

[1]BCC has traditionally stood for "blind carbon copy." "Blocked courtesy copy" corrects the casual ableism and linguistic microaggression of using "blind" to mean lacking knowledge.

style of communication you have already had with those you are thanking. Some people prefer or are impressed by a handwritten thank-you note. You can print your own to match your marketing materials, or purchase professional-looking notecards. You can decide based on the circumstances surrounding each situation what the best choice is. But whether you decide to send a thank you by email or by snail mail, the content should be the same.

Following an interview, there is not much point to writing a generic thank-you note. When I receive a "thank you for taking the time to meet with me. I look forward to hearing from you soon" thank-you note, I tend to roll my eyes and toss it in the recycling. If I remember any of the generic ones it is for the wrong reasons. You need to write a thank-you note with substance that is genuine and, ideally, refers to the conversation you had during your interview. Each note should be customized to the receiver. Take notes at your interviews, because they can be especially helpful for thank-you messages. What key points about the job particularly excited you? What about the area or location appeals to you? Are the shows or schedule especially interesting to you? Did you pick up on a problem they are having that you think you could help with? You don't need to mention all these things in each thank-you note, but they will give you points to mention in the notes you do send. In addition to a job-related comment, you can also mention something more specific to each person. Did someone mention a new baby? A work or personal trip they have coming up? Did someone mention buying a new car or having visited the same hole-in-the-wall restaurant in Chicago that you love? Those are fantastic details to include to demonstrate you were listening and are interested in being a supportive teammate. I have only ever received one really good thank-you note in over twenty years of interviewing people, and I remember not only what it said but how it made me feel. It also reinforced my opinion that the person was the best fit for our job opening. Here is a sample that you can customize to you and your experience.

Dear Zoha Dominguez,

Thank you for meeting with me and answering my questions during my interview for the Technical Director position on Tuesday. I think the style and pace of your productions would be a great fit for my background and experience. I look forward to hearing back from the committee and hope I can look forward to working with you soon. Enjoy your travels in Southeast Asia this summer! It sounds like you have an amazing trip planned.

Thanks again,

Charis Medina

Letters of Recommendation

It is a lot of work for someone to write you a good letter of recommendation, and these letters can be a big factor in getting the job or school you want. You can recognize this effort, make the letter writer's job easier, and get a stronger letter of recommendation if you follow these guidelines when requesting letters.

If an application asks you to send letters of recommendation, you must do so, but you should not send them unless you are asked to. You can request letters of recommendation from the people you have listed on your resume as references, or you can ask other people not on your resume. You have an opportunity to get more people's positive recommendations in front of hirers if your letters and resume references do not match exactly.

The most important thing is common courtesy: be sure to ask your reference if they have time to provide you with a positive letter of recommendation for the type of job you are applying for. There is no need to overwhelm them with other information in your initial inquiry. Asking in person is always nice, but not always possible. An email to them could go something like this:

> Dear Ashwin,
>
> I am applying for a position as a technician on a cruise ship. Would you be able to write me a positive letter of recommendation? I would need the letter completed by [insert date that is at least two weeks away and at least one week before your deadline]. If you can, I will send you more information about the job and my qualifications.
>
> Thank you for your consideration,
> Michelle Greyeyes

Notice that the request includes the type of job you are applying for, asks for a positive letter, and includes a due date that is padded. I know only one person who will get a letter of recommendation out before the deadline; the reality is that letters are often written on, or even a couple days after, the due date. So never give your letter writers the actual date the letters must be in, because you will likely miss that deadline; give them a padded deadline (typically a week earlier), so if they miss it you can still meet the application deadline.

When you request a letter, you will likely get one of two replies: "Yes, of course! Can you give me more information?," or "I'm sorry, I don't have time." "I don't have time" has two potential meanings. The first is that they really just don't have time based on their schedule and when you need the letter—they may have time for a future opportunity, but not right now. Don't ask them again or otherwise try to change their mind. The second meaning of "I don't have time" in response to a request is that the person is not able to give you a positive recommendation but doesn't want to come out and say so. Either way, if someone says they do not have time, trust them and move on. The letter you would get if you try to convince them will either be rushed and lack detail, or will not be the positive letter you are hoping for.

If they say they are willing to write you a positive letter, send them a copy of the specific job description, the name and address of the person to whom it should be addressed, a pdf of your resume, a note of things you think would be good for them to highlight about you or it is important that they mention, and your (padded) deadline (and, of course, don't tell them it is padded). An email response could look something like this:

Dear Ashwin:

Thank you so much for making the time to write a letter of recommendation for me. I have attached a copy of the job description which has the name and address where the letter needs to be sent. I am happy to provide a stamped envelope so you can send it yourself, or you can give it to me to include with my package. I have also attached a copy of my resume to make it easier for you to remember what we have worked on together. I am especially hoping you can talk about how I always meet my deadlines and show up on time, that I'm very conscientious about doing my job correctly, and that I ask questions rather than guessing if I don't know how to do something. Maybe you can reference my backstage decision-making on *Annie Get Your Gun*. In order to make my deadlines I need the letter by March 1st.

Thank you again for agreeing to do this for me. I really appreciate your support.

Michelle Greyeyes

Once you have sent them all that information, you basically have to wait. A few days before the deadline you gave them, it is OK to send a short reminder—below are a couple of examples.

Dear Ashwin:

I have almost all my application materials together for the cruise ship job I'm applying for. Will you be sending your letter directly to them, or should I plan to include it with my materials?

Thanks again.

Michelle Greyeyes

Dear Ashwin:

Thanks again for agreeing to write a letter of recommendation for me for the cruise ship job I'm applying for. Will you be able to get it done by 1st March so I can submit it with all my application materials?

I hope tech went well for you last week!

Thank you,

Michelle Greyeyes

What if your deadline has come and gone and you did not receive your letter? It is OK to get in touch again, depending on what their previous replies have been. They are a person, and presumably a person who knows you well, so don't be afraid to talk to them. Chances are they already mailed it and forgot to tell you, or they feel terrible about missing your deadline and will get it to you very soon. Remember, this is why you didn't give them your real deadline.

If you are applying for multiple jobs at once, you should send your reference the information listed above for each job and ask them to personalize the letter for each job. Sometimes the letter can be exactly the same and they just need to add the name and address of the recipient; sometimes they need to tweak the content a bit. Not everyone will be willing to take the time to do this for you, but the letters are stronger if they are addressed directly to each employer. Some references will prefer to give you a "To Whom it May Concern" letter for you to duplicate and use as needed, because that saves them a great deal of time. These are OK, but not nearly as strong as an individualized letter. A "To Whom It May Concern" letter of recommendation tells the potential employer you are probably applying to many places at once, and might not be very serious about this job in particular. If this is in fact the case it is OK to use these letters, and perhaps your other letters can be personalized. If there is a really big job you are very serious about, perhaps use the generic letter for most applications but ask for an individualized letter for the really important job. Don't use a "To Whom It May Concern" letter for more than a few months. The letter should be dated, and once it is more than two or three months old it becomes stale and you should ask for an updated letter with an updated date.

1 Sample vision board (created by Jason Tollefson)

2 Sample vision board (created by Jason Tollefson)

3 Sample vision board (created by Jason Tollefson)

4 Original image without cropping (photo by Tony Firriolo)

5 Image cropped to full stage to eliminate dead space around the edges

6 Image cropped to highlight center stage, as might be needed by a scenic artist or costume designer

7 Image cropped to highlight a single costume: full body shot with space around the actor so the costume is still shown in context

8 Image cropped to highlight stage-right details: could be used to focus attention on props, scenic art, costumes, or electrics

9 Image cropped to highlight stage-left details: could be used to highlight furniture, scenic art, costumes, or electrics

10 Production photo with background in focus (photo by Tony Firriolo)

11 Production photo with foreground in focus (photo by Tony Firriolo)

12 Composite photo digitally combined with all actors in focus

HOWARD MOSLEY

they/them

CONTACT

HowardMosley@gmail.com
555-123-4567
www.HowardMosley.com
Bismark, ND

SKILLS

Equity Agreements
Gun Safety
Dance Terminology
Dance Notation
Reading Music
Hand Sewing
QLab
Vectorworks
Office Suite

CERTIFICATIONS

AHA CPR/First Aid
Intimacy Training
OSHA Lift
Valid Driver's License
HES Covid-19 Compliance
Stage Combat
Mediation

EXPERIENCE

Stage Managing

Hairspray	Westin Playhouse	Piper Adams	2021
West Side Story	The Shakes	Marlie Boyd	2021
Dreamgirls	Spellman College	Misha Roberson	2021
Half the Sky	Westin Playhouse	Moe Bridges	2020
Caroline, or Change	Spotlight Theatre	Shaina Johnson	2019

Assistant Stage Managing

The Lion King	Westin Playhouse	Ashanti Smith	2020
The Mountaintop	Kimball Theatre	Felix Pitt	2019
Half the Sky	Onstage Atlanta	Susan Anderson	2019
Caroline, or Change	Theatre South	Staci Yandoli	2018

Production Manager

Westin Playhouse	10 show season	Mable C.	2022
Celebration of Arts	City of Austin	Eileen Roybal	2021
Celebration of Arts	City of Austin	Eileen Roybal	2019

EDUCATION

MFA Arts Management   Smith University   Conferred 2020

REFERENCES

Mable C.
  Artistic Director, Westin Playhouse, mable@westin.org
Mary Ryder
  PSM, Onstage Atlanta, mryder@onstage.org
John Taylor
  Freelance Stage Manager, johntaylorSM@johntaylor.com

13 Resume design and layout: Howard (designed by Jason Tollefson)

HOWARD MOSLEY
SM — PM

555-123-4567 ● HowardMosley@gmail.com ● they/them ● www.howardmosley.com ● Bismark, ND

582 Rockaway Ave.
Bismarck, ND 58501

April 23, 2022

Kirsten Blaese
Production Manager
Arrowbear Theatre Festival
926 West Plumb Branch Avenue
Beachwood, OH 44122

Dear Kirsten Blaese:

I am writing in response to your ad in OffStageJobs seeking a stage manager for your upcoming musical theatre season. While I hadn't originally intended to specialize in musical theatre, that is how my career has developed and I think you will find my experience aligns well with your stated needs.

I have a proven track record of problem solving, collaboration, and calm under pressure. Those skills were never more important than on a production of *West Side Story* where we had a series of illnesses passed around the cast which resulted in multiple complex understudy situations. While there were plans in place for one or two understudies to be in at a time, our internal understudy structure was stretch to the max when we had five of our actors go out in one show. Two hours before curtain I remained calm and collaborated with the director to solve the redistribution of crucial roles.

My speed and efficiency were constantly necessary to keep up with a director with a lightning-fast blocking process for a production of *Caroline, or Change*. I also have strong written and oral communication skills and am very comfortable calling complex cue sequences. I enjoy working with the entire team to make sure we run a seamless show. I would be honored to have the opportunity to uphold the artistic vision of your shows. My resume is attached and can also be found on my website.

Sincerely,

Howard Mosley

Howard Mosley

Enclosure

HOWARD MOSLEY | SM
PM

they/them
555-123-4567
582 Rockaway Ave.
Bismarck, ND 58501
www.howardmosley.com
HowardMosley@gmail.com

14 Cover letter and business card: Howard (designed by Jason Tollefson)

LENA SANCHEZ
SCENIC DESIGN

OMAHA, NE
LSANCHEZ@GMAIL.COM

555-123-4567
WWW.LSANCHEZ.COM

THEMED ENTERTAINMENT – HARGROVE SERVICES

CREW LEADER

REFURBISHMENT: FUN-PARK AMUSEMENTS	JOHNNY HARGROVE	2022

SEASONAL OVERHIRE

MAINTENANCE: FUN-PARK AMUSEMENTS	ELIZABETH MOORE	2021

THEATRE

SCENIC DESIGN

BEES AND HONEY	HILLS UNIVERSITY	VERONIKA DALBY	2022
THE HEADLANDS	HILLS UNIVERSITY	KESTER GAINES	2021

ASSISTANT SCENIC DESIGN

ETCHED IN SKIN ON A SUNLIT NIGHT	THE ARTS THEATRE	KESTER GAINES	2020

PROPS MASTER

GREEN GROW THE LILACS	HILLS UNIVERSITY	SHAYNE TRUONG	2020
WOLF PLAY	HILLS UNIVERSITY	AJAY FLOWERS	2019

CARPENTER

STREET OF CROCODILES	THE ARTS THEATRE	KESTER GAINES	2019
FORKED TONGUES	HILLS UNIVERSITY	KENOJUAK ASHEVAK	2018

SKILLS

DESIGN: ARTISTIC RESEARCH, HAND DRAWING, SKETCHUP, DRAFTING: VECTORWORKS, RENDERING
TECHNIQUES: MODEL MAKING, SCENIC PAINTING, CARPENTRY, WELDING, 3-D PRINTING
OTHER: AERIAL LIFT CERTIFIED, ADOBE PHOTOSHOP, QLAB, ISADORA, VALID DRIVER'S LICENSE

EDUCATION

BA TECHNICAL THEATRE	HILLS UNIVERSITY	ANTICIPATED GRAD: 2022

REFERENCES

VERONIKA DALBYR	KESTER GAINES	SHAYNE TRUONG
SCENE DESIGNER	TECHNICAL DIRECTOR	SCENIC ARTIST
HILLS UNIVERSITY	THE ARTS THEATRE	HILLS UNIVERSITY
VERDAL@HU.EDU	GAINES@ARTSTH.ORG	TRUONG@HU.EDU
(555)122-1212	(975)323-6532	(243)645-9856

15 Resume design and layout: Lena (designed by Jason Tollefson)

LENA SANCHEZ
SCENIC DESIGN

OMAHA, NE
LSANCHEZ@GMAIL.COM

555-123-4567
WWW.LSANCHEZ.COM

7834 SUSSEX AVE.
OMAHA, NE 68107

JUNE 4, 2022

SAMERA REYES
ART & DESIGN TEAM
INTERSTELLAR RESORT
346 SAN CARLOS STREET
COLUMBUS, GA 31904

DEAR SAMERA REYES:

WORKING AS AN INTERN WITH INTERSTELLAR RESORT'S ART AND DESIGN TEAM WOULD BE AN AMAZING CULMINATION OF MY COLLEGE CAREER. I WILL GRADUATE FOLLOWING THE COMPLETION OF AN INTERNSHIP AND I CAN'T THINK OF ANY PLACE I WOULD BE HAPPIER DOING SO. WORKING ON A VARIETY OF ELABORATE AND DETAILED LIVE EVENTS, LIKE YOUR YEAR-ROUND INTERSTELLAR HOLIDAY EVENTS, IS MY GOAL AS A SCENIC DESIGNER.

I WOULD BRING STRENGTHS WITH ME THAT I THINK COULD BE OF BENEFIT TO THE TEAM BASED ON YOUR DESCRIPTION OF THE INTERNSHIP. I AM EXTREMELY EFFECTIVE AND EFFICIENT AT COMMUNICATING THROUGH SKETCHING. I USE THIS SKILL TO MAKE SURE THAT EVERYONE ON THE TEAM HAS THE SAME PICTURE IN THEIR HEAD AND, IF SOMEONE ELSE HAD SOMETHING ELSE IN MIND, IT GIVES US AN OPPORTUNITY TO FIND THAT OUT SOONER RATHER THAN LATER AND INCORPORATE THEIR IDEAS. YOU CAN SEE EXAMPLES OF THIS IN MY ONLINE PORTFOLIO FROM MY WORK AS ASSISTANT SCENIC DESIGNER FOR M. BUTTERFLY. MY ATTENTION TO DETAIL IS BEST DEMONSTRATED THROUGH MY DRAFTING; I AM PROFICIENT IN BOTH VECTORWORKS AND AUTOCAD. THERE IS NOTHING BETTER THAN A FINELY DRAFTED DESIGN PACKAGE AND I TAKE PRIDE IN CREATING THEM.

I HAVE SPENT INNUMERABLE HOURS IN THEME PARKS, INCLUDING YOUR OWN. I ALSO DO WORK FOR A CONTRACTOR IN THE OFF SEASON TO HELP REFURBISH AND MAINTAIN THE ATTRACTIONS FOR FUN-PARK IN MY HOMETOWN. I HOPE YOU WILL REVIEW MY ATTACHED RESUME, EXPLORE MY ONLINE PORTFOLIO, AND CONSIDER HOW I MIGHT CONTRIBUTE TO THE SUCCESS OF YOUR PROJECTS WHILE ALSO LEARNING AS MUCH I CAN FROM YOUR TEAM OF AMAZING DESIGNERS AND ARTISTS. IF I CAN PROVIDE ANY ADDITIONAL INFORMATION, PLEASE DO NOT HESITATE TO CONTACT ME.

SINCERELY,

Lena Sanchez

LENA SANCHEZ

ENCLOSURE: RESUME

LENA SANCHEZ
SCENIC DESIGN

LSANCHEZ@GMAIL.COM
WWW.SANCHEZDESIGNS.COM
555-123-4567
7834 SUSSEX AVE. OMAHA, NE 68107

16 Cover letter and business card: Lena (designed by Jason Tollefson)

KIERAN CLEMONS
A PROPS ARTISAN

Longview, TX
(555) 123-4567
kcdesigns@gmail.com
www.kcdesigns.com

EDUCATION

BA Communication Studies & Theatre   Fisk University Longview, TX 2016-2020

PROPERTIES EXPERIENCE

Teatro Dallas
Properties Supervisor
    And Jesus Moonwalks the Mississippi   Katia Porro   2024
Stray Dog Theatre
Props Manager
    What to Send Up When It Goes Down   Kia Divine   2024
Props Assistant
    No Place to Be Somebody   Brandy Clements   2023
Fisk University
Props Carpenter
    The Invaders   LJ Williams   2023
    Edith Can Shoot Things and Hit Them   Desiderio Roybal   2022

SCENIC ART EXPERIENCE

Teatro Dallas
Scenic Artist
    House Rules   Dawn Akemi   2024
Fisk University
Scenic Artist
    Fabulation, or the Re-Education of Undine Joel Ebarb   2022
    Suicide Forest   Reji Woods   2021

RELATED EMPLOYMENT

KISS Events
Décor Specialist: Weddings, Bar and Bat Mitzvahs, Corporate Events 2016-2020

SKILLS

Adobe Photoshop	Foam Sculpting	Period Styles
Basic Welding	Google Sketchup	Upholstery
Budgeting	Molding and Casting	Woodworking

REFERENCES

Mohammed Fateh
    Event Designer   KISS Events   MF@KISS.com   (555)122-1212
Ryca Patel
    Shop Foreperson Fisk University   Ryca.Patel@FiskU.edu (975)323-6532
Yooli Pak
    Scenic Designer   Stray Dog Theatre PakY@StrayDog.us   (243)645-9856

17 Resume design and layout: Kieren (designed by Jason Tollefson)

Longview, TX
(555) 123-4567
kcdesigns@gmail.com
www.kcdesigns.com

41 Cemetery St.
Longview, TX 75604

September 20, 2022

Evelyn Whitefield
Artistic Director
Dearborn Theatre Company
9940 Kent Rd.
Dearborn Heights, MI 48127

Dear Evelyn Whitefield:

I am writing to apply for a position with Dearborn Theatre Company as a properties artisan. I am excited by the thought of working at a theatre that is focused on developing new and original works with a commitment to the development of young theatre professionals. I am a fast learner, hard-working, communicative, and a team player, and I feel that I could be a great addition to your company.

Before returning to school to further my education, I worked for an event company creating centerpieces, decorations, and lighting displays. When I got to college I began as a carpenter which has given me a very strong background for building props. I realized that I liked making smaller things that necessitated creative problem solving and found my place in the prop shop. My other varied training, including work in lighting, sound, scenic art, and costumes have also added useful skills to my props repertoire. For example, when I repaired and reupholstered a récamier, I relied heavily on my patternmaking and stitching skills that I learned in the costume shop. My diverse experiences mean I don't shy away from any type of prop.

In addition to my wide-ranging skills, I am also detail oriented. This is not only evident in my props, but also in my paperwork and budget tracking. I have tracked and managed prop budgets as high as $3500 on a production of The Matchmaker that was overflowing with prop hats, to the show Carver which had hundreds of paper props that I created, tracked, and replaced regularly. My spreadsheets kept all of this information organized and easily accessible.

I would really love the opportunity to meet with you and discuss the job further. Please contact me any time.

Sincerely,

Kieran Clemons
Kieran Clemons

KIERAN CLEMONS
A PROPS ARTISAN

www.kcdesigns.com

(555) 123-4567
kcdesigns@gmail.com
41 Cemetery St. Longview, TX 75604

18 Cover letter and business card: Kieren (designed by Jason Tollefson)

JORGE GARZA
AUDIO TECHNICIAN

SoundsLikeGeorge@hotmail.com   Ocoee, FL   555-123-4567   www.SoundsLikeGeorge.tech

PROFESSIONAL EXPERIENCE (SELECTED)

Audio Engineer and Mixer (A1)	*Hair*	Theatre South	2022
Audio Engineer and Mixer (A1)	*Smokey Joe's Cafe*	Westcoast Black Theatre	2022
Audio Mixer (A1)	Bonnaroo Festival	Superspy Productions	2022
Audio Engineer and Mixer (A1)	*American Idiot*	The Keegan Theatre	2021
Backstage Audio Tech (A2)	Lollapalooza	C3 Presents	2021
Backstage Audio Tech (A2)	Kidzapalooza	C3 Presents	2021
Backstage Audio Tech (A2)	Bonnaroo Festival*	Superspy Productions	2020

UNIVERSITY EXPERIENCE (SELECTED)

Audio Engineer and Mixer (A1)	*Once On This Island**	Alcorn State University	2020
Audio Engineer and Mixer (A1)	*In The Heights*	Alcorn State University	2019
Sound Designer	*The Rez Sisters*	Morris Brown College	2018
Assistant Sound Designer	*Blues for An Alabama Sky*	Morris Brown College	2017

VOLUNTEER EXPERIENCE

Spring Fashion Soiree	Runway to Hope	Peggy Carter	2021
Ties & Tails Benefit	LoveyLoaves Rescue	Juniper Bloomfield	2021

PROFICIENCIES

Consoles: Behringer X32, Midas LS9/M32, Yamaha CL5/M7, DiGiCo SD9, Avid D-Show, Studio Live Al
Software: Logic Pro x, Reaper, Audacity, QLab, IMovie, Vectorworks, AutoCAD, Adobe Suite
Skills: Soldering, Drafting, MAC/PC, Podcasting, Troubleshooting

ACADEMIC ACCOMPLISHMENTS

MFA Sound Design and Technology	Alcorn State University	2020
BFA Technical Theatre	Morris Brown College	2018
Adler Family Graduate Assistantship	Alcorn State University	2018-2020
Kennedy Center ACTF Nomination	Sound Design: The Rez Sisters	2018
Bright Days Scholarship	Academic Performance	2013-2018

REFERENCES

Alejandro Pineda	**Cherri Tong**	**Ollie Moon**
Alcorn State University	Superspy Productions	Theatre South
Director of Production	Production Manager	Sound Designer
Pineda@Alcorn.edu	CherriT@Superspy.com	OMOON@TSouth.org

*cut short or canceled due to Covid-19

19 Resume design and layout: Jorge (designed by Jason Tollefson)

JORGE GARZA
AUDIO TECHNICIAN

SoundsLikeGeorge@hotmail.com   Ocoee, FL   555-123-4567   www.SoundsLikeGeorge.tech

554 Peg Shop Ave.
Ocoee, FL 34761

November 1, 2022

Tobi Mullens
Bloombeat Theater Co.
7800 Vernon Street
New Orleans, LA 70301

Dear Tobi Mullens:

After reading your ad seeking a Staff Audio Engineer on OffStageJobs.com, I knew it was a job I had to apply for. The job responsibilities match what I seek and the requirements align with my experience. After consideration of my academic training and professional work I hope you will agree that I could be a good fit for this position.

I have extensive experience mixing live musicians and singers. Much of that experience is within the live music genre for festivals like Bonnaroo and Lollapalooza, though live mixing musicals was a major component of my graduate school training and I have mixed several productions in the last 2 years including *Hair*, *Smokey Joe's Café*, and *American Idiot*.

With my deep knowledge of equipment, appreciation of a detailed spreadsheet, and experience tracking budgets, maintaining inventories and managing the department's budgets would be a pleasure. In my former staff position I was responsible for both of those tasks which I found to be intertwined. Maintaining an inventory that is well stored, cataloged, and kept in good repair, means that there is more flexibility in the budget because you don't have to continually replace lost or broken equipment.

My experience with the equipment you listed is serviceable. While I am not an expert at the idiosyncrasies of those particular consoles, I have used them before and would be able to apply all of my experience with other Yamaha and Allen+Heath equipment to mastering your equipment in short order.

Thank you for reviewing my application. I have attached my resume and three letters of recommendation. You can find additional information and samples of my work on my website. I believe I have the "desire and competence" you are looking for and I look forward to discussing the position with you in more detail.

Sincerely,

Jorge Garza

Jorge Garza

Enclosures: Resume, Letters of Recommendation

JORGE GARZA
www.SoundsLikeGeorge.tech
AUDIO TECHNICIAN
555-123-4567
SoundsLikeGeorge@hotmail.com

20 Cover letter and business card: Jorge (designed by Jason Tollefson)

Display & Body Fonts That Complement Each Other

Merriweather Sans Extrabold
Merriweather Regular

Playfair Display SemiBold
Raleway Regular

Helvetica Neue Bold Italic
Adobe Garamond Pro Regular

Lobster Regular
Roboto Regular

Alfa Slab One Regular
Gentium Book Basic Regular

Montserrat Bold
Hind Light

Pacifico Regular
Arimo Regular

UNICA ONE REGULAR
Crimson Text Roman

Shrikhand Regular
Fanwood Text Regular

PERMANENT MARKER REGULAR
Overpass Regular

Avoid Double Display or Body Font Combinations

Dancing Script Bold
Shadows Into Light Two Regular

Tahoma Regular
Helvetica Regular

Rye Regular
Vast Shadow Regular

Bonbon Regular
Mountains of Christmas Regular

5

Portfolios

I contend that everyone starting out in theatre and the entertainment industry benefits from having examples of their work compiled for presentation in support of job applications. Even stage managers and audio technicians? Emphatically yes. In fact, I hope you will join my revolution until it is strange for a stage manager *not* to have examples of their work in interview situations. There is a misconception that a portfolio is about what is on the page, but it is actually just an excuse to tell your story, supported by visual aids to demonstrate that what you are saying is true.

Prior to the pandemic we were already in a period of transition, with some people moving away from physical portfolios and toward exclusively web portfolios, but we were stuck in the middle and had not quite left physical portfolios behind. I think this is, at least partially, because of the awkwardness of trying to present a website. The pandemic has made many wonder, reasonably, if they will ever have the opportunity to present their portfolio in person again. With the instant proliferation of video conferencing in 2020, with which everyone is now so comfortable, we may not. I hope we don't see the complete demise of the physical portfolio, because they have advantages that are lost in web and digital formats. As Charlene Gross, who teaches at Penn State, pointed out in an online discussion about portfolios, "a paper portfolio won't freeze up in the middle of your presentation and doesn't require Wi-Fi that may or not be working the day of your interview."[1]

During the Covid-19 pandemic, when meetings and classes all switched to virtual, my students and I settled on the development of a digital "presentation" portfolio in place of a physical portfolio; if designed

---

[1]Charlene Gross, Costume Educators Forum private Facebook group, September 14, 2017.

strategically, the digital portfolio can later be printed as is and placed in a presentation book if that need arises. Even with a web portfolio, you should still develop a presentation portfolio, whether it is digital or in hard copy. Websites are not created to be presented; they are created for solitary interaction, a self-guided tour. Viewing your portfolio by clicking through your website doesn't allow you to present with the same kind of flow you can achieve in your physical portfolio.

If it seems strange to you to have a portfolio because of what you do, then don't call it a portfolio. Instead, put together a few examples of your work that you can share with a potential employer in an organized way, either digitally or in a presentation book. Having pictures of the nature and scale of the projects and shows you have worked on and any related skills shows the interviewer the quality of your work, but more importantly it opens the door for you to tell the story about things that can't be seen in a photograph and you may not have a chance to slip into the conversation: that time the fire alarm went off on opening night and you handled it flawlessly; the time you were A2 and the lead's mic and backup mic went out, and you were able to solve the problem without the audience knowing; the time you repaired a wardrobe malfunction while the actor was off stage and were able get the actor back on stage for their next entrance; that time you retaped the floor before that day's rehearsal, demonstrating your adaptability, because the director and scene designer decided to move the upstage platform three feet to the left; or that time when you did that one thing that was really hard and fixed that thing that was really broken and created a really complicated thing that worked great. Whatever it is, having examples of your work gives you a pretext to make sure they know how great you are. They get to see your paperwork style and how you adapt it to the show's needs, your beautiful welds, your detailed research and sketches, or the clean block diagram for the large audio install you supervised. A portfolio also gives you the opportunity to name-drop by crediting your collaborators. Furthermore, the act of putting together a portfolio, evaluating your body of work, and planning your stories is great preparation for your interview. Having that portfolio with you, even if you don't end up showing it, will give you additional confidence as you walk in the door. So if "examples of my work" works better for you, use that: in the remainder of this chapter substitute "examples of my work" in your head every time you read the word *portfolio*, and when you go to an interview ask if you can show them some examples of your work.

Choosing What to Include

General Guidelines

We discuss the differences between your presentation and website portfolios later in this chapter, but these general guidelines apply to both. Unfortunately, there isn't a magic formula for what to include in your portfolio. You don't want it to be too long or too short, and it needs to highlight your best work and process without being overwhelmingly detailed. There is no secret number of things to include that will be perfect for every situation, but somewhere between four and six is usually a good number to aim for in a presentation portfolio given the time you will usually have to share it. Digital portfolios should feature at least this many, but because of the nature of websites you can include much more if the portfolio is well organized and provides an easy user experience. Your portfolio should always present your best work—if it isn't your best, it doesn't belong in your portfolio. The only time you might consider including very early work is to demonstrate growth when applying for an educational program.

You want to select projects/shows that will encourage potential employers to envision you successfully fulfilling the role for which you are applying. Within those projects/shows, select the materials that best highlight your work. While the specific projects will depend on your exact specialty, you want to demonstrate that you helped realize the designer and/or director's vision. To do that you need to consider the story you want to tell about each project and how it connects to your strengths for the position. Some examples of things you may want to highlight are your attention to detail, incorporating a specialized skill or technique, research and development, trial and error, incorporation of technology, exquisite artistry or skill, efficient time management, leadership, clear use of research or inspiration, etc. Keeping these things in mind will help you decide exactly what to include. When preparing your portfolio for an interview, be sure to review the job description and strategically include projects that highlight exactly what they are looking for.

Including classwork and unrealized designs in your portfolio is fine, and even encouraged, especially when applying for admission to graduate or undergraduate school and in your early career. These projects are especially valuable if they add variety and contrast to your other work—in other words, use the unrealized projects to demonstrate techniques, styles, or skills that you can't otherwise feature in your realized work.

Your portfolio should not merely be a timeline of your work or a summary of your experience. It needs to be a curated presentation that demonstrates your strengths as they relate to the job or academic program for which you are applying. This means you won't present the same portfolio at every interview. If you are applying for a job as a technician, you will want to highlight your technical work and minimize any design work, except as you can relate it to the job for which you are applying and vice versa, as you would on your resume. If you are applying for a job at a theatre that primarily produces shows for young audiences, you will want to highlight work that you can link to that style of theatre. Your goal is to do everything you can to make you the obvious choice.

It is important to remember that your portfolio is not a scrapbook or time capsule. We all have emotional connections to specific shows, but the person you are presenting to won't have that same connection. You have to be able to look at your work objectively, and clearly articulate what skills/qualities/accomplishments it demonstrates. I see many students get caught in this emotional trap when it comes to one of their "firsts" or a project for which they received a significant amount of praise. In most cases those projects were really great for their level of experience at that time, but they have grown past them and that work is not representative of their current proficiencies. It comes as a great relief when I see my former students, now working professionally, begin to remove work they did with me as an undergrad because it is a sign of positive growth in both artistry and maturity. If you review your materials with a mentor and they suggest removing something, trust their advice, even if it was one of your most profound experiences. The magic of the experience doesn't disappear just because it is no longer in your portfolio.

You should list your collaborators for each show or project in your portfolio. Not only do they deserve to have their work credited, but name-dropping here will establish networking ties with the person viewing your portfolio if they are connected to anyone with whom you worked. At a minimum this list should include director, choreographer, stage manager, and all the designers, assistants, and associates. If you worked in a technical position, list anyone that worked directly above you in your area. If you are a designer, give credit to the artists who brought your design to life. A costume designer would credit the drapers, a lighting designer credits their programmer and/or master electrician, a scenic designer credits their charge artist, technical director, and/or prop manager, and so on. In the spirit of crediting the other artists with whom you worked, also do your best to credit photographers and artists whose work you use as research.

Unless your entire portfolio all illustrates the same job title (for example, my portfolio is all costume design), be sure to include your job title. Also, put the production or project name, labels, or captions on all items, and, depending on the position, a bulleted list of important points about the production (more on this later).

Those working in film and on projects for theme parks or other corporate employers may have the added challenge of non-disclosure agreements (NDAs), which can range from preventing you from telling people you worked on a project to only showing public-facing photos. It is important that you read and understand the limitations of your NDA. You may have to find an alternative way to demonstrate the skills you used on the project, such as replacing protected material with fabricated projects that demonstrate the same process and skills.

Photographs

As you select the photographs to include, remember that you have limited space. You cannot document the entirety of every show or project—your goal should be to present the quality and range of your work. First, make sure that each photo you include tells the viewer something different. Multiple angles of one particular scene, or a photo of the work from all sides, give the same information while taking up valuable space that could be used to demonstrate another aspect of your work. Select the one that highlights your work the best to make the most impact.

Always use the highest-quality photos available. If you feel yourself wanting to apologize for the quality, it is not a photo you want in your portfolio. Also, pay attention to the cropping and picture details to be sure the photo is presenting your work as successfully as possible. I especially see this oversight in costuming portfolios with pictures that show or imply poor fit, like drag lines or pulling seams, the performer not wearing the costume correctly, costumes that have not been well maintained and need steaming or pressing, or shoes that need to be repainted or polished. If that's what the show looked like, then that's what it looked like, but this doesn't mean you need to include a close-up of that detail. If when selecting photos you discover they do not accurately represent what things looked like in person, it is acceptable to use photo-editing software to adjust them, but only to the point where you correctly illustrate what it looked like in reality and not so things look different or better than they actually were. To do so would be unethical. Plates 10–12 illustrate how you can edit photos to have all aspects of a production photo in focus.

Give credit to the photographer for photos you are including in your portfolio, by either adding the name to the caption under the photo or inserting it into the image itself, which is usually less visually intrusive. (Accessibility note: if you do this in your website portfolio then you must include details in the alt-text (short for alternative text) for every image, because screenreaders cannot read text that is superimposed over a photo.) Examples can be seen in Plates 22–24. This being said, it is a good idea to take your own photos of your work with a quality camera even if you have access to professional photos from the producer. You cannot rely on marketing or archivists to capture all the work you did on a production. Marketing photos tend to focus on actors' faces, and your needs likely go beyond that. For example, as a draper you really need a full-body shot that includes the hem and shoes, and the props artisan would like a photo of a furniture piece that is upstage the whole show and always seems to have an actor standing in front of it. The only way to guarantee you get the photos you need is to take them yourself.

In addition to quality production photos, you must have quality process photos as well. When taking process photos in the shop or workspace, make sure the visible workspace is neat and proper safety protocols are being used. If you work in a busy shop, be observant of people or projects in the background and adjust as needed.

Photos taken in the shop, even with a good photo setup, do not replace seeing your work on stage, under stage lights, with the work of your collaborators. It doesn't really matter what it looks like in the shop; that's not what you were making it for. The performers on stage, in the convention center, or in front of guests at the theme park—that is your final product and it is important to document it.

Portfolios for Graduate School Applications

A portfolio compiled to apply for an academic program, at either graduate or undergraduate level, will be different from a professional portfolio used to apply for a job because your goals are different. The purpose of your portfolio when applying to schools is not only to demonstrate your current skill levels but also to show the kind of student you are, your process, how you have grown as a theatre artist, and how you incorporate constructive feedback into your work. Laura Robinson, who teaches in the School of Theatre at Penn State, says, "I like to see process from rendering to research to mockup to finished costume."[2] This sentiment can be applied to all areas. Show your thought process and how you made the decisions you made. Show the research that was helpful in shaping your ideas and how it applied to the script. Show how you implemented those ideas and applied your research, demonstrating as much of the collaborative process as possible. Illustrate the process of bringing your ideas to life in support of the play, and show the final outcome.

For stage managers or technicians, illustrating your process may not seem as easy as it is for designers, but it is still necessary and very possible. Begin with including the materials you were provided (renderings, ground plan, elevations, block diagram, props list, research, etc.). Include any preliminary research, sketching, drafting, paperwork, or planning that you contributed. Show your process through photographs, including closeups of your final product (if applicable), and use production photos that show your work in context and demonstrate the scale and quality of the production. You may also choose to include class projects that show growth, and discuss how your instructors helped you develop. For example, a picture of your first welding joint and a picture of your much better welding joints now, or the same concept with renderings, sketches, joinery, paperwork, soldering, zipper insertion, scene painting, distressing, etc., work great in this instance (though should be avoided in your professional portfolio). This type of work shouldn't be your whole portfolio, but could be a last example. As Heather Meyer Milam, assistant professor of Costume Technology at Indiana University, says, "I want to know I can teach them and they will be receptive to growth."[3] If you come to the interview demonstrating how you have grown through the influence of your mentors thus far, it will strengthen your application. Holly Poe Durbin, professor of Costume Design at UC Irvine, adds, "I like to see a sketch book or original items from an art class or hobbies that show an interest in artistry of any kind, not just show work. I've been fooled by undergrad projects before where I discovered that their teacher drew improvements for them or the project was copy work

[2]Laura Robinson, Costume Educators Forum private Facebook group, November 7, 2019.
[3]Heather Meyer Milam, Costume Educators Forum private Facebook group, November 7, 2019.

[and not identified as such]."[4] Unrealized projects are also absolutely fine; just follow the same idea of demonstrating your process. They really want to get to know how you think and problem solve.

Shawn Boyle, projection and lighting designer and faculty at Yale School of Drama, says, "If you are applying to work for me, I look at your portfolio in a completely different way [compared to a student portfolio] because if I'm going to hire you, you are, in a sense, an extension and representation of me and the way that you present your work is how I assume you would represent me."[5] For a student, he wants to know that you can be taught. He suggests that you ask before your interview if there are certain things they are hoping to see in your portfolio that would help facilitate conversation.

Breakdown by Specialty

While this subsection gives you ideas of what to include depending on your area of specialization, I encourage you to read all the subsections rather than just skipping to those that most interest you. Even if you don't think they apply to you, they may give you ideas that connect to your work. At any point in this process you may change your mind about what materials to include. You might have too much of one thing and need more of another. You even may discover this after you've used your portfolio in an interview or when sharing it with a mentor for feedback. That is normal and expected. The materials in your portfolio will continue to evolve as you and your career do.

Technical Positions

Stage Manager (Including Assistant Stage Manager, Production Assistant, Event Manager, etc.)

When a stage manager has examples of their work it gives them the opportunity to talk about intangibles (like problem solving, delegating, and soft skills) that interview questions may not provoke. While you are likely very attached to your color-coded and overly tabbed show bibles/prompt books and could find anything they contain within in a matter of seconds, they tend to be overwhelming to the rest of us, and few people

---

[4]Holly Poe Durbin, Costume Educators Forum private Facebook group, November 7, 2019.
[5]Shawn Boyle, personal interview with the author, March 2, 2020.

actually want to look at an entire show book. That doesn't mean people aren't interested in getting a glimpse into your process or paperwork style. Put together some examples of your work that are well organized and concise, and include visuals of the show for context. This way you can highlight your contributions and skills without overwhelming people with details. It also allows you to tell the stories that are going to help you stand out as a great candidate. You want to include at least a couple of production photos to show the scale and quality of the production. A full-stage, full-cast photo works well (though avoid curtain-call photos). Other photos can be used to lead into a discussion of some aspect of the production that you want to highlight. Was there an actor wearing a full-head bunny mask with limited visibility that you had to account for when calling cues to ensure their safety? A production photo of that will illustrate your story. Were there children in the show who impacted the rehearsal schedule or atmosphere in the rehearsal room? A production photo of them gives a visual while you discuss how you accommodated child performers.

Beyond photos, you can include excerpts of your paperwork to support other aspects of your stories. Perhaps include a section of a rehearsal report indicating the schedule changes necessitated by an imminent hurricane, and discuss how you helped navigate that challenge. If you want to talk about how you handle rehearsal injuries, you could include a rehearsal report where a performer was injured. If you were calling a show when the fire alarm went off you could include a copy of your "in case of emergency" script, which will allow you to talk about how you kept your cool and followed all your safety protocols. If there was something really unusual about the show for which you had to create a tracking system, include a copy (or excerpt) of that system. You get the idea. Include one or two artifacts that will provide a visual and give you an excuse to tell that story. If you include paperwork that was created by someone else, indicate that, so you aren't inadvertently taking credit for their work. Always include title blocks on drafting. If you were an ASM or PA, a bulleted list of your responsibilities will clarify exactly what you contributed to the production without having to list them verbally as part of your presentation.

Audio, Video, Projections

Much like in other technical areas, those who work in these positions want to use their portfolio to communicate their technical knowledge, troubleshooting prowess, and interpersonal skills. Audio, video, and projections technical portfolios tend to be much more equipment-focused than other types of portfolios. A bulleted gear list is an important item. If your interviewer is in the same field (as·opposed to an artistic director, for example), they will be interested in your gear list, but it can also serve to remind you if you are asked about it and don't recall a specific piece of equipment or software in the heat of the moment. Include paperwork provided to you and/or of your own creation, such as speaker plots (plan and section views), block diagrams, acoustical analysis, rigging, labor breakdown, shop orders, projector plans, computer networking, etc., that you can use to talk about your significant contributions to the show. Always include title blocks and scale on drafting. Absolutely include production photos. This gives context as well as the scale, quality, and general feeling of the show, so the viewer can put together what you are saying and evaluate your success as a collaborator. If you were involved with mic placement, include photos of the different approaches you used, especially in collaboration with hair and makeup.

It is difficult to evaluate the skills of a mix engineer or other audio technicians without the use of recordings of the show, but recordings of most shows, even for portfolio purposes, are illegal. Gordon Firemark, an entertainment attorney in Los Angeles and former theatrical sound engineer/designer, puts it plainly: "The basic general rule is that it is unlawful to make or use recordings of any material without the permission of the copyright owner. There are really no meaningful exceptions." Unless you are doing something like an original musical without Equity actors and can secure permission from everyone involved, you can't record your work. Bringing an illegal recording to an interview will not curry favor with your potential employer, but demonstrating an awareness of the legalities may help you.

Costumes, Wigs, and Makeup

As a technician/craftsperson like a stitcher, first hand, cutter/draper, crafts artist, milliner, tailor, wig artist, makeup artist, etc., consider which of your skills you can highlight with the portfolio, the story you want to tell, and how it connects to your strengths for the position. First and foremost demonstrate that you created what the designer designed. Include a copy of the designer's rendering (including swatches) next to a photograph of the finished piece. Credit the designer in the label/caption. Renderings do not need to be large; in fact, your work should always be most prominent on the page. If the design changed during the process, explain this, and how you adapted to ensure you were delivering the designer's intent. Any sketches you may have done as part of your planning are a good way to illustrate your methods. Include photos of key points in the creation process, but do not feel compelled to document every small step. Take photos of every step so you have a variety to choose from, but only include the major development points. For stitchers, first hands, drapers, etc. that would include photos taken at the end of the fitting showing the marked and pinned alterations, and close-up shots of finishing details—an exquisitely installed zipper, hand beading or embroidery, well-placed piping, boning channels, or perfectly matched plaids. Also include production photos of the costume. Some people advocate photos using a dress form, but it doesn't matter what the costume looks like on a dress form; it matters what it looks like in context, on the actor, under show lights, in front of the scenery with accessories, makeup and hair. If you are unable to see a detail due to lighting or angle in the production photos and you feel it is important, a close-up photo taken on a dress form to show that element is a good solution. If the show has not opened or production photos have not yet been taken, use a photo of the most recent fitting so at least we see how well the costume fits.

Costume shop managers will want to include items similar to those above plus documentation of time and labor budgeting and scheduling, not only as a demonstration that you can do these things, but also as an excuse to talk about your philosophy and approach to both. How did your budgeting or scheduling contribute to a more successful outcome? How did you have to adapt to accommodate the needs of the show? Include paperwork that opens the door to talk about this. What unique challenges did this production or season present that you were able to solve? Include visuals so you have something to reference when telling the story. A bulleted list of key points about the production or season gives additional information that you don't necessarily have the time to verbalize or space to illustrate, but will still get the facts into the viewer's head as another means of understanding your work. Items on this list could include budget, number of days or weeks in the shop, number of labor hours, size of staff, number of actors, number of costumes, any wardrobe responsibilities, number of quick changes, and any other important details specific to the project.

If you want to include design work on the last page or two of your portfolio you can, but only if you can use it to tell a story about why it makes you a better technician/fit for the job. There can be a prejudice against technicians who have design experience—assuming that while they may tolerate being a technician, they are only doing so until they can get a design gig, at which point they'll walk away from the technology job; or they will be miserable working as a technician, leading to lowered morale and poor quality of work. I have not observed that same bias in reverse: technology experience for designers is generally viewed as an asset. Another way you could handle this is to include your design work in a separate digital presentation or, if in person, a small (8.5 inch x 11 inch) portfolio that doesn't get shown unless you are specifically asked. This way you show that it is obviously not your focus but you have the skills if called upon.

Electrics

As we get into the less concrete areas it becomes more challenging to illustrate your work; however, there are plenty of things you can include. Start with whatever you were supplied by the designer and any paperwork, drafting, or updates you did as part of your position. If you had to troubleshoot anything during the install, focus, or tech, provide a visual that allows you to discuss this. Did the space create any particular challenges? You don't need to include a photo of you on a ladder to prove that you were at focus, but if there was something particularly challenging to focus, a visual of that would be fine. Include a bulleted list of key points about the show to help to demonstrate scale and scope. Items could include number of instruments (automated and conventional), number of electrics, number of dimmers, practicals, number of cues, console type, etc. Always include title blocks on drafting.

Scenery

Carpenters, master carpenters, scenic artists, and properties artisans all contribute to the look of the final production and, like those in technical costume positions, want to demonstrate that they delivered their portion of what the designer asked for. It is important to include any ground plans, elevations, sketches, and/or research images you were given to guide your work, as well as production photos of your work to demonstrate your success. Along the way you should include documentation of your process and steps: your own drafting or sketches, research, samples, and/or photos of your work in progress. Include a photo of that beautiful weld, circular staircase, mitered corner, or rabbet joint, your planning and cut list, the table legs you turned, that amazing painted wood grain, etc. Don't go overboard with these details, though; use them to supplement production shots that show your work in context. Always include title blocks on drafting.

Those in leadership positions in scenic areas (technical director, assistant technical director, scenic charge, prop manager, etc.) should include budgeting and planning documents (or at least excerpts from them), drafting and/or sketches you received from the designer, and examples of your own drafting and/or sketches, with a focus on particular pieces that you plan to discuss in your presentation. While a full set of drafting cannot and should not be in your actual portfolio, you may benefit from bringing a complete drafting package for one show as a separate item in case it can be useful to answer a question or if the hirer wishes to see more. In your portfolio, include things that will allow you to talk about how you planned the build, how this build was unique, and how you planned labor and work calls. Use photos that allow you to talk about problems that arose in the build, load in, tech, or strike, and how you resolved those issues. Include a bulleted list of important details about the show, such as special technology like winches or turntables, number of scene changes, number of active flys or drops, budget, number of labor hours, size or style of space and/or scenery, length of build, size and experience of crew, etc. You do not need to talk about every item on the page, but the viewer likely will read them as long as you keep them short and easily digestible, and they can be a good filter through which to consider your work.

Show Crews

Whether you are focused on a career running the show or want to include your crew work as a supplement to another specialty, there are great ways to present your work in a portfolio. Include paperwork you created or used to do your job that helps to communicate the scope and scale of your responsibilities. This could include run lists, ground plans, prop placement, scene-change breakdowns, etc. Include production photos that help to illustrate your work and the scale of the show. For example, you can highlight your work on a quick change by including a photograph of the actor in the before and after costumes. This gives you an opportunity to discuss the details and logistics of the change, including time, exit and entrance, underdressing, quick rigging, etc. The same general idea can be used to demonstrate scene changes and complicated prop shifts.

Designers

Designers should choose one production to present, from beginning to end, illustrating the highlights and noteworthy aspects of the project. For this fully documented production, include a short statement or bullet points that the director gave you to guide your design. Include research and initial sketches. Show your final designs and how they grew from your research and early ideas. Show key points from initial ideas, research, and rough sketches through to final designs, construction/installation, and end result. This production will obviously take more space in your portfolio than the others, but you don't want it to be overwhelming—two to four pages in a presentation portfolio should suffice to accommodate the additional detail. The remaining entries should all be one double-page spread. In all cases, be sure you include at least one full-stage production photo. This will show the quality and scale of the production and help illustrate the success of your collaboration with other areas. In addition to any realized designs, you can include unrealized designs, class projects, personal projects, painting, drawing, and digital art. Work to match the style of the organization where you are interviewing. If the work you would be doing is concert style, showing box sets might not highlight the kinds of skills they are looking for. When putting your portfolio together for a job, focus more on what you can do than what you have learned. Below are some specific guidelines by area.

Sound Designer/Composer

As a sound designer or composer there are numerous things you want to include (either in full or in part, depending on length) as applicable to the production: preliminary paperwork and planning, research, descriptive cue sheet/breakdown of cues, speaker plot (plan and section views), mic placements, block diagrams, special orchestra requirements or characteristics, and anything else unique to that show. If you worked with any permanently installed equipment, include information or photos of that and discuss how you were able to use the system to your advantage. There are absolutely people interested in your gear list, so include it as bulleted points on the page. Finally, production photos of key moments in the show you plan to discuss provide a visual to help your viewer understand how you supported the action, mood, and feel, or provided reinforcement.

Just as audio mixers are restricted from making and having recordings of their work, so too are sound designers if it involves copyrighted material.

> Any sound designer who works on a show in which grand rights haven't been properly licensed shouldn't expect to have any way to showcase their work anyway. Grand Rights is only the Producer's right to *perform* the work live in a theatrical environment … No recordings allowed there anyway … That'd be a different license. Now, if the Producer has obtained proper permission to record the show, the sound designer (and others) should be able to negotiate for the right to use clips from that recording for portfolio/demo-reel purposes. But make sure that's included in your contract, or as a separate written permission.[6]

---

[6]Gordon Firemark, email exchange with the author, February 27, 2020.

Entertainment attorney Gordon Firemark adds:

> [I]f a designer creates a particularly special sequence of cues or a soundscape, they should seek and obtain permission [from the rights owner] to make a short recording just to show off that work product. As long as it's not intended for any kind of commercial use, and isn't made available to the general public, owners aren't likely to have objections. Now, of course, if a designer builds a special sound-effect [or composition] him or herself, then he/she is its owner and can do with it, as he/she pleases … as long as other authors' and designers' work isn't used without permission, and no Equity performers are included.

If you have any cues or compositions to which you own the rights, you should absolutely use them. Shawn Boyle, a lighting and projections designer, suggests including a QR code[7] on any printed pages so you or the viewer can pull it up on a device. Remember, bringing an illegal recording to an interview will not impress a potential employer, but demonstrating an awareness of the legalities of recording as well as your knowledge of grand and small rights may help.

Costume Designer

Fitting an entire show's costume renderings into a portfolio presentation, along with research and photos, takes a tremendous amount of planning. You don't want each show to drag on to the point that the viewer gets bored. Select a few choice renderings to feature at a larger size, with smaller versions of your other renderings. This will help direct focus to the most important things. Include evocative research used for color palette and/or overall mood, as well as character-specific research and inspiration. Keep character research in proximity to the designs it inspired. Resist the urge to group each type of material on separate pages. People want to be able to see your thought process and how your research translates through to renderings and the final production, so don't force your viewer to flip or scroll back and forth to find the connections. When selecting rough sketches for inclusion, those that went through substantial changes will help illustrate how you respond to directorial input. If they are identical to the renderings, the space may be better used for other material. Unless a significant design change is illustrated and you plan to tell a story that relates to them, there's no need to include fitting photos in designer portfolios. Do include general budget

[7]A QR code can be read by a smartphone camera to direct you quickly to a website for more information.

information, but don't commit space to a complete budget breakdown unless there is a story you need to tell where that level of detail would be illustrative. The budget versus amount spent is sufficient. Select production photos that show characters on stage together with scenery and lights. Include the full costume from hat to heels. Unless you need to show something in detail, dress-form photos are not helpful. The costume was made to fit an actor, not a dress form, and it was designed to be viewed in context on stage. Lastly, and most importantly, be sure the costume looks good in all the photos you choose, and that you aren't highlighting poor fit or construction issues.

Lighting Designer

As a lighting designer you want to demonstrate that the words and visuals you communicated to the director were directly translated into your design. People hiring you want to know that if you present evocative imagery in a design meeting, you will be able to deliver that same feeling onstage. Research paired with production photos illustrating how you can translate a story and establish the mood are great things to have in your portfolio. When it comes to documentation, there are two types of people: those who want to see your plots and supporting paperwork, and those who don't. Try to strike a balance between the two, and be prepared to share more with those who want it. Descriptive cue sheets, magic sheets, small-scale plots and sections, and shop orders/gear lists should be included for every show. A bulleted list with interesting bits of information like number and type of fixtures, number of scenes, number of cues, type of console, etc. is also helpful to spur discussion.

Scene Designer

As with the other design areas, you want your portfolio to tell your story and demonstrate your process. The first show in your portfolio should tell as complete a story as possible. To that end, in addition to production photos you'll want to include things like research, thumbnails, rough sketches, storyboards, models (digital or well-lit photos of physical), sections, elevations, paint elevations, etc. Once you have demonstrated your whole process and a complete design package, the other items you present can focus on one or two key factors you want to emphasize, with photos and supporting documentation. You can demonstrate your collaboration with the director, showing how your ground plan evolved in the early stages of the process. As you go through your career you may find less of the supporting documentation is necessary.

Projection Designer

As the newest recognized design area, portfolio expectations are still being established in this field. Projection and lighting designer Shawn Boyle says he's looking for a portfolio that demonstrates where ideas come from, how those ideas evolved, and the final outcome, and acts as an "invitation for conversation."[8] Storyboards, projector plots, elevations and sections, descriptive cue sheet, labor breakdown, budget, shop orders/gear lists, photos of set (or model) with and without projections to show how they transform the space, information about the control system, any system integration with other areas, content contact sheets, resource lists, a bulleted list of software used, content sources, number of images/videos, etc. can all contribute to these goals. If you are a content creator, include examples of that work as well. To show video and/or animations in a physical portfolio, a QR code on the page will allow you or the viewer to pull up your content on a device. It is important that you stay within the legal limitations of recording live productions and do not run afoul of the law.

Assistant and Associate Designers

If you are looking for a job as an assistant or associate, or have worked in one of these roles and want to highlight that work as a supplement to your main body of work, your goal should be to demonstrate how you made the designer's job easier and contributed quality work to the project. Include examples of paperwork and documentation you created and/or maintained. Depending on your area, this could include dressing lists, swatching, instrument schedules, magic sheets, file organization, calculations for projectors or acoustics, focus charts, prop lists, block diagrams, etc. Include research contributions, copyright documentation, reference photos, load in and focus contributions, etc. Because responsibilities can differ from designer to designer and show to show, provide a bulleted list of your responsibilities. Include production photos, especially as they relate to your contributions, and a full-stage photo to give the viewer an idea of the scope and quality of the overall production. Demonstrate your ability to participate in the creation of the work.

---

[8]Boyle, note 5.

Presentation Portfolios

Unless you have figured out how to leverage and master either a long-scrolling or a scrollytelling website to meet the needs of both a presentation and a website portfolio, you will be much more effective at presenting your work with a presentation portfolio separate from your website portfolio, because traditional websites are not made to be presented. Examples of presentation portfolio pages and corresponding website portfolio pages can be seen in Plates 30, 32, and 34–40 with additional examples on the companion website.

Planning Your Design, Order, and Layout

The aesthetic and layout of your portfolio will communicate as much about you as does the work itself. People equate a sloppy portfolio with sloppy work habits. Aesthetically, your portfolio should match your letterhead, resume, and business cards in fonts, colors, and any graphics or logos. These items work together as your branded marketing package and professional persona to give a memorable impact.

Your first decision is choosing between portrait and landscape orientation. In a physical portfolio, portrait is preferable for numerous reasons, with the strongest being it is just plain easier to hold and present when the pages turn like a book instead of bottom to top. If you think you will most often be presenting your portfolio in a physical format, live and in person, consider building your digital presentation portfolio in this same manner so it can be printed as is. However, when presenting over video conference, a landscape layout provides a more optimal viewing experience because of the aspect ratio of computer screens. Whichever layout you choose, it is best to stick with only one orientation and not switch back and forth between the two.

The single page you see when you first open the portfolio should serve as a title page that includes your name, what you do (job title), and your contact information. It should match the aesthetic you have established for your marketing materials. Some people choose to include an iconic image from their work, like a particularly powerful production photo. Remember that if you are applying for different types of jobs (like lighting and projections, or design and technology) you are going to need a different title page depending on the job you are applying for.

Once you have determined what you are going to include in your portfolio you need to decide the order in which it appears. Chronological or reverse chronological (like your resume) is not an ideal organization plan. You want both your initial and final entries to leave a favorable impression on the viewer, and neither of these temporal options is likely to accomplish both these goals. A ranked approach is a far better way to go. We know, of course, that all of this is your best work, but still, let's rank them from best to merely fantastic. Suppose you have four productions to include and you rank them "A" through "D," with "A" being your strongest work and/or the work that you can mostly articulately connect to the job for which you are applying, moving through "B" and "C" to "D," which is still a great example of your work. This gives you *An Octoroon* (A), *Bubbling Brown Sugar* (B), *Ceremonies of Dark Old Men* (C), and *Dutchman* (D). You could put the shows in this "alphabetical" order from "best" to "least best," but the downside is that as you move through the portfolio you are getting farther away from your most impressive work, and may not leave as positive a lasting impression as you hope. I suggest the following approach instead. The first thing in your portfolio should be the best, most complete representation of your process from start to finish, so in our example that would be *An Octoroon*. Following that, your second entry should be *Dutchman*. It might be less impressive than the others, but viewers will still have *An Octoroon* in their mind while looking at it. From there you move up the ranks so the work gets stronger with each entry. This means that *Ceremonies of Dark Old Men* is next, which is stronger than *Dutchman* and helps to reassure them that your work on *An Octoroon* wasn't a fluke. End with *Bubbling Brown Sugar*, so you have a strong finish and confirm the confidence they had in you from the beginning. If you have more than four pieces to present, just make sure they still follow this convention.

If you have a piece or two of work that relates to but is outside of your main area, you can include it either at the end of your main portfolio or in a supplement. If you put it at the end, make sure that it is not a letdown after viewing your primary work. For example, a scene designer or technical director who also includes examples of scene painting or sewing skills must make sure they are reasonably good examples of these skills. You don't want the last thing they see to be weak. Also be sure that you use your presentation to relate the additional work to your primary job. And remember, just because you have done it, doesn't mean it belongs in your portfolio.

Once you have established the order, you need to decide the general page layout so you can remain consistent. Having your job title, the show, collaborators, etc. all in the same location on each page helps the viewer find the information they are looking for quickly and limits frustration, which helps inspire positive feelings toward you.

Unless all the items in your portfolio fall into the same category (like draping, sound design, or master electrician, for example), the title of a page should be what you did on the show, not the name of the production. This seems to be very difficult for people to accept, as we all tend to think the show is the most important thing, but this is about you, not the show. The viewer needs to know which lens to look through when evaluating your work. If you were a stage manager on one show, a production assistant on another, on a third you were an ASM (assistant stage manager) and mainly interfaced with costumes, and next you were an ASM but mainly dealt with props and scenery, it is really important to know this right away as I begin to look at your work. If your career has developed so that all the work in your portfolio is the same thing, you can use the show title as the title of the page.

Decide where you are going to place your title on the page and then keep that consistent throughout the portfolio, although you only have to include this on the first page for each show and it doesn't need to take up space on subsequent pages. An upper corner, especially upper left, is a good location because as English readers we are trained to start in that corner of a page. Near that you should place the title of the show in a slightly smaller font. Be sure it is formatted to indicate it is a play title, using either italics, small caps, or some other styling. The location/producing organization should be near this as well. Then decide where on the page common elements like your bulleted lists can go.

With the locations of these consistent items determined, you can sketch your plan for all your pages based on the materials you have decided to include for each individual show. You want to tell your story with your layout. For designers, start with the information you were given: guidance from the director, and the script. Then illustrate how you developed that into the design of the show. Do this in such a way that the viewer can see how your research and inspirations connect to the final product without having to flip back and forth between pages. For technicians, start with the information you were given by the designer, like renderings, ground plans, or paint elevations. Include process photos of how you used that information to create the items (construction process, fitting pictures, install, etc.) and a production photo of the final outcome. Keep renderings and paint elevations on the same page as the production photo so it's easy to evaluate how closely you delivered the design. Use scale to help tell your story. Your work, the most important thing potential employers look at, should be the largest item on the page with the other materials smaller, thus indicating their supporting role.

There are some general page layout and design tips.

- Establish a margin all the way around the page and don't put anything in it, just as if you were typing a paper. It doesn't have to be large; it just needs to be consistent.
- Consider creating layout templates so your job title, show title, producing organization, bullet point lists, QR codes, etc. are in the same place on each page. This will save you time rather than having to rebuild each page from scratch.
- Arrange items so it is clear where someone should look and how they should move through the page in the order you want them to see things. Keep in mind that most people looking at your portfolio will instinctively look to the upper left first.
- Do not use all the available space. Keep some "white space" to give the eye a place to rest between items.
- Keep things clean and linear as much as you can. Things that are too jumbled make for a confusing experience for the viewer.
- Slight overlapping can help group similar things. For example, perhaps your research images are grouped and slightly overlapped, or your research images and sketches are reduced and overlap with your final design to connect them visually and indicate how to view these items. The relationships will be clearer if you have some "white space" between the different groupings. Be careful not to overdo this, or you will cross into a scrapbook aesthetic.
- One larger good photo is much better than several smaller photos, even if the multiple smaller photos show the item from every angle. Make sure every picture on the page provides unique information and doesn't duplicate any of the other items you have included.
- Make sure to label *everything*, and be consistent in how you do so throughout the whole portfolio. If you left justify, then left justify all items on every page. Be descriptive: "Act" and "Scene" are not particularly helpful as captions on a production photo. Include a label that helps the viewer know what to look at in the image or paperwork; tell them why they are looking at the item.
- A drop shadow or glow behind photographs helps them pop out from the page and gives the page depth.

- The colors, fonts, and graphics you use should match the marketing materials you designed.
- Your background shouldn't draw attention to itself. Stick with neutral colors. Most portfolios default to a black background, but you might consider a dark grey to help provide some definition to your photos. If your presentation primarily features paperwork, for example as a stage manager or technical director, a lighter neutral background will reduce the contrast and make your work easier to look at.
- Whatever background and font colors you choose, use them consistently throughout the portfolio.

The Construction Process

If you have the skills and long-term access to the software, Photoshop is a good choice to build your pages digitally. If you are a Photoshop novice but are determined to learn, make sure you give yourself plenty of time. It is also a good idea to identify a Photoshop mentor, someone you can call to get help when you get stuck. If Photoshop is not an option for you, there is a much more practical option: PowerPoint (or Keynote for Mac users). Most people have both access to and experience with PowerPoint, and it can do the basic things that you need to create portfolio pages. Whichever software you choose, you need to be able to change the page size and dimensions; change the background color; import, crop, and resize images; insert text and bullet points; change font, style, and colors; and insert drop shadows and/or glow effects to objects on the page.

If you ever need to present your portfolio in physical format, it is a very good idea to print a draft so you can check to be sure everything prints as you expect and you haven't lost photo quality as you edited the digital files. Catching errors in less expensive drafts will hopefully reduce the number of full-color reprints you need to do. When you are satisfied with your portfolio in physical form, print your final pages on photo paper. The quality of paper you use makes an incredible difference in the print quality: photos that look cloudy when printed on regular paper often pop when printed on photo paper (see Plate 41).

Printers and paper brands vary widely in color rendition and quality, so printing some pages on different printers will likely result in unmatched prints. When you find the printer on which your work looks best and the colors are most accurate, it is advisable to continue using that printer for the entire portfolio.

Supplemental Materials

You may have additional material that you want to be ready to present to provide further information in case it can help you during an interview. This could range from full-size drafting files to a secondary area of work not in your main portfolio. Prepare these materials in a separate, easily located portfolio or file. This is one of those "back pocket" things that you only bring out if the interviewer says something like, "Do you think you could send me more examples of [whatever it is that they want to see]." If you are ready for this moment, you can reply with, "I have that right here and can show you now." It will be obvious that this isn't part of your formal presentation, and your preparation will impress them.

Selecting Your Case

If you present your portfolio in physical form, you should not feel pressured, or really even compelled, to buy a high-priced portfolio case. It helps to know that items typically called *portfolios* don't usually have any pages and are made for carrying loose artwork; what you want is called a *presentation book*, and I use the term *portfolio* simply because that is the standard terminology in our discipline. The most popular portfolios today have a flexible, solid-black plastic cover with plastic sheet protectors permanently attached to the spine, and range in price from $10 to $30 depending on the brand, the number of pages, and the size. You can often find them locally at art and craft stores, with more variety and price points available online. Common brands include Itoya, Filexec, Blick Basic Series, Amazon Basics, and Alvin. Features you should look for include sturdy, acid-free plastic pages that won't rip and are securely attached to the spine so they won't fall out, and enough pages to accommodate the amount of work you plan to include without having too many extra pages left over.

You need to decide what size and orientation of portfolio to use—if this doesn't match the size and orientation you have created for your digital presentation, you may have to redo all the pages before printing. For stage managers I recommend portrait orientation of either 8.5 inches × 11 inches, which is standard paper size in the US, or 9 inches × 12 inches. Keeping it small is less intimidating and more relatable; going for 9 inches × 12 inches gives you more flexibility when laying out your presentation and reads more like a portfolio, but also means you have to print your pages on

11 inch × 17 inch paper and trim them to fit. But either decision is fine: you just need to choose what is best for you. Whatever you do, avoid the temptation to use traditional sheet protectors in a three-ring binder—this doesn't come across as polished and professional.

For designers and technicians it can be a little more complicated. Going small, like 9 inches × 12 inches, won't give you the space you need to present the work big enough for the hirer to see specific details clearly, and a single show could easily fill an entire portfolio at this size. On the other hand, sizes like 18 inches × 24 inches or larger are difficult to transport and present, not to mention more costly. For designers and technicians, my favorite physical portfolio is 14 inches × 17 inches; this has enough room to include all the steps in your process as well as large photographs, renderings, and detailed drafting without having to run on over pages and pages for a single show.

Website Portfolios

A website portfolio is accessible from anywhere, easily and quickly updated, and when designed well communicates an important level of professionalism.

What Is Good Design?

Think about how you interact with websites, and what annoys you or makes you give up. Do you read paragraphs of text or skip past them? How many times are you willing to click to get to what you are looking for? How do you feel when the navigation links move and you have to figure out where they are? What about when a website automatically starts playing music? Or a website that is very obviously out of date? Or a page that goes on and on and on? How about overly "creative" websites that make finding anything overwhelmingly complex? These aesthetic, layout, and functionality aspects all contribute to what is termed "user experience" (abbreviated as UX), and when designing an online portfolio good UX should come before anything else. The last thing you want is to find your portfolio featured on one of the lists of top-ten worst internet sites (e.g. www.webpagesthatsuck.com). Examples that demonstrate the desired characteristics can been seen in Plates 29, 31, and 33, with additional examples on the companion website.

- Websites that prioritize UX share certain characteristics.
- Clear and consistent navigation and layout.
  - An attractive and limited color palette (two or three colors), which should match your marketing materials and have sufficient contrast.
  - Limited font choices (again, two or three at the most) that also match your marketing materials and are chosen with readability in mind. A font size no smaller than 16 point is best.
- A professional aesthetic that is representative of your style and genre.
  - A clear visual hierarchy delineated through size, color, and placement helps guide the UX.
- Well-organized, quality content that loads quickly.
  - Leave enough negative space to allow the eyes to find what they need easily and have the opportunity to rest. Line spacing of at least 1.5 helps to improve UX.
  - Use one good larger photo rather than several small ones, especially if multiple photos don't provide additional information.
  - Provide labels or captions that help the viewer know what to look at in the image or paperwork.
  - Provide paperwork that opens as a pdf in the browser and does not require downloading to view it.
- A home page that can be fully seen without scrolling.
  - Use a visually clean and linear arrangement to avoid confusing or overwhelming the viewer.
- A simple and unambiguous navigation bar with no superfluous links.
  - Avoid layouts and designs that make the viewer search for hidden or "creative" links that are not obvious.
- Accessibility for all users on desktop and mobile devices.

What You Need to Know to Create Your Website

We are lucky to be living in a time with so many options for creating websites. Gone are the days when you had to write HTML code or hire a web designer to create a custom site. While these options still exist, most people will find that one of the WYSIWYG[9] design platforms makes creating your own website manageable.

If you search online for "how to make a portfolio website" you will find links to dozens of articles and blogs about the features you need to consider when selecting a content management system (CMS). A CMS is the website/app you will use to upload and store your digital files; create, lay out, and edit your pages; and revise and update your digital portfolio as needed. The CMS gives you a drag-and-drop interface and does all the coding for you. It also will typically serve as your hosting service, eliminating the need to search out and learn to use another service.

There is a seemingly unending choice of programs. Some of the most commonly used are Wix, Weebly, SquareSpace, and WordPress, but there are many, many others. What you want to look for when test-driving your options is ease of use, available template designs, level of customization possible, level of technical support, and available features like number of pages, storage size, cost, and reliability. Any reputable CMS that provides hosting will be able to give you a percentage uptime number, allowing you to compare it to other companies—it doesn't do you much good to have a website if the hosting service keeps going offline.

Explore the websites for several different companies and read their reviews. Almost all of them have a free version, so when you have narrowed your shortlist down to two or three, try them out by going through their tutorials and making a page or two using your images, fonts, text, etc. to see which you find easiest. You don't need to complete your entire portfolio to know if you understand how to use a site and if the product you end up with is what you want.

Consider the options that become available as you subscribe to the paid versions of each service. Most of them offer tiered pricing, so you can grow your website as your business and career grow. Free versions typically include ads for the service, an assigned URL which includes the company name, limits on storage space and number of pages, and limited or no search engine optimization (SEO).[10] These limitations are pretty workable when you are just getting your site up and running, but in time you will probably want to transition to a paid site to take advantage of the additional features.

---

[9]WYSIWYG (pronounced WIZ-E-WIG) stands for "what you see is what you get." WYSIWYG applications allow you to edit and adjust the layout of your site by moving elements visually while the software handles the computer code behind the scenes.
[10]The better your SEO, the more likely you are to appear in search results and the more people are likely to see your website.

Paid versions usually include a personalized URL in addition to more pages and storage space.

While you don't need to have your own web address (URL), especially when you are just starting out, it is a good idea to do so as it projects professionalism. Another advantage of registering a URL is that most services include a matching email address, which further enhances your professional image. You want your URL to be something that is clearly connected to you. Your name is a good starting point, and it can reference what you do if you want. Be careful about being too specific. You never know which direction your career may take, and while you can always get a new URL if you need to in the future, it is much easier to stick with the same one. If you are going to add anything to your name, consider keeping it more general, like www.sboyledesign.com or www.ryancoletd.com.

When you have a URL in mind you need to check if it is available. Any web hosting service will have a domain search function you can use to see if your choice is already taken. Be ready with variations. Another, possibly less desirable, option that might appeal to you is to explore something other than the regular .com top-level domain (TLD) suffix. A common alternative is .net, but since ICANN[11] began accepting applications for additional TLDs in 2012, options like .design, .lighting, .management, .makeup, .me, .show, .td, and others have become available. If you have a URL that also exists as a .com, chances are very good that people will end up there instead of on your website that ends with .design or one of the others. These TLDs are not widely available, so you will have to do some research to find where you can register a URL with one of them.

If this is all still just too much for you, hiring a web designer is absolutely an option. Keep in mind not only the expense of having your website created in the first place, but that you will also have to pay for every update or change. In the long term, this could get expensive. A compromise approach could be to have a web designer create your website using one of the common online WYSIWYG services, and then turn it over to you to update and maintain. Or maybe you have a friend who can help you out in exchange for some pizza and fresh-baked chocolate chip cookies. Ultimately, taking charge of your website updates will give you the ability to ensure that it is accurate and current.

---

[11]ICANN stands for Internet Corporation for Assigned Names and Numbers, which is the non-profit governing body that decides things like which TLDs can be created.

Planning Your Website

If you sit down at the computer and expect to have a portfolio sorted out in a couple of hours, you will likely end up disappointed. You need to make a plan before you begin. To understand the latest trends in digital portfolio websites you should spend some time looking at other people's sites and taking note of the features that you do and don't like. Make notes, and bookmark the pages you really like. Be sure to note color palettes, organization, navigation, photo quality, and completeness. Would you interview or hire this person based on this website? The aesthetic of your website is going to match all your other marketing materials, so you aren't looking to take an aesthetic from one of the sites you look at; rather, you are looking for layout, functionality, and content. There is a worksheet on the companion website that can help you collect your thoughts. Once you have a feel for good and not-so-good portfolios, you can put together a plan for your own.

Make a list of what you plan to include on your website. Remember, everything that goes into a presentation portfolio goes into your digital portfolio, including bulleted lists, captions, photos, paperwork, etc. You may need more info on your web page, since you won't be there to talk people through it, especially when it comes to demonstrating process. Most web portfolios will include your bio, resume and/or CV, contact information, and portfolio materials. Make an outline of all the items you plan to use. Here is an example from my website.

A. Splash page with links to Teaching, Writing, Design, and About (linked from my name)
B. About
    a. Bio
    b. More detailed contact info
    c. Resume link
    d. CV link

C. Educator link
    a. Teaching philosophy
    b. Downloads of syllabi
    c. Downloads of teaching projects

D. Designer link

    a. Portfolio menu with link to production archive

        i. Production archive with links to shows I have removed from my main portfolio page

        ii. Show 1

            1. Research

            2. Sketches

            3. Process photos

            4. Renderings and production photos

            5. Link to preview video

            6. Link to review

            7. Bullet list

        iii. Show 2

            1. Research

            2. Sketches

            3. Process photos

            4. Renderings and production photos

            5. Link to preview video

            6. Link to review

            7. Bullet list

        iv. Show 3

            1. Research

            2. Sketches

            3. Process photos

            4. Renderings and production photos

            5. Link to preview video

            6. Link to review

            7. Bullet list

        v. Etc. etc. etc.

E. Author link

    a. Latest book

    b. Other book

    c. Articles

    d. Articles

    e. etc.

You may find planning by way of a flowchart (see Figure 3) is helpful either in addition to or instead of the outline.

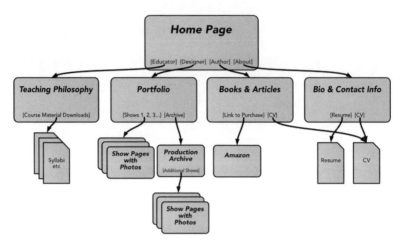

Figure 3 Website flowchart example

The layout of my website will probably not match your needs, but there are several other layout options illustrated in Plates 25–28.

Compiling and Preparing Your Content

Once you have a plan, you need to gather your digital materials, organize them, and edit them in preparation for use on your website. If you already have a naming convention and organizational schema that works for you, then by all means continue to use it. But if you are like most people and things are arranged a bit haphazardly on your computer, I recommend you establish a plan for keeping your portfolio materials organized. Begin with a folder labeled something like "Website content." As you begin filling this folder, establish a naming convention that will help your files remain grouped without the need for folders. Let's say you are collecting scene design materials for the show *Stop Kiss* by Diana Sun. You could abbreviate the title to SK, so all of the materials for this show would begin with SK and thus would be grouped together in your folder. Then add a descriptive name so you know what the file is later without having to open it. Keep things short. Establish abbreviations for the different types of materials—for example, r for research, d for design, re for rendering, p for photo, pw for paperwork, etc. So your list of materials may look something like this:

sk_r_color.jpg
sk_r_centralpark.jpg
sk_r_skyline.jpg
sk_r_apartments.jpg
sk_re_groundtexture.jpg
sk_d_sketch.jpg
sk_d_groundplan.pdf
sk_d_elevations.pdf
sk_d_model.jpg
sk_p01_kiss.jpg
sk_p02_apartment.jpg
sk_p03_hospital.jpg
sk_pw_budget

Creating individual folders for each show or project is an option, but this format gives you at-a-glance access to all your files and ultimately saves you a lot of time.

Photos and renderings should be in JPG format. Paperwork you would like to show as paperwork and not as an image should be in PDF format, although some CMSs do not easily support this. If you want a thumbnail of the paperwork to use as a link, you will likely have to make a JPG of it as well.

You need to do some prep on your photos to make them work best in the online environment. This is called image optimization. You need to balance the file size with the quality of the photo. In general, the higher the quality of the photo, the larger the file size, and the larger the file size, the longer it takes to load on your webpage. The three aspects of each image that are important for web use are file size (how much space the file takes up where it is being stored, which can be reduced by making adjustments to the image), resolution (how many pixels are squeezed into every inch of the picture—the higher the resolution, the more pixels per inch and the larger the image can be made without it becoming "pixelly"), and cropping/image dimensions (adjusting the edges of the photo to eliminate extraneous visual information, allow the viewer to focus on the important aspects of the image, and reduce the actual image dimensions of length x height to a workable size).

By default, most digital cameras create images that are far larger than you need or want. If you use photos straight off the camera, you will likely run up against storage limits with your CMS and make your website load slower than necessary, especially on a mobile browser. You can check the file size of your images by using *Properties* or *Get info*, depending on your platform, or set your folder to display file size when in detail format. SquareSpace suggests in its support documents that photos should ideally not exceed 500 kb per image for best performance, but it supports photos up to 20 MB. Other sources suggest under 300 kb, and some even say under 125 kb per photo. The smaller the image's file size, the faster a web browser will be able to display it. This effect is cumulative, so on a photo-heavy page like a portfolio it can really affect the load time of your site. People who study these things seem to agree that around 50 percent of users will give up if a web page takes more than three seconds to load, and that percentage goes up with every additional second. We aren't a very patient bunch.

To edit your photos you need some sort of software. Photoshop is the industry standard when it comes to photo editing, but it is very expensive and also overkill if all you need to do is crop and adjust the image dimensions and resolution. And it's by no means the only option: there are less expensive or even free options like Affinity Photo, which is nearly as powerful as Photoshop, Pixlr, an online option offering both free and paid versions, and GIMP, a free open-source image editor. You can find tutorials online with step-by-step instructions on how to do everything you need in whatever software you choose.

A quick side note before you begin editing your images. Save a backup copy of the image before you make any changes, and store all these "originals" somewhere separately from your website materials. You never know what your image needs might be in the future, and having the original image may make it far easier to meet future requirements.

Dpi stands for dots per inch, a classification typically used for print purposes. Computer screen resolution should technically be expressed in pixels per inch (ppi), but the two are often used interchangeably. Most computer screens display images at 72 dpi; any resolution higher than this won't provide any improved image quality when viewed on screen. Printers, however, typically have an output resolution of 300 dpi, so higher-resolution images will look noticeably better when printed, especially at larger sizes. If you anticipate you or your user needing to download and print any of your images, you should increase your image's dpi to provide a better product. The great thing is that resolution doesn't affect the file size of the image, so this is simply a matter of personal choice and user experience.

The first real step in optimizing the file size of your images is to consider the dimensions of the photo. My phone, which is in no way the latest model, takes photos that measure 4,032 px (pixels) by 3,024 px, which can produce an image nearly 60 inches wide! But this image file is also over 2 MB in size, over four times larger than even the most generous recommendations for photo size when loading on to a website. When editing your photos, a good guideline is to set the widest image dimension (width for landscape photos and height for portraits) to 800 px. This size will still produce a nice-looking image on a typical computer screen without overly affecting the download speeds.

While cropping your photo is more about aesthetics than file size, it will make the image smaller, thus reducing the file size a little as well. When deciding what to crop, consider the subject of the image and crop to draw focus to that element. That doesn't mean focusing solely on that element: viewing your work in context is important too, so even in a costume photo you'll want to be able to see the scenery and lighting. But if there is dead space along an edge of the image or patron heads along the bottom, crop them out; see Plates 4–9 for examples of ways to do this.

After making these changes, check your file size. If it is below 300 kb you probably don't need to adjust things any more; but if it is over 300 kb you may need to consider compressing the file to reduce its size further. One of the reasons we use the JPG file format for photos is that it allows for this compression—using fancy computer algorithms the actual image data can be reduced. Search the web for "compress photo file" and the name of the software you are using to find step-by-step instructions. This produces a smaller image file, but if done too much it can result in a noticeably lower image quality, often seeming blurry, pixelated, or fuzzy. Because of this, only choose this option if you really need to.

When uploading your images to your CMS, be sure to note the alt-text or caption for the image. The alt-text is what a screen reader will read aloud for those who experience websites auditorily and not visually; it is also read by search engines and can improve your SEO. Often the default is the file name, but you should include a better description to increase accessibility. Also review what your CMS is using as the caption on your photos, as it often defaults to the file name for that as well and you definitely want to change this.

Putting It Together

Once you have your flowchart planned, your materials gathered and organized, all your text and bullet points written, and your images optimized, the only thing you have left is to upload your content into your CMS and begin creating your website. Allow yourself plenty of time for this process.

It just plain takes time, and you will be learning how the site functions simultaneously. Make full use of the CMS tutorials and help documents. Get feedback from knowledgeable friends and colleagues, and make adjustments until you have finalized everything. Then put a reminder in your calendar to update your portfolio at least every six months. Keeping your portfolio current is a sign of professionalism.

6

The Interview

Interviews cause some people a lot of anxiety, feelings of self-doubt, and visions of failure or embarrassment. Here's a secret: the interviewer is probably nervous too! When Ryan Gravilla, principal lighting designer for Walt Disney Entertainment, is interviewing people, he says, "I'm nervous because I'm rooting for them. I want them to be successful! I try to put them at ease as much as possible so we can just talk."[1] Additionally, most interviewers do not have any interview training and are mimicking their own past interview experiences.

Everyone seems to focus on what the interviewer will think of them, and overlook the fact that interviews are not just for the employer. They are a great opportunity for you to learn more about the job and potential employer. Interviews help you figure out if this is actually a job you even want. It isn't an interrogation, it's a conversation; a chance for you to learn more about each other. By keeping these three things in mind you will find interviews are quite valuable. You may even be able to enjoy them.

1. Be prepared.
2. It is just a conversation with a person.
3. You are also interviewing them.

What to Expect at an Interview

Fear of the unknown is at the root of most people's anxiety surrounding interviews. Understanding the anatomy of an interview will help you feel more confident.

---

[1] Ryan Gravilla, interview with the author, October 2, 2020.

Before the interview you will need to spend some time preparing. Don't expect to be able to walk in cold and perform at your best. An actor wouldn't go to an audition without preparation, and neither should you. The most important thing you need to prepare as you begin your job search is answers to the most common interview questions, which we go over in detail later in the chapter. You should also practice your answers out loud. Just as actors need to say their lines aloud to get muscle memory of them, you need to do the same.

In a notebook you plan to take with you to the interview, make a list of important points you want to mention and a list of questions you want to make sure you get answered (there are suggestions later in this chapter). When the interviewer asks if there is anything else you want to add or ask, instead of staring at them wide-eyed hoping you can think of something, you can check your notes to be sure you have communicated your important points and asked your questions.

When the recruiter calls to schedule the interview, ask questions to help you prepare: with whom will you be meeting, will anyone else will be joining the interview, and how long should you block out in your schedule? If it is an in-person interview, are there any special directions or parking details, and whom you should contact if you have difficulty finding the location.

If feasible, a few days prior to your interview try a practice run to the location. This can alleviate the anxiety of not knowing where you are going on the big day, boost your confidence, and help you accurately plan to arrive ten minutes early.

In addition to bringing enough copies of your resume for everyone attending the interview (plus one for you to look at because it is not unusual for you to forget everything you have ever done!), take along your portfolio and business cards. It helps to create a checklist of what you need to have with you.

- Directions to the interview location.
- Phone number of contact person in case you get lost or have questions.
- Sufficient copies of your resume.
- Notebook and pen for taking notes (with your key points and questions already written in it).
- Portfolio/examples of your work.
- Business cards.
- Small bottle of water to help you fight off dry mouth.

Once you've arrived, most interviews follow a standard format. You will check in with someone and let them know you are there. Sometimes your interviewer will come to greet you, or you may be escorted by someone else. Be sure to greet everyone you meet graciously and professionally. Your interview has begun the moment you enter the location; indeed, truly it began the moment they contacted you to set up the interview. The interviewer will certainly check with support personnel you engage with to be sure that you were professional and pleasant. Once seated you should give each interviewer a copy of your resume. If there have been any updates since your application, let them know it is updated. Get out your notebook. If you did not bring water with you and you are offered, take it. You may not want to be "a bother," but you need to override this instinct. This water may be your lifeline! It can give you something to do with your hands, help you overcome a case of cotton mouth, and taking a sip of water is a good way to stall if you need to think or just slow yourself down during the interview. Take the water.

Once everyone is settled the interviewer may jump right into questions, provide you with more information about the job, or continue with small talk. The important thing to remember is that these are just people you are conversing with about a shared common interest. You both want the same thing. You want this job and they want you to be perfect for this job. It isn't adversarial. They aren't trying to trip you up or catch you in anything. They want you to be brilliant. If you are perfect for the job it makes their life so much easier; they can confidently conclude the interview process and move on to the next item on their to-do list. Realize also that you hold as much power as they do. Just because they offer you the job doesn't mean that you must take it. You need to find out if this is a job and an organization that you are interested in. Think of the interview as a collaborative process where everyone is working toward the same goal. It will shift your frame of mind and positively impact your performance in the interview.

During the interview you will learn things about the job or company that you want to remember, and the notebook you brought with you is ideal for this purpose. It is absolutely OK to take notes, and in fact it is encouraged! It shows you are interested in the job and serious about this opportunity. You can also use the notes you take to help you write substantive thank-you notes following the interview.

Remember that an interview is just a conversation; it is OK to ask questions as they come up as part of the discussion. If your questions don't fit into the conversation fluidly, write them down in your notebook to remember them. If you aren't asked if you have any questions toward the end of your interview, let them know you have questions to be sure you get the information you need. You are interviewing them too, remember. You can't make an informed decision about which job offer to take if you don't have all the information. It is typically a red flag if you don't ask any questions, but be careful not to ask questions that have already been answered, or it will seem you were not listening.

The interviewer will likely ask to see your portfolio, although if they forget be sure to speak up and offer it. Sometimes the interview will include a tour and introductions to various staff. You won't be expected to memorize the floor plan or remember every name of every person you meet. The point of the tour is to give you the feel of the workplace and an opportunity to picture yourself working there. Typically they will show you the office or workspace you will have if you are hired. If the tour takes place at the beginning of the interview, you will then be shown to the place where your interview will take place. If the tour happens at the end, you will likely be walked to the exit and the interview is over. If this is the case be sure to ask your questions and show your work before you leave the interview room.

Worst-Case Scenarios

Some of the worst-case scenarios people have given me include giant sneezes, tripping, spilling something on themselves or the interviewer's desk, having a spider or mouse crawl on them, and forgetting what they were going to say. I can't guarantee these things will never happen, because they might (well, probably not the mouse), but if they do it isn't actually a big deal in terms of your interview. Imagine if one of these things happened to you in a non-interview conversation (you probably don't have to imagine it because it is likely that sometime in your life something like this actually *has* happened to you). So if you have a very big sneeze, just take care of the situation, wash your hands if necessary, apologize, and move on. Going back to the idea that these are just people you are talking to, they have also sneezed at an inopportune moment. If your roles were reversed, would you think that they would be a terrible employee and you shouldn't hire them because they had a giant sneeze? No. You would feel compassionate and do what you could to help them. What if you trip? They will ask if you are OK and you can either play it cool and say yes or, if it fits your personality, make a comment with a smile about what a bad interview impression you must be making. These things happen, and they aren't going to stop you getting the job.

Another thing I hear is "I'm just not good at interviews." I don't accept that. This is simply an attempt to excuse yourself from preparing and performing well. Then if you don't get the job you can tell yourself, "See! I'm really terrible at interviews!", and if you do get the job you can dismiss it and think "I don't know how I got that job since I'm so terrible at interviews." The only reason you will be terrible at an interview is if you don't prepare. We tend to dislike things that we don't know how to do well, and the solution to that is to do your research and prepare answers ahead of time. With preparation you can confidently walk into the interview knowing you can answer anything they ask.

Personal Appearance and First Impressions

While most interviews in our field don't require a business suit, neither should you show up in your shop clothes. There is a range of acceptable dress depending on the type of position you are applying for. The general rule is to strive to dress a degree or two better than you would expect your daily attire to be on the job. You should probably never dress below business casual when going for an interview: showing up to an interview in blue jeans and a t-shirt sends the message that the position isn't important to you. Blue jeans are not interview attire. The same goes for shorts, although skirts are fine. Choose clothes in which you can both sit and stand comfortably without readjusting them.[2] Pay particular attention to the comfort of your footwear. Some interviews will include walking tours of facilities, and you don't want to be limping around due to uncomfortable shoes.[3] Another thing to avoid at an interview, and in the workplace in general, is any type of cologne, perfume, body spray, or scented lotions. These can cause allergic reactions in many people, and you don't want to be the cause of anyone's medical distress. You should be freshly showered and groomed. It is good practice for everyone in work settings to avoid clothes that show the back,

[2]Nikki Blue-Emens, personal communication with the author, January 31, 2020.
[3]Heather St. George Gibson, personal communication with the author, January 31, 2020.

chest, stomach, or undergarments. "Your work should stand out more than your appearance."[4]

Body modifications, including tattoos, piercings, colorful hair, and unique fashion sense, are more acceptable in many workplaces in our industry, although you are unlikely to find such things shown in any online sites discussing business attire. But there are corporate employers with very strict appearance standards who don't allow anything they consider outside their brand. The descriptions below are mostly representative of these more restrictive environments, and your interview is probably not the place to test the limits.

Business professional. Dark, solid-color, or subtly patterned full suit with skirt, dress, or pants with belt, freshly pressed professional shirt with subtle jewelry, scarf, or tie. Conservative, polished, closed-toe dress shoes with or without a heel. Stockings, dress socks, or tights should match the pants or skirt (no white socks!). Minimal subtle accessories (watch, bracelet, cufflinks). Manicured nails. Optional cosmetics should be neutral and natural looking. Understated briefcase or purse. Professional padfolio and pen.

Business casual (note that this is different from casual business or casual). Neatly pressed khakis, slacks, skirt, or dress at least to the knee. Optional sport coat or sweater. Twin set, polo shirt, cardigan, button-down-collared shirt, blouse with subtle jewelry or scarf, or a freshly pressed dress shirt and tie. Well-maintained closed-toe dress shoes or boots with or without a heel. Stockings, dress socks, or tights should match the pants or skirt (no white socks!). Minimal subtle accessories (watch, bracelet, ring). Manicured nails. Optional cosmetics should be neutral and natural looking. Understated briefcase or purse. Professional padfolio and pen.

Casual business. Typically comfortable clothing that is practical for your job responsibilities. Can include nice jeans or cargo pants without holes, dresses, casual pants, and skirts. Shirts can be with or without a collar, including sweatshirts and sweaters. Work boots, athletic shoes, or sandals are typically acceptable. All clothing should be in good repair without rips or fraying. A wider range of colors and patterns are acceptable in a casual business environment. Clothing worn for exercise or lounging is generally not appropriate. Casual business attire should not be worn to an interview even with a company that has a casual business, casual, or "shop clothes" dress code.

---

[4] Rebecca White, personal communication with the author, January 31, 2020.

Casual or "shop clothes." Most importantly, follow all safety-related clothing choices when working in a shop, on stage, backstage, etc., including rubber-soled, closed-toe shoes or boots, long pants, tied-back hair, eye and hearing protection, no jewelry, etc. Jeans are expected, and those with holes and covered in paint are not frowned upon, nor are bright colors or logo t-shirts. While the recommendation still stands not to reveal your back, chest, stomach, or undergarments, many of the other workplace standards do not apply. Casual or "shop clothes" should never be worn to an interview.

The vast majority of my former students tell me they have had no problems with visible tattoos because all their employers have been open to creative expression through appearance. One former student, however, had a full sleeve and neck tattoo and almost lost their summer job stage managing at a theme park because of this. They ended up being the only person working outside in the Florida sun wearing a black turtleneck under their assigned work uniform. When they returned to school the following fall they had begun the time-consuming, expensive, and painful process of having laser removal of the neck tattoo because they were offered another position they wanted to accept and it would be impossible to cover it. It hadn't occurred to them that they might want to work somewhere that didn't accept their tattoos. You never know how you or your priorities will change, so if you decide to make any permanent alterations to your appearance be sure to consider how placement and subject matter may affect your future employment options.

It is against the law for employers in the United States to discriminate against you based on race, religion, sexual orientation, gender identity, and disability, among a few other grounds. Unfortunately, white appearance standards continue to be considered "the norm." While even the strictest of employers are finally starting to realize that white standards cannot be applied to everyone, people of color still receive a range of negative responses to their completely appropriate appearance choices—in addition to, of course, their skin color. Even in our generally open-minded industry, bigoted and racist people are still making hiring decisions that discriminate against our Black, Asian, Middle Eastern, and other colleagues of color. Demand better from your employers and hiring committees.

Your appearance is obviously going to make a first impression, but so will the way you greet people. Look people in the eye and repeat their name out loud when they are introduced. Experts say that is the best way to help you remember their name. If you, like me, struggle with remembering names, especially when introduced to several people in a group, try being open and admitting that you may need to ask their name again at some point. No need to be embarrassed. I have even found that embracing this difficulty takes the pressure off and allows me to focus on the conversations more fully, so I generally have an easier time remembering their names. Most people are glad to hear that you are a normal person who has the same struggle they do. It makes you relatable, and the honesty is often refreshing.

If interviewing or working internationally, be sure you understand the local cultural norms you need to follow. In the US, prior to the global Covid-19 pandemic handshakes were expected at interviews and networking events, but many are now rethinking the handshake imperative. It is possible that the handshake is a thing of the past, as it becomes more commonplace for people to decline to give or receive them for health reasons. If you will not be shaking hands, have a plan for what to say if approached so you don't compromise your stance in a panic. My planned response is "It's so nice to meet you" or "It's so good to see you," adding, "After Covid I don't shake hands any more," all with a friendly smile. If you offer a handshake and the person declines, replying with a friendly smile and "I understand" will suffice. The guidelines for handshakes below should be considered in the context of public health.

Shaking hands creates an instant impression. Prior to a handshake your hands must be clean and dry. If you are meeting a group of people it is customary to shake hands with everyone in the group. Unless there is a compelling reason to shake a person's left hand (the person's right arm is in a cast or they only have a left arm), handshakes are done with the right hand and should be "web to web." That means you offer the other person your right hand with your palm facing to the left, not angled up or down, and the web of skin between the thumb and pointer finger should contact this same part of the other person's hand. This helps to avoid the awkward "dead fish" handshake where someone just grabs your fingers and squeezes. The finger squeeze is especially painful for people who wear rings, and pain should not be part of a handshake! A tighter handshake is not a better handshake, but quite the opposite—it is often viewed as "aggressive" rather than "confident." The standard number of arm pumps is three (think "rock, paper, scissors" if you have a hard time remembering; bonus is you will likely give a more genuine smile). Your whole arm is involved in a handshake, from your wrist to your elbow to your shoulder. Limiting motion to any one joint makes for a stiff and awkward handshake. You want your movement to be fluid without flailing. Don't touch or grab the other person with your free hand; this is viewed as aggressive even if your intent is friendly.

If you plan to be a handshaker, practice. You will never know what your own handshake feels like. Review these tips and shake hands with as many friends and family members as possible. Ask for feedback about what your handshake feels like, and adjust as necessary.

What Makes a Good Answer to an Interview Question?

Answering interview questions isn't as straightforward as it may seem, and perhaps that is one of the reasons why interviews make people so nervous. There is a strategy to answering interview questions well, and once you understand the strategy you can answer any question an interviewer asks with confidence. Even if you are asked yes-or-no questions you should not give yes-or-no answers; giving concrete examples from your experience allows the interviewer to imagine you in the position for which you are applying.

You can search online and find several mnemonic devices to help you remember the key components to good answers. One of the most common is STAR: situation, task, action, and results.

To apply this system, first describe the *situation* you were in: I was working on a large-scale musical in an unfamiliar venue; I was on the load-in team for a large convention and we had three hours before the floor opened; I worked on a major cruise line for six months; I was a technician at an outdoor venue in a theme park; I was assisting on a show with an out-of-town designer; I was on a bus and truck tour filling multiple roles, etc. Provide the context so the interviewer knows what frame of reference to use.

Next, explain the *task* you need to accomplish, which will typically present some kind of challenge: I had to troubleshoot the projections system; I discovered that I get seasick and had to figure out how to work through that illness; I couldn't find the venue technician to let me into the locked booth; the fabric store was out of the fabric the director had approved; the artistic director came into the final rehearsal with a list of changes; I needed to back paint the set but the black paint would arrive a day late, etc.

Then explain what *action* you took to accomplish your task, what did you do? I made a detailed Gantt chart to plan every step of the project to meet the tight deadline; I swatched new fabrics that were as close to the original choice as possible; I created a unique and detailed tracking sheet to be sure that everything would get where it was supposed to be in time; I went through a troubleshooting process tracing the system from inputs to output, and discovered a bad connector; I had the actor wear their Act II pants for the rest of Act I because there was no way to make the repair in time; I called the understudy to prepare to go on in case the actor couldn't finish the show; I followed the chain of command in reporting the problem, etc. Include some detail to explain even better what you did. Use "I" statements for everything *you* did. We absolutely work in collaborative teams, but your team is not applying for this job, you are. Be sure to take ownership of your decisions and actions. Give credit to those who participated without downplaying your own contributions.

Finally, what was the *result* of your actions? Because of my quick decision-making the shop remained on schedule and everything was ready for tech; the director was able to address the actor's concerns; despite my best efforts to find a new source we had to go with the less-desirable fake fish; by remaining calm during the crisis I was able to lead my crew through our emergency procedures and get everyone out of the building safely.

Some people add another R to the end of the STAR method to make STARR. The extra R is for *reflection*, which can be a valuable addition. What did you do well? What did you learn that you would do differently next time? For example, I was able to reflect on where the communication broke down and I now take steps not to let that happen again; they later told me how much they appreciated my apology and accepting responsibility for my mistake; I'm so glad I took the time to read the manual so I was prepared for that type of malfunction; I have added that step into my master list so it is now always part of my process; that experience taught me that I really don't want to be a designer.

These ideas come from the behavioral interview technique, which says your past behavior is the best predictor of your future behavior. So if you explain how you have done things in the past and how you would or would not do them again, the interviewer gets a more in-depth view. But interviewers don't always ask good questions, don't ask their questions in a behavioral style even though that's the type of answer they are looking for, or don't even ask the right question for the information they want. If your interviewer asks you a hypothetical or a yes-or-no question—Have you ever gone over budget? What would you do if you went over budget?—it is best to describe what you did when you encountered that situation rather than give a one-word answer. If you later decided you should have behaved differently, explain that. But if you have not had the experience they are asking about, only then is it OK to give a hypothetical or related response. Using the budget scenario, describe how you would track expenses and what you would do if you thought you were going to go over budget. Or describe what you do to manage your personal finances and how you could transfer those skills to a production budget. If you just answer that you haven't done the thing they are asking about, they learn nothing positive about you.

The words you say are obviously important when it comes to answering interview questions. The interviewer is also going to read your body language, tone of voice, and facial expressions. Changing non-verbal cues, even when using the same words, can completely change the message you are sending. Keep this in mind as you practice and prepare.

What Are They Really Asking?

You never want to be caught without an answer during an interview. To be prepared, you need to take the time to consider the most common interview questions and construct written answers to each of them. Why write them out? You'll put more thought into them by doing so and are less likely to skip any by telling yourself you know how to answer it already. It also helps to ensure you aren't telling the same story more than once, and you use the full diversity of your experiences. You'll never be asked all the possible questions, but you never know where an interviewer's interests lie. Having a document to review and update as you go through your career will save you time in your future interview prep. You can also use it to seek feedback from your mentors as you revise and perfect your plan.

To know you are telling the best story for the question, you must know what the interviewer is actually asking with each question and what kind of information is going to satisfy and impress them. Most people who conduct interviews do not actually have any training in interviewing people and just make it up based on their own past interview experiences, so they don't always ask questions that will get them the information they are really seeking. It is important for you to figure out the question behind the question. Remain focused on giving your potential employer information that will be helpful to them. Be honest. Being honest doesn't mean you have to reveal all the details about every experience. It means don't lie. Don't stretch the truth. You can be honest without being open. You don't have to tell them everything, but everything you tell them must be true.

Here are a few examples of questions you may be asked, and underneath each is a note of what the interviewer really wants to learn from you.

- So, tell me a little about yourself.
    - This will likely be the first question in 90 percent of your interviews. The biggest thing the interviewer wants to do is start the conversation. Your answer provides a first impression of sorts, and sets the tone for the rest of the interview. They don't want to hear about being a tree in the third-grade school play. They are evaluating what you find important enough to include in your introduction. You can use a version of your elevator pitch to answer this question.
- Why are you interested in this position?
    - Is this really a job you are interested in, or was it one of the dozens of applications you sent out just fishing for anything? What do you think you would like about working at this company?
- What aspect of [job you are applying for] do you hate or appeals to you least?
    - The employer knows what the job entails. If you hate the very thing they know you are going to have to spend a lot of time doing, they may decide you won't be happy in the position or won't do it very well. That doesn't mean you should be vague or wishy-washy about the things you don't like to do. Remember that not getting a job is sometimes a gift, especially if it would have made you miserable.
- What do you think your weaknesses would be for this position/the kind of position you are seeking?
    - Do not give a fake answer like "I care too much" or "I work too hard." Be honest about a couple of the areas that aren't your strongest, and then put them in context. They want to hear about how you compensate for these weaknesses, which helps them understand how you will respond to new challenges on the job. End your answer on a positive note.
- What unique experience or qualifications separate you from other candidates?
    - Assuming that everyone they are interviewing has the same general skills, they want to know what additional benefit you would bring over someone else. Do you have advanced training in something, do you use unique software, do you have a long history doing this type

of work, do you have certifications? They are also testing your level of understanding of the position: if you list things that are normal and not unique for this type of position, that will tell them you may not understand this level of work.

- What do you see yourself doing five years from now?
  - The subtext of this question is have you thought about how you want your career to progress? Does this job make sense for you based on your longer-term goals? Do you understand the typical job ladder for your career goal and how this job fits into your planned path?
- Describe a situation where you made a big mistake on the job.
  - Everyone makes mistakes, including the person interviewing you! Do not pretend you are perfect: that's a sure way to cause the interviewer to question your sincerity. They are evaluating how you fix things when you mess up, and how you adjust your approach to avoid that mistake again.
- Describe the worst boss you have ever worked with.
  - *Never* put anyone down in an interview—or ever. Some people will test you hard on this point; they will mention someone you have worked with and say something negative about them, trying to see if you will take the bait. Don't do it. Use this as an opportunity to talk about challenges you have faced with supervisors (generically) in the past and how you handled them appropriately. Employers know that if you are willing to badmouth your previous employer then it is likely you will do the same to them when you move on to your next job.
- Have you ever gone over budget?
  - If you are managing a budget for them and don't have enough to complete the work, are you going to keep spending and let them know once you are already over budget, or will you come to them early to alert them of the problem and discuss solutions?
- Tell me about an occasion when you disagreed with a supervisor's decision or policy.
  - When you get mad at your boss, how are you going to handle it? Are you going to storm off? Are you going to backstab or gossip? Are you going to handle it professionally? Do you understand which decisions necessitate going over their head and which don't?

- What are your salary requirements?
    - ○ This is absolutely a question you need to be prepared to answer, and there is a lot of strategy involved. Are your salary expectations reasonable? Can they get away with paying you less than they are willing to pay? This is discussed later in this chapter in the sections on negotiation and setting your fees.

Visit the companion website for a comprehensive list of questions and what they mean, as well as example answers for all the questions.

Some interviewers like to use scenario-based questions rather than behavioral questions.

- What would you do if your supervisor told you there wasn't time to follow safety protocols when making a last-minute fix in the truss above the stage before the show?
- As the stage manager, if you found that one of your performers was ill just before curtain, what would your steps be in resolving this?
- How would you handle a situation in which you were given conflicting notes (on a costume, a set piece, light cue, etc.) by a show director and artistic director?
- What would you do if you suspected a co-worker was stealing from the company?

Some people subscribe to a more "creative" interview style. Interviewers who use this approach say they are looking for insights into your personality and how you respond to the unexpected.

- Who is your favorite superhero and why?
- From these animal pictures, which animal do you think best describes your leadership style and why?
- Do you have a theme song or motto?
- What kind of dog would you be if you were a dog?
- Which Hogwarts house are you in?

Remember to Interview Them

Too many people envision interviews as an all-powerful employer asking questions, deciding who they want to hire, while completely forgetting the interviewee also must decide if this is a job they want. The potential employee has as much, if not more, power in the interview dynamic, but to take advantage of this power they must ask questions and collect information. To be most effective you need to do some research: spend some time reviewing the job description, the company website, and any other information you can find ahead of time. A day or two before your interview, make a list in the notebook you plan to take with you to the interview. Write down any questions you have related to the company and the specific position for which you are applying. Toward the end of your interview they should offer you an opportunity to ask any remaining questions (if it seems like they are planning to wrap up without doing so, let the interviewer know that you have questions you would like to ask before you leave). This is your opportunity, and you need to take advantage of it.

Interviewer: Thank you so much for coming in. We will be in touch soon.

You: Before I go, I have a few questions I would appreciate the opportunity to discuss.

or

Interviewer: Do you have any questions before we wrap up?

You: Yes, I do. I'm going to look over my notes to see which ones haven't already been answered.

Don't ask any questions that could be answered on their website (that shows lack of preparation) or were answered in the course of the interview (which shows inattentiveness). If they answered part of your question or you have a follow-up, it is good to acknowledge the part they have already answered. For example, "I know you said that I wouldn't be expected to work very many weekends. To give me a better idea of what that means, can you tell me how many weekends the last person who held this position worked during this past season?" Avoid questions that can be answered with yes or no, and if this is your first interview for the position don't ask about money or benefits unless the employer brings it up first.

Below is a list of possible questions you might find helpful when deciding if the job is a good fit for you. You should limit your list to eight to ten questions, knowing you may not be able to ask them all. You will likely only have time for three to five, so you'll need to prioritize in the moment those you need the answers to right now. Keep in mind that if you make it to round two you will have the opportunity to ask additional questions. Also note that the questions you ask provide the employer with information about you as a potential employee. Adapt any of the questions below to your situation, the type of job, and the type of company you are applying for. Be sure to use correct terminology.

- What would you say are the company's strengths and weaknesses (or the specific department you would be working for)?
- In what ways does your organizational structure differ from what I would find at other theatres (companies, convention centers—insert what is appropriate for this employer)?
- What concrete actions is the organization actively taking to pursue diversity?
- What policies does the organization have that establish an inclusive environment?
- Do you support employees using their correct pronouns and including them in introductions and email signatures?
- How will my work be evaluated?
- What do you think are the most important skills required for this job?
- Does this position have any responsibilities that might be unexpected for this job title?
- What training should I expect to receive?
- How do you select your season?
- How are projects budgeted?
- What are the biggest challenges of this position?
- What are the biggest challenges the organization is facing right now?
- What are the next steps in the interview process?
- What does it look like during the busiest and toughest times for this role?
- Would I need to travel for the position?
- What kind of hours are needed for me to meet quality expectations?
- Is overtime expected and/or allowed?
- Could you tell me a little bit about the person I would report to directly?
- If I were hired for the position, what would be the ideal starting date?
- How long have most people stayed in this position? Did they move up within the company or leave the company for other opportunities? (If this is for summer stock you can ask about people returning to work another season instead of staying in the position. The moving up is still a good question.)
- How is information documented and shared across projects and departments?

- Is there anything else I can tell you about myself that would help you with your decision?
- Do you have any concerns about my fit for this position that I might be able to address?
- May I ask why the last person left the job?
- What mistakes have people made in this position?
- What could I do in this position that would make your life easier?
- Why is this position open right now?
- How long has this position been open?
- How many people have held this job in the last two years?
- What would be your number one priority for me coming into this role?
- What have you identified as the most important things you are looking for in a candidate?
- What improvements or changes do you hope a new person will bring to this position?
- Does the company have any traditions that you enjoy or think are interesting to share?
- What are some reasons people like working here?
- What do you wish you had known before you joined the company?
- Who should I stay in touch with as things move forward?
- How big is the team I will be working with?
- What is your typical rehearsal and production schedule?
- What tools/equipment/software are you primarily using or would I have the opportunity to use here? You could also ask about specific equipment or software by name.

There are things you should not ask at a job interview. Consider why these examples would not be in your best interest, and use them to help you evaluate any other questions you think of asking.

- What kinds of shows do you do?
  - You should have already researched this on their website. This question shows lack of preparation or interest in the job.
- How soon can I take vacation time?
  - This will send a bad message about your work habits. Vacation time is considered part of your benefits package and could be negotiable. It is something to discuss in a subsequent interview or after being offered the position. If you have a pre-existing commitment, like an upcoming vacation, family reunion, wedding, or other kind of trip, wait until you are offered the job to discuss it. In almost all cases

anything you have planned prior to accepting a job will be approved without consequence as unpaid time off.

- Can I set my own hours?
  - This will send the message that you may not want to work when the work is scheduled. You can certainly ask what the typical work hours are, and in answering that you will find out if setting your own hours is something they allow.
- Can I work from home?
  - Companies that don't typically have employees work from home tend to be suspicious of people who wish to do so, but after the lockdown periods for Covid-19 many more companies are open to it.
- How many times can I be late before I get fired?
  - This will tell them that you have a problem with punctuality and might not be reliable.
- Can I bring my dog to work?
  - When asking about the work culture they will likely mention if people bring their dogs to work. If not and you are still curious, this is something to ask on a second interview or even after you have started in the position and have a chance to feel out the environment. If you have a legitimate service animal, you don't have to ask as they are legally obliged to allow it.
- Will I have to take a drug test?
  - This would be a red flag to companies with strict drug policies. You could ask what the procedures are for starting the job and their answer would likely include this information.
- Does this company monitor internet usage?
  - The only reason you would want to know this is if you plan to do something of which they wouldn't approve. You will be told about computer policies after being hired. Don't use company computers or Wi-Fi for goofing off, and you won't have a problem.
- Did I get the job?
  - Any form of this question like "so when do I start?" or "Can I start today?" will be off-putting to the interviewer and crosses the line from confident to obnoxious. You can ask about the timeline for the rest of their hiring process, and if you are offered the job you can ask when you could begin.

Illegal Interview Questions

In the United States there are topics that are illegal for an interviewer to ask an applicant either directly or indirectly.[5] The lists are quite similar in Canada and the UK, but you should always look up the laws in the country (and even US state) in which you are interviewing. Being illegal, you might think you'll never be asked these sorts of questions, but that isn't the case. Federally protected categories in the US are listed below.[6]

- Race, color, ethnicity, and national origin.
- Birthplace, country of origin, and citizenship.
- Religion.
- Sex, gender, and sexual orientation.
- Pregnancy status.
- Physical or mental disability and health condition.
- Age (40 or older) and genetic information.
- Marital status, family structure, and number of children.
- Military status.
- Arrest record (though convictions may be considered if they are related to the line of work and the same standard is applied to all applicants evenly).[7]

Some states have additional protected categories or limit discriminatory employment practices even further than the federal laws.

Most of these federal protections only apply to employees, so if you are an independent contractor you are not covered unless you live in a state that has

---

[5]The number of employees and length of their employment impacts if protections affect private companies. Additional information can be found at https://www.eeoc.gov/employees/coverage_private.cfm, accessed February 19, 2020.

[6]These protected classes are established and defined in various US federal laws: Title VII of the Civil Rights Act of 1964 (42 U.S.C. § 2000e), Titles I and V of the Americans with Disabilities Act (42 U.S.C. §§ 12101–12113) as amended by the Civil Rights Act of 1991 and the Americans with Disabilities Act Amendments Act, The Rehabilitation Act (29 U.S.C. §§ 791, 793, 794), Age Discrimination in Employment Act (29 U.S.C. §§ 621–634), Genetic Information Nondiscrimination Act (42 U.S.C. § 2000ff), Uniformed Services Employment and Reemployment Rights Act (38 U.S.C. § 4311), Section 1981 of the Civil Rights Act of 1866 (42 U.S.C. § 1981), Equal Pay Act (29 U.S.C. § 206(d)), and The Immigration Reform and Control Act (Pub. L. 99–603, 100 Stat. 3359 (1986)), in addition to applicable sections in Title VIII Aliens and Nationality (8 U.S.C.). They can be found at https://uscode.house.gov/browse.xhtml accessed February 19, 2020.

[7]US Equal Employment Opportunity Commission, https://www.eeoc.gov/laws/practices/inquiries_arrest_conviction.cfm accessed February 19, 2020.

extended these protections to such workers.[8] The only federal protections you have as an independent contractor are found in the Civil Rights Act of 1866, s. 1981: "Equal rights under the law."[9] This section provides protection based on race, color, and ethnicity (including harassment) when making, performing, modifying, enforcing, or terminating contracts (among other things),[10] and courts have determined that this includes making contracts with independent contractors. The other federal employment protections for age, disability, religion, etc. do not apply to independent contractors.

Questions that give an interviewer information regarding protected topics are illegal even if asked as part of small talk, because the information could be used to discriminate, consciously or unconsciously. All questions must relate to the requirements of the job. Table 11 shows examples of illegal and legal questions related to federally protected classes; state laws may limit questioning even more.

Many of these questions arise as part of getting to know a new person, and may be asked accidentally as small talk. That doesn't make them legal, but it does complicate your decision on how to respond. You have a few options, with the only constant being that you shouldn't be hostile, even if you choose to call them out.

There is nothing illegal about answering an illegal question, but answering does not change the fact that the question is illegal. In fact, you may be causing harm to other people who have reasons not to answer illegal questions by reinforcing the view that the line of questioning is appropriate. You don't want to get a job because someone else was discriminated against. You should also consider whether you want to work somewhere that makes hiring decisions based on illegal and discriminatory practices. For example, if it is not a child-friendly workplace or it will be a hostile environment for you as a non-binary person, this may not be the place for you. You do not have to answer an illegal question. You have other options, and you should prepare yourself for how to respond so you don't blurt out an answer you didn't intend.

If you are asked a question where answering would result in revealing protected information, one option is to ignore the fact that they just asked an illegal question and redirect your response to your qualifications and expectations for the job. For example, if asked "Will it be a problem for you to have a [man/woman] as your shop supervisor?", respond with "The

[8]US Equal Employment Opportunity Commission, https://www.eeoc.gov/employees/coverage.cfm, accessed February 19, 2020.
[9]Civil Rights Act of 1866, accessed February 19, 2020, https://www.fjc.gov/history/timeline/civil-rights-act-1866.
[10]Section 1981 of the Civil Rights Act 1866 (42 U.S.C. § 1981).

Table 11 Illegal interview questions in the US

	Illegal	Legal
Marital status, family structure, children	• Are you married? • What does your spouse do for a living? • What is your maiden name? • What is your father's last name? • Are you single? • Do you live with your parents? • Who do you live with? • How will your spouse feel about the amount of travel required for this job? • Who will take care of your children when you travel for work? • Do you own a home? • Do you have children? • Are you planning to have children? • Are you pregnant? • When is the baby due? • How old are your kids? • Do you plan to stay home with your kids? • Have you figured out your childcare arrangements? • What are your plans if you get pregnant? • Do you prefer Miss or Mrs.?	• Have you ever worked under a different name? (Only OK if asked of all candidates regardless of gender.) • What are the names of any relatives who already work for our company or work for a competitor? • Are you able to perform the duties listed in the job description? • Are you able to work the hours required by this position? • Will you be able to work overtime? • Are you able to be at work by 7:30 am every day? • How long have you lived at your current address?
Race, color, ethnicity, national origin, birthplace, country of origin, and citizenship	• What is your accent? • Is English your first language? • Where did you grow up? • Where are your parents from? • Where do you live? • Where did you get your beautiful skin tone?	• Are you authorized to work in the US? • Are you able to provide proof of employment eligibility? • What languages do you speak fluently? (If applicable to the job.)

	Illegal	Legal
Physical or mental disability or health condition	• Do you have any health problems? • How did you get that limp? • Do you drink? • What accommodations will you need to do this job? • Have you ever had a workplace injury? • Do you have a medical condition that would affect your ability to do this job? • How is your mental health? • What happened to your arm? • How tall are you? • How much do you weigh?	• Are you able to meet the demands of this job safely, with or without accommodations or modifications to equipment, surroundings, etc.? • Our equipment has a safety weight limit of XYZ from the manufacturer. Will you be able to operate this equipment within the safety limits?
Religion	• What holidays will you need off? • Can you be fully available on weekends? • What religion are you? • Do you attend church? • Were you raised in the church? • Do you drink alcohol or caffeine? • What religious affiliation was your school? • Why do you cover your head? • Can you work during Ramadan? • What fraternity or sorority were you in? • What clubs do you belong to? • Do you belong to a church?	• Are there any shifts you cannot work? • Are you able to wear the work uniform? • Are you a member of any professional organizations like USITT, IAAPA, TEA, etc.?

	Illegal	Legal
Age	• When did you graduate from high school? • How old are your kids? • How long until you plan to retire? • Do you think you are overqualified for this position? • Do you live with your parents? • What is your birth date? • Who do you live with?	• Are you at or above the legally required age for this position?
Sex, gender, and sexual orientation	• Are you male or female? • How do you identify? • Do you think a woman/man can do this job? • Will you have a problem working with a team of all women? • Will it be a problem for you having a woman as a boss? • Is this your maiden or married name? • Who do you live with? • Were you in a fraternity/sorority?	• Questions related to gender are only legal if there is a bona fide occupational qualification (BFOQ) to justify them.
Military status	• Have you ever been in the military in another country? • Can you provide a copy of your discharge papers? • What was the condition of your discharge from the military?	• What training or work experience do you have that relates to this job?
Arrest record	• Have you been in trouble with the law? • Have you ever been arrested?	• Have you ever been convicted of embezzlement or larceny? • Were you ever disciplined by a former employer for not following company policy?

qualities I appreciate most in a supervisor are … " If they're smart, they'll realize their mistake and not press the issue. If they do, you could respond quizzically with "I'm not sure why that matters" or a flat "I don't think you are supposed to ask that type of question."

If you don't see a way to sidestep their direct question, you could answer the question with a question, redirecting it to the job.

Interviewer: "How much do you weigh?"
You: "Are there weight requirements or limitations for this job?" *or* "I should fit safely within any weight requirements the equipment has, if that's what you are asking."

Interviewer: "What do your kids think about you taking this touring job?"
You: "Why do you ask?" *or* "I don't get any outside pressure about my job."

You can also be intentionally vague or cheeky with a smile, if that is your style.

Interviewer: "Where are your parents from?"
You: "They grew up in a really small town."

Interviewer: "What is your heritage?"
You: "I've always wanted to do DNA testing. It sounds so fascinating!"

Interviewer: "How do you identify?"
You: "Just as a person."

Interviewer: "When did you graduate from high school?"
You: "If I told you that then you'd know how young I am!" *or* "Are you trying to figure out how old I am?", *or* just flat out ignore that they asked a question at all.

Interviewer: "Where did you get your beautiful skin tone?"
You: "Thank you so much! That is kind of you to say."

Deciding how to answer these types of questions may take you as much time as deciding how to answer the legitimate ones. Just as you will for standard interview questions, write out how you plan to answer these so that you only give out the information you choose.

Portfolio Presentations

Presenting your portfolio in an interview situation is not as easy as flipping through the pages and reciting each show's name in order. I think the biggest mistake people make when presenting their portfolios is wrapped up in the phrase "portfolio presentation." This implies that the focus is on the materials in the portfolio itself, resulting in portfolio presentations that go something like this:

> Hi, I'm Jovani. The first show in my portfolio is *Blood at the Root*. I was the scenic artist for this production in the Margeson at Orlando Shakes. I painted this tree and I also did all the graffiti on these lockers and I helped with the texturing on the floor in this picture. The next show in my portfolio is *A Hero Ain't Nothin' but a Sandwich* which I did when I was in college. This was the first show I ever painted on and I'm really proud of it …

The problem with this kind of presentation is that by focusing on what is on the page, you neglect the true point of the presentation, which is to help the person who is viewing your work get to know you: your approach, your thought process, your collaboration, your problem solving, your skill. Throw out that lackluster presentation, and instead use your "portfolio presentation" to demonstrate who you are as an artist and collaborator. Don't tell them what is on the page, tell them *why* it is there. Show them what you can *do*, not just what you have *done*. With that in mind, here are some common pitfalls to avoid.

- Don't say anything about the title page. This awkward single page only exists because you need something as a buffer at the top of your presentation, and in a physical portfolio the title uses up the first page so you can start off with a double-page spread. It can serve as a visual introduction if you are asked to leave your portfolio unattended, but when you are guiding the presentation just move past it and give your opening while doing so.
- Don't read your portfolio to them. Based on the previous chapter, you have taken care to label each page clearly with your job title and show. You have included captions and a breakdown of your responsibilities. By providing this basic information, you are absolved from having to recite it aloud.
- Don't ever use the word "just." You chose the materials in your portfolio for a reason, and you shouldn't undercut your work. If you realize that the material really is "just" then it doesn't belong in your portfolio.
- Don't apologize for your work. If you feel the need to apologize for something in your portfolio, then you should probably remove it.
- Don't tell them what is in the photos. They can see it. Telling them "This is a yellow dress I made for the play *The Yellow Dress*" gives them

absolutely no additional information about you or your skills. Telling them "the chiffon overlay on this dress has French seams along the princess lines, and I'm quite pleased I was able to stitch them without any puckers or tucks" tells them something! It tells them *why* you included that dress in your portfolio, and exactly what they should be looking at. Always tell them why you included something, what you contributed, or why it is a good example of your work.

- Don't say it was your first time. Your interviewer knows if you are just getting out of school. You don't have to remind them continually of your inexperience. Pointing out that something was your first time is like apologizing for your work. It implies that they should overlook any shortcomings. If it is in your portfolio then you did it and you did it well, no matter how many times you have or have not done it before.

- Don't introduce each show or project with "The first show is … The next show is … ". Transitions are a prime opportunity to set up your next show or project and make sure your viewer knows what to focus on.

Now, let's talk about what you can do to transform your portfolio presentation into an effective display of your talent and skill …

If a portfolio presentation was only about showing pictures, you could send them a link to your website and be done. The reason why portfolio presentations happen in person is so you can explain the process you went through to create each project. They want to know about challenges you faced and how you overcame them. The portfolio is really just a prop. It gives you an excuse to tell your best stories so you can give them the information you need them to know.

There are a few key moments in your presentation: the opening, transitions between shows, and the conclusion. These require additional planning and will have the biggest impact. These moments, where you must shift your train of thought, are invariably the points at which people stumble if they don't have a plan. These are the parts that you should script out and commit to memory. Of course, you also need to plan the details you will discuss about each show. You will likely speak more fluidly if you create bullet points rather than a full narrative. Here is an example of how a substantive opening to your portfolio might go as you move past the title page to the first show.

I'm excited to tell you about my work, which, as a designer, is rooted in my detailed research, my strong visual communication skills, and my collaborative approach to the process. I'll show you examples of those strengths as we go through my portfolio so you can see how these things impact my work.

With an opening like this you have now set in your interviewer's mind key aspects of your work, and they will be looking for these as you continue your presentation. They know what you consider your strengths to be, and you have used the few seconds getting into your portfolio to provide substantive information. If there are any characteristics or details in the job description you can highlight, that will be even more effective. This strong opening is lost, however, if you then revert to the typical presentation style of "my first show is … ." A strong presentation needs substantive transitions between shows that, ideally, refer to the strengths you highlighted in your opening. Continuing the example above, as you turn to the first show remember that your job title and the name of the show are clearly printed across the top of the page, so you don't need to take the time to verbalize that information.

> I use white models to communicate visually in the early stages of the design process, to address problems and find solutions. This allows me to resolve problems before we are too far along.[11]

This transition will have your viewer interested to see what you are talking about and will focus their attention on your white model progression. Don't fill the time turning the page with awkward silence or meaningless verbal crutches. Use it to state your rationale for including the next project and what it demonstrates about you as a professional. Then use details and examples on the page to provide the visual evidence to support your claim. The talking points that follow that transition might look something like this:

- Director inspired by Vilhelm Hammerhøi's Danish paintings.
- Director emphasized small, intimate show, but wide/tall proscenium made that a challenge.
- Adjusted proportions, widened downstage, used ceiling line to stop eye.
- Might not have caught concern without white model—like to use this every time.
- Work to find a way to communicate visually in the method the director understands.
- Fit in oversized space; connection to the audience; director's blocking needs.

---

[11] Enid Montalvo, portfolio narrative, April 25, 2019, adapted with permission.

Verbally presenting these bullet points would go something like this:

> The director was inspired by Vilhelm Hammerhøi's Danish paintings, and wanted the set to reflect that style. I incorporated the architectural aesthetic I found in my research [reference the research you have included on the page] to do the initial ground plan and sketches [reference these in portfolio]. To communicate better with the director, I built this white model [reference image in portfolio]. When the director and I went over it we decided that I needed to make adjustments to help evoke a more intimate feeling due to the theatre space being wide and tall. I adjusted the proportions, constrained the upstage areas more, and added a faux ceiling to help stop the eye from traveling too far up [reference image in portfolio]. I really love doing a white model early in the process, especially for directors who need that additional visual. I think it is important to figure out the form of visual communication the director needs and meet them where they are. Ultimately this leads to a better outcome. In this case I was able to compensate for the oversized space, maintain the needed connection to the audience, and meet the director's blocking needs.[12]

There were probably a lot of other great things about this design that you could talk about, but you have a limited amount of time so you have to prioritize. You can and should include things on the page that help illustrate your full process, even if you don't plan to talk about them. The viewer will still see them, and can ask questions if they wish.

After presenting the first production in your portfolio, you use your next page turn to transition to the next show:

> I love research and incorporating the details I find into my designs.

Then you discuss your bullet points (remember your job title and the show title are right at the top of the page).

> This break room at a Detroit stamping plant in 2008 allowed me to implement realistic details from my research, including the dingy color palette, scuffs and dents on appliances, rusty furniture, decaying pipes, and aging paint on the walls. The image of the hard hat was so prevalent in my research that I used the imagery to demonstrate visually the decline of the plant, with the number of hard hats on the rack shrinking to show the reduction of the workforce due to the recession.

---

[12]Ibid.

Repeat this pattern until you have discussed all the shows in your portfolio. Your final task is to wrap it up neatly with a meaningful conclusion. I cringe every time someone gets to the end of their portfolio and says awkwardly, "aaaaaand … that's all I have. Do you have any questions?" That isn't the impression you want to leave with them. Close by reinforcing the strengths you highlighted.

> I'm ready for the challenge of this position. My research, communication skills, and collaborative drive, in addition to my other skills, could be a great asset to the team.

You can find other sample openings and transitions on the companion website if you need additional inspiration for developing your own.

The last piece to put this all together is practice. I don't understand why people resist this step. If you are serious about giving a really strong presentation, if you are serious about getting the job, you will practice. If you don't practice, don't be surprised if you fall back into the old habits of "and the next show in my portfolio is … ", thereby negating all your preparation.

When you practice, it is important to practice aloud. Talk through your presentation over and over. Actors don't rehearse for shows by reading the script in their head, and you can't rehearse for this presentation by reading your outline in your head. Present it to a family member, roommate, or your dog. Record yourself and watch the video to see where you stumble, then rehearse those parts more. If you will be presenting a physical version of your portfolio, practice with your portfolio facing away from you. This means you will be seeing it upside down as you hold it in front of you and look down. If you always practice with it facing you, you may be thrown off by suddenly looking at everything upside down. Practice creates comfort, comfort inspires confidence, and that confidence will come across to your viewer.

Follow Up

As soon as possible after your interview, be sure to send thank-you notes to everyone you met, following the guidelines in Chapter 3. The most anxious questions I am asked by job seekers are those that come once the interview is over and the thank-you notes are sent. "What should I do now? I interviewed last week but haven't heard anything." People are often hesitant to follow up after an interview for fear of coming across as desperate, anxious, or annoying. First, think back to the interview. Did they tell you when you should expect to hear from them? Has that much time passed? If you were given a date, then wait a few days after that deadline before reaching out to them. Do not contact them before then. If they said you would hear from them in three weeks then, unfortunately, you must wait an anxious three weeks. If you weren't given a timeline then wait at least a week after your thank-you note should have arrived before sending a follow-up. An email follow-up (sent at least a week after the thank-you note) could go something like this:

> Dear Jerome Washington:
>
> Thank you again for interviewing me for the assistant stage manager position for your summer season. The more I reflect on our conversation last week the more excited I am about this job. Please let me know if you have any other questions for me and if you are close to making your final decision.
>
> I look forward to hearing from you.
> Sincerely,
> Khadijah James

If following up by phone is more appropriate, which it may be, depending on the main means of communication when setting up the interview, your opening to the phone conversation or voice mail could sound something like this:

> Hi Jerome Washington. This is Khadijah James. We spoke last week about the assistant stage manager position for your summer season. I am calling to find out when you expect to make a final decision and if I am still being considered for the job. I'm hoping to get my summer plans solidified soon.

If leaving a voicemail, add: "I look forward to hearing from you. You can reach me at [give phone number and/or email]."

If you have sent a thank-you note and a follow-up and still haven't heard anything, there isn't much point in following up again. Any more contact will cross into the "being annoying" category. This doesn't mean you won't get the job; it is still possible, but you should direct your energy elsewhere unless and until you hear back from them. Unfortunately, some employers will just ghost you even after an interview. Some are simply too frazzled to get back to you, and others will wait until after they have filled (or are offering you) the position. While simple courtesy would dictate that all applicants are communicated with and at least notified when the search is complete, that just isn't always the case.

Another source of anxiety can be when you have interviewed in multiple places or have multiple interviews scheduled, and receive an early job offer. What you do will depend on the specifics of your situation. If this is the job you really want, it is OK to negotiate and accept the offer, then let the others know you have accepted a position and need to cancel your interview. If you aren't sure this is the best of your options and want to wait until you find out about other positions, it is absolutely OK to contact the other interviewer(s) and let them know you have an offer on the table. This is a circumstance where you can bypass whatever timeline the employer has given you. You can communicate this new information to them in a message something like this:

> Hello Esme Anders:
>
> I have just received a competitive offer from another theatre for the upcoming season, but I'm still interested in the chance to work with you. Can you tell me if I am still being considered for the props manager position and when you might be able to give me a final answer? I need to reply to the other company in the next couple of days.
>
> Thank you so much for your consideration. I look forward to hearing from you.
>
> Sincerely,
>
> Fraya Chung

Job offers are typically accompanied by the company's request for a very quick reply, but just because they want to know in the next twenty-four hours does not mean you have to accommodate that timeline. You can tell them that you need to consider all your options and you can let them know within a week, or whatever number of days you need to do your interview, hear back from the other company, or just figure out which job you want. It is a good idea to take your time anyway, even if you are pretty sure you want the job. Remember that you will need to negotiate their offer, so you could begin that process while waiting to hear about any other job. Letting the preferred company know they may lose you to another offer will likely get them to make their decision sooner, or at least tell you that you are no longer being considered and thus release you to take the offered job with confidence. It can be an anxious process, but open communication will demonstrate your professionalism and leave a good impression with all potential employers. You never know: the place you turn down today may be your employer in the future.

Phone Etiquette

At some point in this process you will probably have to communicate by phone with potential employers. Using good phone etiquette demonstrates maturity and professionalism, and can build the potential employer's confidence in you and your ability to represent the company.

The first thing is to ensure that you have a professional outgoing message on your voicemail. While your favorite song or faking people out by just saying "hello" may have been fun as a student, you are entering the professional world now and need to represent yourself as such. Include your name in the message, so potential employers aren't left wondering if they have reached the correct person. Do what you can to eliminate any questions or stress for the person who may want to hire you.

When placing a call you have an obligation to identify yourself to the person answering the phone. If this doesn't come naturally for you, it is a good idea to get into this habit before making your first job search calls. Don't just demand to speak to someone. The dialogue should go something like this.

> *ring* *ring*
> Receptionist: Hello, Magic Fingers Puppet Workshop.
> You: Hello. This is Pat Munoz. May I please speak with Riley Lawson?
> Receptionist: Yes. Hold on and I'll transfer you.

There is also specific etiquette you should follow when answering the phone. Always answer as if it is your next employer calling. One of the most efficient ways is to identify yourself right away.

> *ring* *ring*
> Pat: Hello, this is Pat.
> Caller: Hi Pat. This is Riley Lawson with the Magic Fingers Puppet Workshop. Is this a good time to talk?

This approach eliminates some back and forth identifying who is talking. If you prefer to find out who is calling before identifying yourself, that is OK too. That exchange could go something like this.

> *ring* *ring*
> Pat: Hello?
> Caller: Hi. This is Riley Lawson with the Magic Fingers Puppet Workshop. May I please speak with Pat?

Pat has at least two options: "Hi Riley! This is Pat," *or* "This is [insert Pat's pronoun]."

When answering the phone you should decide if communicating your pronouns is important. This may be the case if you have an ambiguous name or otherwise want to avoid being misgendered. Either way, it is a good idea to practice your planned approach out loud so you can answer naturally in the way you intend.

If the person calling you isn't using proper phone etiquette, you must decide how you would like to respond. The commonest way that people calling you will violate phone etiquette is by asking for you without identifying themselves first.

> *ring* *ring*
> Pat: Hello?
> Caller: Hi. Can I talk to Pat?

At this point you need to decide if you want to identify yourself immediately or find out who is calling first. If you want to know who is calling before you identify yourself, your response could go like this.

> *ring* *ring*
> Pat: Hello?
> Caller: Hi. Can I talk to Pat?
> Pat: May I ask who is calling?
> Caller: This is Riley Lawson with the Magic Fingers Puppet Workshop.
> Pat: Hi Riley. This is Pat *or* This is [insert Pat's pronoun]. I'm so glad to be talking with you. I've been looking forward to this all day.

While searching for jobs, you should always try to answer your phone, even if you don't recognize the number; it may be your next employer calling to set up an interview. Job searches are a lot of work for the employer, so make it easier for them by answering the phone instead of having them leave a message. They will appreciate it. However, only do so if you can give the call your full attention; not while driving or in the middle of a meeting, class, or scene shop, for example. When answering, be sure to use proper phone etiquette.

Phone Interviews

For many years the first round of hiring procedures was a phone interview; indeed, some jobs were filled based on the phone interview alone. After the global eruption of video conferencing in 2020 you will probably do far more video interviews, but it is still wise to be prepared for the unique aspects of phone interviews just in case.

If they don't email you to set up the appointment, their first call is likely intended to set up a mutually convenient time to speak later. If they do call and ask to interview you right then, it is a good idea to schedule for another time even if you are just sitting on your couch watching Netflix, so you can be prepared and have all your materials in front of you. Ask how long you should block out in your schedule for the interview, and be sure to specify a time when you have at least an additional ten or fifteen minutes before for set-up and thirty minutes following the scheduled time in case your interview goes on longer or your interviewer is running behind schedule. Plan to do the interview from a private, quiet location without distractions that could prevent you from listening or answering clearly. Avoid places that have anything you will feel the need to apologize for, like people talking, power tools, traffic, or your barking dog.

Prior to the scheduled time, be sure to review the job description, research the company, and make a list of questions you have about the job. Have all of this in front of you during your phone interview, along with a pen and notebook to take notes. Having the job description, your prepared answers, your resume, and your portfolio spread out in front of you means you can access the information you need to get you back on track even if you blank from the excitement. Don't read your prepared answers, or even mention that you are looking things up as you talk; simply use them as a cheat sheet if you need to remember what stories you planned to tell. Ideally you will have rehearsed your answers out loud so much that they just come naturally to you, but if they don't it is better to be prepared and not need them than to need them and not have them.

Other things you should be sure to have immediately available during your phone interview are charging cords and power adaptors for your phone and computer, water, and headphones.

Don't be surprised if you find yourself standing or pacing during a phone interview. While standing seems to be generally encouraged to help you feel more confident, some people discourage pacing. But as long as you aren't pacing so much that your voice changes or you sound out of breath, go ahead and pace. People who get especially nervous can benefit from letting some of their nervous energy out through movement, and pacing slowly is much better than clicking a pen or bouncing your leg vigorously.

Take notes during the phone conversation by hand, if possible. The noise of your keyboard may make it sound like you are attempting to multitask during the interview. If typing notes is your only option, consider mentioning this to them so they know the typing noises are related. Taking notes helps keep you engaged in the conversation, because you must listen in order to write things down, and it can also help dissipate nervous energy. Your notes will also likely help you later, because many people report that their memory of a phone interview seems to disappear the moment they hang up. During the interview, If you don't understand the question or want to clarify that you understand what they mean it is OK to ask them to repeat the question or for you to repeat back what you think they are asking. Avoid doing this for every question, as it will make the interview longer than necessary and doesn't reflect well on your listening skills. If you have a poor phone connection, be sure to tell them about it as soon as you notice it, so they know that any difficulties are technology related.

Some recommend dressing as if you are at an in-person interview even though nobody will see you, because it can put you in the right frame of mind. If you think this might help you feel more confident and present your best self, then do it. If you feel being in your pajamas will make you more successful, then do that. The right choice is whatever works best for you.

Video Interviews

Nearly everyone is familiar with video conferencing technology, and more organizations are taking advantage of it to conduct their first round of interviews rather than traditional phone interviews. Some even use video interviews instead of in-person interviews. You can apply most of the guidelines for phone interviews here as well, but the element of video brings with it additional challenges.

Well in advance of your interview, make sure you have all your logistics in place and have an opportunity to test your set-up. When scheduling the interview, be sure to find out which platform they plan to use so you can download it, register your account, and understand how it operates. Don't forget your username and password! Having to reset your password as the clock is ticking toward your meeting time is a terrible way to start an interview. It is also a good idea to exchange phone numbers with the person interviewing you, so you have an alternate way to get in touch in case either of you has trouble with technology on the day of the interview. Knowing you are well prepared will do a lot to stave off pre-interview anxiety.

Contentwise, prepare for the interview in the same way you would prepare for a phone interview (see above). Logistically, there is more to do. First, select a location that has a neutral, non-distracting background, effective front lighting, strong internet access, and electrical outlets. Find a comfortable chair that does not swivel or roll, so you don't absentmindedly move your chair back and forth during the interview. If you are doing your interview at home, a blank wall with minimal decor is the best option. Alternatively, a large swathe of closed curtains, or even a temporary backdrop, can work—just make sure anything you set up isn't going to fall down during the interview! Avoid things in your setting that may be distracting to your interviewer, like bookshelves, souvenirs, collections, a messy desk, pets, housemates, dirty dishes, laundry, etc. Be mindful of the time of day and how natural light may help or overpower you on video. Do not sit in front of a bright window. Avoid bedrooms if possible, but if that is the only option then remove any indications of it being a bedroom from the camera's view. If you do not have a suitable place in your home, investigate using a private study room in a library or a friend's home or office. If all else fails, you can use the background blur effect or a virtual background. Even more important for a video interview than a phone interview is making sure your location is private and quiet without any visual or audible distractions.

Your computer or other device must remain still during the interview, so the camera does not shake or move around. Place your device on a table (or in a stand if necessary for stability). It is OK to use a tablet or phone as long as it is well supported and you use it in landscape orientation, so your image fits the orientation of their computer screen. The camera should be at or slightly above your eye level, so you may have to get creative in setting up your space. Having the camera below eye level distorts the face. Double-check what is visible on the wall behind you once your camera is positioned, and make any necessary adjustments.

Video conferences require you to dress in appropriate interview attire. As tempting as it may be to be professional from the waist up and in pajamas from the waist down, don't do it. There is always the possibility that you will forget to turn your camera off if you need to stand up to retrieve something during the interview, and your secret will be revealed. Because you will be on video, strive to wear solids rather than patterns to reduce distractions, Avoid extremes like bright red, all white, or all black. Have a backup outfit in mind in case when you camera-test your first choice you discover it doesn't read well.

At the location you've chosen, wearing the outfit you plan to wear, and armed with your technology, username, password, and non-rollie chair, schedule a camera test with a friend or family member on the video conference program you will be using for your interview. During this practice session you want to make sure that your internet stays strong, the lighting is effective, your devices are all plugged in, your clothing and background are not distracting on camera, you have silenced your phone and all alerts on your computer, and your camera, headphones, and microphone are working and at the proper angle. If you wear glasses, adjust the camera and/or lighting angles to minimize the visible reflection of the computer screen in your lenses. This is the time to troubleshoot any non-functioning technology so you can avoid these problems at your interview.

With the environment set, turn to your computer screen. Either clear your desktop or maximize the window so nothing else is competing for your attention on screen. Once you know the camera is set up correctly, either hide your personal video feed or adjust your windows so the video feed of you is small and immediately below the camera. During the interview you will look directly into the camera: this is how you make "eye contact" with the interviewer, because you will appear to be looking directly at them. If you want to be able to glance at yourself while talking, having your video immediately below the camera allows you to take infrequent glances at yourself without displacing your eyes from the camera too much. Don't allow yourself to do this too often, however, or the interviewer may think you are not focused on them. Run through a few trial questions in advance so you can get your windows correct and practice when to look at your screen and when at your camera. When the interviewer is talking, you have two options. You can continue looking directly into the camera to give the interviewer the sense that you are looking them in the eye. This will, however, cause you to miss all non-verbal cues from the interviewer, like facial expression and posture, so you may find it makes communication more difficult. The other option is to look at the video feed of the interviewer while they are talking and then up into the camera while you answer their question. You could adjust the display windows to have the interviewer's face close to your camera as well as your own. Your practice session is a good time to test these options out and develop your plan, so you aren't fussing with all the windows while your interview is going on. Practice starting a screen share so you can show examples of your work during the interview.

Continue your practice session or schedule additional sessions until you are comfortable with the technology and confident in your ability to communicate effectively through video conferencing. Consider recording your practice sessions so you can review them to see ways you can improve. Create a checklist if you are concerned you will miss any of the finer details of preparation on the day of your interview. And, just like other forms of interviews, have notes ready about the questions you want to ask and the important points you want ensure you communicate.

On the day of your interview be sure to clean off your desk or table except for the information and tech you need in front of you for the interview. Keep all your devices plugged in, and be set up, logged in, and ready to go at least ten minutes early just in case you encounter any difficulties. Open any windows you anticipate needing to reference or screen share.

Sit with good posture, smile, and gesture normally, although the video feed may have trouble keeping up if you are gesticulating too wildly. You can refer to your notes as needed, but try not to read from them or refer to them too often, since this will reduce the amount of eye contact you can make. It's also fine to take notes while they are talking. Let them know you are doing this so they understand why you are looking down so much.

Informational Interviews

Not every interview will have a job on the line. Informational interviews are an invaluable tool that is not used often enough—many people don't even know they are an option. An informational interview is an opportunity for you to meet with someone in the industry whom you admire, respect, or aspire to be. This is someone you think has information, experience, perspectives, or contacts that could help you along your career path. Informational interviews preferably take place in person, but if proximity does not allow this then a phone or video interview is acceptable. Informational interviews are most often conducted by those who are still completing their education or just entering the job market, although they can be undertaken at any point in your career, especially if you are trying to figure out how to advance, make a career change, or make a lateral move into a different industry.

Once you have identified someone you would like to talk with, setting up an informational interview is as easy as contacting them and asking if they would meet with you so you can ask them questions about their career path. Writing a formal letter makes a good first impression, and you can follow up with an email a couple weeks later. If you don't have their mailing address and an email is your only option, it could look something like the example below. Be sure to add your own relevant details to make the letter more compelling, including the name of the person who suggested this contact.

Subject: Request for Informational Interview

Dear Harmony McChesney:

My name is Camden Munoz and I'm a student at State University studying Costume Design. My shop manager, Henrik Abernathy, suggested I contact you. I'm trying to figure out my next steps after I receive my undergraduate degree, and wonder if you could take some time to talk with me about your career path and opportunities in the industry. I think I might want to have a job like yours someday, and would love any advice you may have on how to achieve my goal.

Could we set up a meeting in the next few weeks? I would be happy to take you to coffee or lunch as an expression of my appreciation.

Thank you for considering my request, and I hope to talk to you soon.

Sincerely,

Camden Munoz

If the interview is granted, you must ensure you are well prepared so the person doesn't come to regret saying yes or feel like you are wasting their time. Most people actually like to talk about themselves and give people advice—it is flattering to have someone reach out to you because they view you as an expert in your subject area. I find that the vast majority of these types of requests are granted, and can lead to great things for the person asking the questions. Mentoring relationships, jobs, wonderful advice, and a string of new contacts are just some of the positive things that can come out of an experience like this. Bring a couple of copies of your resume, and absolutely bring your portfolio. Always start off with a version of your elevator pitch so they learn a little bit about you. Bring a prepared list of questions, grouped by topic and in order of importance. Below are sample questions that you can customize to suit you.

- How did you get into this line of work?
- Where did you get your education and training?
- Did your training prepare you for the work you do now?
- Did college prepare you for the job market?
- What have been the highlights and lowlights of your career?
- Would you follow the same career path if you had it to do all over again?
- Do you have a portfolio? Would you show it to me? How do you decide what to include in your portfolio?
- If you work freelance, how do you set your fees?

- Have you hired any professionals to help you, like a CPA or tax preparer, business attorney, financial planner, agent, manager, or any others not listed? If so, why did you decide to hire them? How did you pick the person?
- Do you exclusively work in theatre and the entertainment industry or do you work in other industries as well?
- What opportunities or jobs did you turn down? Were those good decisions?
- Are you a member of a union? If so, how has that helped or hindered your career?
- How has mentoring had an impact on your career?
- Do you plan to remain on your current path?
- What is on your five-year plan? Ten-year plan?
- How has your career differed from what you expected?
- What is the best advice you were given about your education and/or career?
- How long have you been in your current position?
- What is the hardest part of your job?
- What are the best aspects of your job?
- What is something most people don't know about your job?
- How does your job impact your life outside work, either positively or negatively?
- Are you responsible for hiring people? If so, what do you look for?
- What advice would you have for someone like me who aspires to do what you do?
- What experience or skills do I need to have?
- Where can I find job openings for the kind of work that you do?
- What networking tips do you have?
- Do you have any tips for negotiating?
- What are the current employment trends in your segment of the industry?
- Could you give me some feedback on my portfolio?
- Is there anyone else you think would be helpful for me to meet or contact?
- Would you mind if I keep in touch and update you on how my career progresses?

No matter how the interview goes, it is crucial that you send a thank-you note following an informational interview. The person who gave you their time had no obligation to do so, and you need to thank them sincerely. In your note, mention specific points from your conversation that you found particularly poignant or helpful. Then, with their permission, stay in touch. You may be able to establish a meaningful, long-term mentoring relationship.

If the person won't meet with you, the interview doesn't go well, or for some reason you and the interviewee just don't "click," that's OK. Take what you can from the experience and move forward. Under no circumstances should you badmouth the person in public or private. Our industry is small and interconnected, and you don't want your comments to travel through the very short grapevine back to the person. This could end up having a negative impact on your future prospects.

Graduate School Interviews

Whether attending URTA or just conducting your own research/interviews, choosing a graduate school is a very important decision. In some ways, the dynamic is flipped: you are looking to hire a school to educate you. In addition to preparing for a portfolio review, you need to have a list of questions to help you make that decision.

- Is the curriculum fixed or flexible?
- I am especially interested in learning X. Is that something I can pursue at your school? Do you have faculty members who can mentor me in this area?
- Is the program a design program, a technology program, or a combined program?
- When will I get my first major assignment, and how many major assignments can I expect to have?
- Am I able to freelance while in school?
- What opportunities does your city or region offer me for professional work or networking while in graduate school?
- Do you offer assistantships, and if so how much of the tuition and fees do they cover?
- If I receive an assistantship, how much will I be paid and how much am I required to work in exchange for that funding?
- What will I do for my assistantship work hours?
- If I am on assistantship, when will I receive my first paycheck?

- If the assistantship does not cover all tuition and/or fees, when is the remainder due?
- If I receive an assistantship, am I guaranteed the same funding for every semester I am in the program?
- Do you require a thesis project?
- Do you require a written thesis?
- Do you require an internship?
- Do you require a GRE[13] score or minimum GPA?
- How many students are in the program, and how many are you going to accept this year?
- Do you accept students every year?
- Who are the faculty members I will be learning from, and what kinds of professional connections do they have?
- Are the faculty always in residence, or are they often away working on productions?
- Will I have the opportunity to assist faculty members on their outside production work?
- What do people do during downtimes in the area?

You should also be prepared for them to ask you questions (remember, it's a conversation). Spend some time writing out your answers to common questions like these, to be sure you are prepared and ready to respond when asked.

- Why do you want to go to graduate school?
- What are you hoping to get out of your graduate education?
- What do you enjoy about making theatre and about your specific area (costumes, scenery, lighting, sound, projections, etc.)?[14]
- What do you see yourself doing in five years?[15]
- How do you handle stress?[16]
- What are your experiences and expectations from the director–designer collaboration and/or from the designer–technician collaboration?[17]

---

[13]The Graduate Record Exam (GRE) is a standardized test required by some graduate programs; see www.ets.org.
[14]Laura Robinson, Costume Educators Forum Facebook group, November 7, 2019.
[15]Judy Adamson, Costume Educators Forum Facebook group, November 7, 2019.
[16]Ibid.
[17]Janice Benning Lacek, Costume Educators Forum Facebook group, November 7, 2019.

- What kind of theatre do you want to make? What kind of theatre does the world need?[18] (These ideas may be requested in the form of an artist's statement.[19])

These questions help the recruiter from the grad program know if you are seeking what their program can offer. Heather Meyer Milam, a Costume Technology faculty member at Indiana University, adds: "Do they *know* what they want and what sort of career they hope to grow into? I want to know I can teach them and they will be receptive to growth. I readily recommend other programs if mine isn't the right fit."[20]

Academic Job Interviews

The initial application and interview process for academic positions is like that for most other jobs, including phone or video interviews. The process takes considerably longer, however, so you must adjust your timeline expectations. Academic positions use search committees. Every university is different and every search committee is different, so there may be some variance in the process from what I describe here.

Faculty positions are always filled using a search committee process, while staff positions may or may not have a formal search committee. Search committees are typically made up of faculty and/or staff who are familiar with the responsibilities and demands of the job for which you are applying. You should expect that initial phone or video interviews will be with the entire search committee, which may range in size from three people to as many as seven. There is always a committee chair, so you will have one point of contact, and the department administrative staff will likely work with you to schedule your interviews.

After reviewing all the written applications, the search committee narrows the pool and does initial phone or video interviews with those candidates. Depending on the position and the number and quality of applicants, this could be between five and ten people or even more. Ask who the members of the search committee are when setting up your initial interview. This allows you to research those with whom you will be speaking, which can help guide

---

[18]Ibid.
[19]Alyssa Opishinski, Costume Educators Forum Facebook group, November 7, 2019.
[20]Heather Meyer Milam, Costume Educators Forum Facebook group, November 7, 2019.

the questions you have for them and calm your nerves by eliminating one of the unknowns. The committee typically asks the same questions of all the candidates, and narrows its list based on how those initial interviews go. References will be checked at some point, but the timing of this can vary.

The process may end here for staff positions like technical directors, costume shop managers, staff electricians, etc. Some schools can afford to bring the finalists in for on-campus interviews, but others make their hiring decisions based solely on phone and/or video interviews and will expect you to do the same. If this is the case, you can expect to have more than one phone and/or video interview before an offer is made. Feel free during your initial interview to ask about the process and what you can expect going forward.

If you are applying for a position for which on-campus interviews are being held, the committee will create a list of its top candidates (typically three) following phone interviews and reference checks. If anyone on the shortlist declines the on-campus interview, the committee moves down its ranked list until it has at least three candidates scheduled for visits. The cost of the on-campus interview, including transportation, hotels, and most meals, will be paid by the university. Depending on spending regulations at the institution, they will either pay your expenses outright or require you to make your own arrangements and then reimburse you. They will work with you to find dates that are mutually agreeable. Once the dates are set, they start building your agenda. It is important to let them know if you have any specific needs during the visit—perhaps time each day at a computer to check email for your current job, or times for specific breaks due to medical needs or because you are a nursing mother. They will likely let you know what to prepare ahead of time, and give you a copy of your itinerary (if not, be sure to ask); it will typically include the names of those you will be meeting as well as the person who will pick you up from and return you to the airport. Getting your schedule in advance gives you an opportunity to research these people prior to your visit, which makes small talk easier.

There are two types of presentations you will likely be asked to prepare for your visit. The first is a sample class in the area you teach, often on a subject of your choosing, although they may assign the same topic to all the candidates for easier comparison. Be sure to ask if they have a preference on the level of the subject matter. Are you "teaching" majors or non-majors, and do they want a first-year class or a class with upper-level content? It will also be important for you to know what technology is available in the room you will be using. Students will be recruited and often begged to attend. I have seen teaching demonstrations with zero students (I "taught" five faculty members in mine), and some with standing room only. There is no way to know ahead of time who your exact audience will be, except that members of the faculty and search committee members will attend.

You may also be asked to prepare a formal portfolio presentation. You should expect to show your portfolio a few times in one-on-one or small-group settings, but some campus visits will include a talk about your work to a large group. Ask about available technology, and plan your presentation accordingly. Teaching a class and/or presenting your portfolio replaces what is typically referred to as a "job talk" for other academic disciplines.

Campus visits for faculty positions will be at least one very full day, and some spill over into a second day. Campus visits for staff members are less involved and will likely only involve two or three meetings, a campus and facilities tour, and probably a meal or two. A teaching demonstration may still be required if the position involves teaching classes. Faculty interviews require you to meet a lot more people. The day typically starts with an early breakfast meeting, followed by a non-stop schedule of meetings: the department chair, members of staff (administrative and/or production), the full faculty (or at least those who are interested and available to come), undergraduate and graduate students (also typically very poorly attended), the dean or their representative, and multiple meetings with the search committee (often beginning and ending your visit). Among these meetings they will fit in your presentations, as well as both lunch and dinner meetings and a tour of the campus, theatres, and shop facilities. Interviews may include meetings with Human Resources and a library representative, and in rare cases a neighborhood tour with a real estate agent. You may also be given an opportunity to attend a rehearsal and/or performance depending on the production calendar. Your day can easily begin at 7:30 am and not end until after 11 pm.

By the time you've made it to a campus interview, the committee has already determined that you have the education, experience, and skills to fill the position. From your phone or video interview the members found you personable and engaging; what they are trying to determine when you are on campus is if you would be a good colleague. Do they want to work with you? Will you fit in? How do the students respond to you? How do you respond to the students? Can you fill the needs of the department? Are you philosophically aligned with the department? If a tenure-track position, are you on a path that would allow you to achieve tenure successfully? In theatre and the entertainment industry we spend a great deal of time working and collaborating with our colleagues, much more than in other academic departments. Compatibility both artistically and personally is of significant importance and a major factor in decision-making.

As with any job interview, remember that you also have a decision to make—you are interviewing the department. You can pretty much guarantee that there is some sort of conflict within the department. Academic departments are rife with drama (pun intended), and you need to determine if their drama is manageable. Be sure to ask lots of questions to get to know the departmental culture. Ask some of the same questions to multiple faculty and staff members, and compare their answers. Refer to the list of questions to ask at an interview (see earlier in this chapter) for ideas, and remember that students are a great source of information.

There are also some questions you may ask in an academic interview that would differ from those asked in a traditional job interview. Kathryn L. Cottingham, from Dartmouth College, compiled a comprehensive list of questions that would be applicable in an academic interview. Here are some examples from her list.[21]

- What is the long-term plan for this school/institution, and how does this department fit into that plan?
- What is the outside perception of this department?
- What are the expectations for the summer?
- What is your biggest frustration in the department or university?
- What are the schedule and mechanisms for faculty evaluations?
- How much of the department is already tenured?
- What are the unwritten criteria for tenure?
- Are there tensions among the subdisciplines?
- What are current plans for future hires?
- How often does the department meet to discuss departmental business?
- Do you feel that faculty/staff have an adequate say in day-to-day operations and major decisions?
- What kind of students do you attract?
- How big are classes? Are teaching loads weighted by the number of students in the classes?
- What are the non-teaching expectations?

---

[21]Search for the complete list at "Interviewing for an Academic Job," www.dartmouth.edu, accessed February 5, 2020.

- What are you looking for in this new position? (Pay attention to whether there is agreement or opposing ideas.)
- Is there travel support? How often? How much?
- Are there any upcoming curriculum changes?
- What's it like to live here?
- What else does a newcomer need to know?
- What do you wish you had known prior to working here?

Dining Etiquette

Interviews can extend past a meal break, and you will attend formal meals or receptions at conferences or networking events. Employers may want to see what you are like in a more social setting, especially if your position is one that will include meals or cocktails with clients or the public. It is important to feel confident and comfortable in these situations, so you don't draw unwanted attention. You want people to remember what you had to say, not your poor table manners.

If you remember nothing else, follow these three rules and you will survive any dining situation.

1. Be discreet. Avoid drawing attention to yourself.
2. When in doubt, follow the lead of the interviewer/person who invited you.
3. It is not about the food. It is about a lot of other things, but never about the food.

Of the three, it is the third that people respond to incredulously. "I get a free meal and I'm not even allowed to enjoy it?" You are in an interview or networking situation, or trying to close a sale with a potential client. *That* is the point of the meal. If you focus on your food, you are going to miss out on all the ways this experience can benefit you. In fact, it is common advice to eat before you go to business meals, so you won't be hungry and will be more inclined to engage with people rather than your plate.

As a job candidate you are likely going to be introduced to the table upon arrival. It is customary to rise, if seated, when being introduced. Your interviewer or host will likely indicate where you are to sit, but if not, do not sit down first. Wait for others, or ask which seat you should take. Sit up straight and don't cross your legs at the table.

Once everyone is seated, place your napkin in your lap without drawing attention to yourself. Once in your lap, it shouldn't go back on the table until your host signifies the end of the meal by doing so. If you need to get up from the table during the meal, leave your napkin in your chair as an indication that you will return. If you drop anything on the floor during the meal (napkin, silverware, etc.), don't retrieve it. Ask the server for another.

It is acceptable to drink water or tea already on the table or served when everyone is seated. At a round table it might be confusing to determine which drink is yours, but this simple trick allows you to identify your drinking glass and bread plate inconspicuously. Touch your pointer finger to your thumb with each hand, forming a circle, while extending your remaining fingers. Your right hand will form the shape of a lower-case *d* while your left hand will form the shape of a lower-case *b*, indicating that your drink (d) is on your right and your bread (b) is on your left. If someone at the table starts with the wrong glass, don't point it out; just follow their lead. Always return your glass to the same spot; don't rearrange the table.

When passing the breadbasket before the meal, etiquette dictates you offer some to the person on your left, take a piece for yourself, and then pass it to the person on your right. This is true for anything you pass around the table. To eat your bread, tear off small bite-sized pieces by hand. If you want butter, remove some from the serving dish and place it on your bread plate. Butter and spreads should never go from a serving dish directly on to your food, and no food should go from the serving dish directly into your mouth. Once on your side plate, butter one bite of bread at a time just before eating, not the entire roll.

When ordering your meal you can ask the server clarifying questions about the menu. However, if you have dietary restrictions it is best to discuss these with the server away from the table. When possible, call ahead or speak to the server upon arrival, so you are ready to order with everyone else. If the meal is a catered event it is acceptable to inform your host of your limitations ahead of time, with an apology for any inconvenience. Eat what you are able, and remember rule number 3. If ordering from a menu, never select the most expensive item, nor order appetizers or dessert unless encouraged to do so by the host. If you don't know how to pronounce a dish, indicate to the server by pointing at the item on the menu. Choose foods that are easy to eat with utensils, not your hands. Stay away from dishes with lots of sauce, that require a bib, or would compel you to lick your fingers. Also avoid foods you don't know how to eat or that would, in any way, make it difficult for you to follow rule number 1.

Wait until everyone at the table has been served before you begin eating. Do not turn your plate from how the server placed it in front of you. If your food is too hot, focus on conversation until it is cool enough to eat. If your food is too cold it is best to eat it anyway, unless doing so would be a health risk—in which case you can unobtrusively inform the server.

You can find guides online which label every piece of a place setting, from the champagne flute to the seafood fork, though it is unlikely you will encounter this level of formality. When it comes to the question of "which fork do I use?", work from the outside in. If you are still unsure, wait for someone else to begin, then follow rule number 2. Once used, a utensil should never be placed back on the table. Rest it on the dish for which it was used. As courses are completed, the utensils intended for that course are typically removed from the table. There's no need to "save" your fork for the next part of your meal.

Speaking of utensils: use them. Even with a food you might normally eat with your fingers at home or in a casual dining situation, use your knife and fork. There are two styles of knife and fork use: American and Continental. If you are not familiar with these styles you are encouraged to look them up, pick one, and practice it prior to an important meal.

No matter what style you use, only cut one bite at a time, not your entire salad or steak. Placing your silverware on your plate in resting position between bites allows for easier conversation. Try to keep pace while eating so you don't finish significantly before, or after, the rest of the table. If you do fall behind and your host has finished their meal, it is time for you to be "full" even if you haven't eaten all the food on your plate. (Rule number 3!) When finished, place your fork and knife on your plate, side by side, with the knife blade facing towards you and the handles at 4:00 pointing towards 10:00. If eating American style the tines of the fork should face up, if Continental style the tines should face down. Leave all unused utensils on the table; the server will remove them if they are not needed for the next course.

If an item is served on a service plate, that plate should be passed around the table along with the food. When asked to pass the salt or pepper, always pass both even if they only asked for one. And never use them before passing.

Taking small bites you can chew and swallow quickly allows you to be ready to answer questions. Remember rule number 3: this is not about the food. If you need to leave the table, simply say "excuse me" without any additional information. They don't need to know you are going to the bathroom or need to blow your nose. If you are served something you don't like, try to eat it. If you are asked if you liked the food, remember rule number 1 and reply with something like "It was fine, thank you." If there is something wrong with your food—you find a hair in it, or it is undercooked—don't draw attention to yourself or to the issue. Either eat around the problem, decide you are full, or subtly mention it to the server. If you have something in your mouth that you can't or don't want to swallow, like a piece of gristle or a fishbone, proper etiquette dictates that you should remove the food from your mouth in the same way it went in. That means if it went in with your fork, it comes out with your fork. The idea is that this will not draw any attention to you because people will just see your fork going back and forth to your mouth. Spitting something into your napkin draws unwanted attention, and then you can't really use your napkin any more. If you must pick something from your teeth, excuse yourself from the table first.

When you have finished eating, do not push your plate away or stack any of the dishes. They will be removed by the server. If you order coffee after the meal, use no more than two packets or two cubes of sugar. People notice. Oh, and they also notice how many times you go back to the buffet. You will know the meal has ended when your host places their napkin on the table. You should then follow suit.

Receptions and Networking Events

Receptions and networking events are typically more casual, with small servings of food, little or no seating, and possibly a bar, but remember that they are still business meetings. The point of these types of events isn't the food and certainly isn't the alcohol. Hand shaking is typical at this type of event, so you should always have a hand free. If you plan to shake hands, hold your drink in your left hand so your right hand stays clean and dry. If you have food, hold the plate in your right hand and eat with your left, only switching the plate to the other hand if shaking hands with someone. If there are high-tops or seating it is fine to have both food and a drink, because you can put them down on the table, but if not then choose one or the other so you always have a hand free to greet someone, exchange business cards, etc. Remember that your goal is to connect with people and network.

When conversing with someone, give them your full attention. You should not be scanning the room looking for the next conversation. If nametags are provided, place yours on your right shoulder so it is in line with your hand if shaking hands and easily seen. If at a conference with lanyard-style name tags, be mindful if they are only one-sided and get flipped around. A good tip is to place one of your business cards on the back of the pouch, so even when it is flipped your name is visible.

In small groups or a one-on-one setting for drinks or coffee there are some other things you should keep in mind, according to Benjamin Parrish, a freelance stage manager in New York City: "Don't order a drink with too many ingredients, a stupid name, or a crazy color. If you order coffee, ask the server for cream and sugar when you order, otherwise you could be interrupting your pitch to ask for milk." He also suggests that you "observe the pace at which your companion is consuming their drink; they should finish first, and you should be a sip or two behind them."[22] Don't order more than one drink, even if they do and even if they are picking up the tab.

Above all, follow the three fundamental rules. If you do, this event may just lead to your next job.

---

[22]Benjamin Parrish, personal communication with the author, February 4, 2020.

7

Talking About Money

You were probably taught that it isn't polite to talk about money. Over the last century, corporations have succeeded in making this idea so pervasive that not talking about money is an accepted cultural norm in the US, and many people even believe it is illegal to do so. It's not. It's well past time for people to break this gag order and get comfortable talking about money. Not doing so makes it too easy for employers to perpetuate discriminatory pay rates, like paying those who work in the scene shop more than those who work in the costume shop, or offering female electricians less than their male counterparts. President Barack Obama said it best when speaking on Equal Pay Day in 2014: "Pay secrecy fosters discrimination and we should not tolerate it."[1]

> Congress enacted the National Labor Relations Act ("NLRA") in 1935 to protect the rights of employees and employers, to encourage collective bargaining, and to curtail certain private sector labor and management practices, which can harm the general welfare of workers, businesses and the U.S. economy.[2]

> You have the right to act with coworkers to address work-related issues in many ways. Examples include: talking with one or more co-workers about your wages and benefits or other working conditions … Your employer cannot discharge, discipline, or threaten you for, or coercively question you about, this "protected concerted" activity.[3]

---

[1]Obama White House Archives, April 8, 2014, https://obamawhitehouse.archives.gov/the-press-office/2014/04/08/remarks-president-equal-pay-equal-work, accessed August 15, 2020.
[2]National Labor Relations Act (NLRA), 29 U.S.C. §§ 151–169 v.
[3]National Labor Relations Board, https://www.nlrb.gov/about-nlrb/rights-we-protect/whats-law, accessed August 15, 2020.

A termination clause for discussing pay is against the law. But beware, as this protection applies to employees, not independent contractors.

Setting Your Fees

If you flipped ahead to this section hoping I could reveal the secret that would make this entire process easy and anxiety free, I'm sorry to disappoint you. Setting your fees is *tough*, and you may always wonder if you are charging the right amount or if you could have asked for more and gotten it.

One of the many advantages union membership provides is that the union sets a minimum acceptable salary—the operative word being *minimum*. You are always free to negotiate a higher fee, so you still should go through the process of figuring out what your fees or daily rates should be even if you are covered by a union.

The first piece of information you need is the market rate for what you do. What are other people in your area with similar levels of experience being paid? It can be challenging to find this information, but you have a great resource: your network. Reach out to friends and co-workers and ask. Ask in social media groups, at conferences, and at networking events. Keep in mind that pay can vary drastically by region and city, so the numbers you get from your friend who works in Chicago aren't really applicable for a job in Birmingham. Depending on the segment of the industry you are in, you may be able to find salary data reports online, especially for non-profit theatres.[4] Any information you can get about what people are being paid for the job you want to do will be helpful.

You might expect that to figure out your hourly freelance rate you would just take a round number of what you would like to make in a year, divide by twelve months, then divide by four weeks, then divide by forty hours a week, and the number you come up with tells you what you should charge per hour. For example:

$40,000 a year divided by 12 months = $3,333 per month divided by four weeks = $833 per week divided by 40 work hours in a week = $20.83 per hour.

---

[4]GuideStar is one example. It compiles financial information from more than 1.8 million US IRS-recognized non-profit organizations. Other organizations compile this data regionally as well.

Unfortunately, for a freelancer it isn't that simple. If you charged based on this calculation, you'd quickly realize that you wouldn't have enough money for your rent, car payment, health insurance, and food for you and your cat because every penny you brought in would end up going toward expenses related to running your business. This simple calculation only really tells you what your hourly rate would be as an *employee* making that annual salary where the employer subsidizes a lot of the costs of your employment (including paid vacations). To support yourself as a freelancer taking on all the employer expenses, your actual rate has to be around 2–2.5 times the number you just worked out.

To calculate a livable rate, begin with your target annual salary. Let's continue to use $40,000. Robert McGuire, publisher and editor of *Nation 1099*, a web-based publication "devoted to supporting professional freelancers who want to get better at the business side of their work," suggests you label this amount as "Owner's salary" to differentiate it from the costs of doing business, overhead, and being self-employed.[5] Employer expenses may include studio or office space, marketing, invoicing and accounting software, specialty project software, regular computer upgrades, internet and web hosting, supplies and materials, equipment and tool purchase/maintenance/repairs, phone bills, utilities, travel, postage, shipping, parking, tolls, legal and professional services like tax prep and attorney fees, etc.

Then you need to add in the costs of being self-employed, like retirement savings, health insurance, and self-employment taxes, which could include state and local in addition to federal depending on where you live.

And don't forget paid holidays, vacation days, and sick days. Your business cannot survive without you. If you turn every waking hour into work hours you will burn out, or perhaps worse, look back on your career and regret the personal sacrifices you made. Calculations for this are up to you. Twenty paid days off a year (five sick days, ten vacation days, five national holidays) would equal about 8 percent of your salary. If you adjust the number of paid days off, that percentage will obviously change as well.

McGuire advises that you should anticipate being booked for only about 80 percent of your time, to account for slow periods as well as time spent marketing, in professional development classes or conferences, networking, and business activities you cannot directly bill for like updating your website/

---

[5]Robert McGuire, "How Do I Set Freelance Rates?", *Nation 1099*, September 6, 2020, https://nation1099.com/how-do-i-set-freelance-rates/, accessed September 7, 2020.

portfolio, answering emails, invoicing, bookkeeping, etc.[6] You need to include the cost of 20 percent of your hours that you cannot bill for but which you still need to do and get paid for because they are part of running your business.

If we take all these considerations into account and work them into our calculations based on our $40,000 salary goal, the result might look something like Table 12.[7]

Table 12 Sample calculations for determining freelance rates

Owner's salary		$40,000.00
Owner's expenses		$50,260.00
Overhead, cost of doing business, etc.	$10,500.00	
Retirement savings (20%)	$8,000.00	
Health insurance	$6,000.00	
Self-employment taxes (minimum 16%)	$6,400.00	
Twenty paid days: holidays, sick, and vacation	$3,360.00	
Unbillable hours (20%)	$8,000.00	
Business profit (20%)	$8,000.00	
Total business income needed to generate $40,000 take-home pay		$90,260.00
Minimum hourly rate for 40-hour work week (2,080 work hours a year)		$43.39
Minimum day rate (our industry typically uses 10-hour days for day rates)		$ 435.00

All this figuring is geared toward paying yourself that $40,000 we started with. This is your personal salary for working as an employee of your business. And do you know of any businesses that survive if they don't also make a profit? Your business should make a profit that can either be paid to you as a "bonus" or be reinvested back into the company to help foster future growth, or a bit of both.

There are a couple of other schools of thought on how to set your fees. One strategy I referenced earlier is to take the initial calculation we made

---

[6]Ibid.

[7]This example does not constitute financial advice. These are loosely contrived numbers used only to demonstrate the process you need to go through using your own financial information. Consult a financial professional to determine how your finances may or may not fit into this calculation.

that gave us an hourly rate of $20.83 per hour and multiply that by 2 or 2.5. Doing so gives you an hourly rate between $41.50 and $52. The rate we calculated in Table 12 falls within that range. This might not be the best formula to use when you are just starting out, because you want to be well informed about all the expenses involved in your business, but it may prove a useful shorthand at some point in your career.

Another approach is to multiply your desired annual salary by 1 percent to get your minimum day rate.[8] Using this calculation, our $40,000 annual salary figure results in a $400 day rate, which is pretty close to our more detailed calculation. However, the additional $35 a day calculated in Table 12 can make a huge difference over the course of a year. Depending on the number of days you work, you could lose out by $5,000 every year.

The most radical pricing recommendation I've come across is from Jake Jorgovan, a "Serial Entrepreneur, Author, Podcaster and Business Advisor."[9] His suggestion for coming up with a price to present to your client is this: make it up. He says to base your made-up number on three criteria.

1. Do you like this client? (Is the project boring? Are they likely to be very nitpicky? Is this a project you have always wanted to do?)
2. How much are they willing to pay? (Ask them what their budget for the project is, and if it is at least X amount. Give them a wide-ranging ballpark figure depending on the scope.)
3. How much value are you providing to the client? (Are you providing a service that is very important to them? If so, they will be willing to pay more.).[10]

It is important to note that once you have calculated your minimum hourly rate, don't share it with your clients. This is information for you to use to provide quotes based on the scope of work, and can be used to evaluate any job offers you receive for independent contractor work. You also have to keep in mind that not every client will be willing or able to pay what you charge. The sad reality is that fees in most of our industry, particularly the non-profit sector, have not changed all that much in the last ten or even twenty years. Julie Englebrecht is quoted on the website Costume Professionals for Wage Equity saying, "I have made a relatively similar amount each year for the past twenty years though it buys far less than it did particularly since health

[8]Marion McGovern, *Thriving in the Gig Economy* (Wayne, NJ: The Career Press, 2017).
[9]Jake Jorgovan, "About," https://jake-jorgovan.com/about, accessed September 6, 2020.
[10]Jake Jorgovan, "Unconventional Pricing for Creatives," https://jake-jorgovan.com/blog/unconventional-pricing-for-creatives, accessed September 6, 2020.

insurance is a much greater cost now. And I work juggling crazy hours at three to four jobs all the time."[11] As artists we have been duped into accepting whatever we are offered and are expected to be grateful for the opportunity. We cannot operate that way if we want to make not just a living, but a life.[12] With an understanding of how to calculate a livable wage, you are empowered to ask for what you need and get what you are worth.

Negotiating

The inordinate number of books, blogs, podcasts, and websites about negotiating can be overwhelming. Each expert has a list of absolute dos and don'ts, and many of them will directly contradict each other. *Getting to Yes* by Roger Fisher, William Ury, and Bruce Patton (who all teach in Harvard's negotiation program) has been a standard since it was first published in 1981, and is the root of a lot of commonly accepted ideas about negotiating.[13] There are two other sources that I have found valuable. The first is *Slate's* "Negotiation Academy" podcast.[14] This series of eight ten- to fifteen-minute podcasts covers topics like how to get started, setting time limits, dealing with jerks, and the gender divide. The second, which in many ways directly contradicts both aforementioned sources, is *Never Split the Difference* by Chris Voss and Tahl Raz (Voss is a former FBI hostage negotiator).[15]

What it comes down to, in the midst of all of the contradictory guidance, is that there is no one way to negotiate and every negotiation is different. Planning your negotiation strategy should begin when you go for your interview. Remember that list of questions you prepared prior to your interview? It should include questions like the ones below that will help you

---

[11]Julie Englebrecht, "Doing the Math on 'Success' in the Theatre," Costume Professionals for Wage Equity, February 21, 2019 http://cpfwe.org/2020/02/21/doing-the-math-on-success-in-the-theatre/, accessed September 7, 2020.

[12]Inspired by Maya Angelou, "I've learned that making a 'living' is not the same thing as 'making a life.'"

[13]Roger Fisher, William Ury, and Bruce Patton, *Getting to Yes*, 3rd edn (New York: Penguin Putnam, 2011).

[14]*Slate's* "Negotiation Academy" podcast, https://slate.com/business/negotiation, accessed August 9, 2020.

[15]Chris Voss and Tahl Raz, *Never Split the Difference: Negotiating as If Your Life Depended on It* (London: Random House, 2017).

at the negotiation phase if you get the job offer. (This is another reason why it is important to take notes at your interview!)

- Who makes the hiring decisions?
- What size staff does each area have?
- How is overtime handled?
- Who sets the work hours and what is typical?
- What are the housing options?
- What is your timeline for offering contracts and having the staff finalized?
- How are salaries determined?
- What is the biggest challenge when hiring for this position?
- What happens if you don't find anyone?
- What kind of training do you provide for new employees?
- When are prelim and final designs due?
- When are tech rehearsals and opening?

Why are these questions helpful? Because knowledge is power. When you receive their offer you will have basic information to negotiate not only the dollar amount but also lifestyle and working conditions. If you wait to ask these questions during the negotiation conversation, the person you are working with may be more guarded. At the interview they will likely be more relaxed and talk more freely, because it seemingly doesn't cost them anything to give you information.

A complete job offer, at minimum, should include the following details.

- The job and title they are offering you
- The compensation they are offering, either hourly or salary
- Start date and, if seasonal, end date
- Work hours per day and/or week
- Days off
- Overtime compensation
- Job perks like housing, meals, per diem, travel, training, tuition, etc.
- Benefits such as health insurance, retirement plan, etc.
- Job classification as an employee or as an independent contractor

Once you receive the job offer you have to decide if you will accept it for the package they are offering. If your response is "*Of course* I'm going to take it! It's a job!", you are not alone. But don't make a hasty decision you may later regret. Once you have accepted an offer, you are not only accepting the job but also the conditions of employment. Negotiations should take place before you accept the job or contract.

During negotiations is also the time to bring up needed time off for plans you made before you were offered the job, like weddings, vacations, etc. Employers rarely refuse these kinds of days off when brought up during negotiations, unless they are in direct conflict with the event you have been hired for. They understand that any plans made prior to accepting the position can't follow the company time-off policy, but if you neglect to bring them up during negotiations they are likely to adhere to their standard policy.

Don't ever accept a verbal offer. If you are offered a job over the phone, ask them to follow up with everything in an email so you can review it. If, for some reason, they can't or won't do that, then you should take detailed notes and follow up with an email detailing your understanding of their offer, asking questions about any topics on which you need more information, and requesting that they confirm you have the details of the offer correct. Only once you understand the complete offer and they have confirmed can you begin to evaluate it. Take some time to weigh the pros and cons. Ask the employer when they need a response. A day or two is not unusual. They want to get this wrapped up and move on to the next item on their to-do list. If the time they give you is insufficient, tell them what you need: "Oh, that's very soon. I need a little more time to evaluate your offer and figure out if I can make it work. How about Friday next week?" If you are entertaining other offers or have another interview scheduled, it is OK to let them know you have these on the table. "Thank you so much for this offer. I am waiting to hear back from another interview and need some additional time to be able to check in with them prior to making a decision." They will likely be able to accommodate you unless the time you are asking for is unreasonably long.

Evaluating a job offer is not just about how much money they've offered you; you also need to think about how much the job will cost you in hidden expenses. These can and will vary depending on whether you are considered an employee or independent contractor. Are there travel or commuting expenses? Will you have to maintain two residences? Do you need to provide any specialized equipment for which you would typically receive a rental fee? If you are being paid as an independent contractor, you need to factor in your additional tax liability (see the section on taxes and business deductions). Looking beyond fiscal matters, is there a physical or emotional cost to taking this job? Do you think this is a company you would be happy working for? Compare what they are offering you with what your needs are, your value as an employee, what the job will cost you, and your knowledge of the industry.

There is a huge problem in the theatre industry with misclassification of employees and extremely low compensation, sometimes illegally low. We must work together to demand living wages and reasonable work hours. You are entitled to be paid appropriately for your skilled labor. The practice of calling a new worker an "intern" and paying them $100 a week is disgusting. Even worse are those places that expect you to pay them! Not only does this practice keep wages down across the industry, it also excludes anyone who can't afford to work for free. This classist system disproportionately affects minorities and people from lower socioeconomic populations, keeping them from getting a foot in the door. The result is a privileged, predominantly white workforce. We all have a responsibility to shine a light on these practices and demand higher wages for ourselves and others at every level of our industry.

Knowing what you're worth and what you're willing to say "yes" to in a negotiation are the beginning and end points, but it's often the stuff in the middle that gives people the biggest butterflies. I get one of two responses when I bring up the actual act of negotiating: fear and loathing.

Starting with fear, it is possible to turn fear into excitement and have it work for you, not against you. In a journal article Alison Wood Brooks reports on the findings of her study:

> Individuals often feel anxious in anticipation of tasks such as speaking in public or meeting with a boss. I find that an overwhelming majority of people believe trying to *calm down* is the best way to cope with pre-performance anxiety … Compared with those who attempt to calm down, individuals who reappraise their anxious arousal as excitement feel more excited and perform better.[16]

She says that turning your fear or anxiety into excitement can be as easy as repeating "I am excited" out loud, and this simple act will lead you to "feel more excited [and] adopt an opportunity mind-set (as opposed to a threat mind-set)." This shift from fear to excitement helps you to perform better than allowing your fear to remain or trying to force yourself to calm down.[17]

---

[16]Alison Wood Brooks, "Get Excited: Reappraising Pre-Performance Anxiety as Excitement," *Journal of Experimental Psychology: General* 143(3) (2014): 1144–58, https://doi.org/10.1037/a0035325, accessed August 9, 2020.
[17]Ibid.

The number-one thing people say they are afraid will happen if they ask for more is that the employer will rescind the job offer. I had a student tell me that for her last job offer the supervisor suggested an hourly rate and asked if it was acceptable. She said "yes" because she was afraid that if she said it was not acceptable she wouldn't get the job. The employer literally asked her if she wanted to be paid more and she still said no! While I'm sure you can find urban legends of offers being withdrawn, it is extremely rare. You would have to be so rude and demanding that they would second-guess your fit in the organization and reconsider their desire to work with you. Asking for more money or other perks does not come anywhere near that level, and this is not something you need to be worried about.

After fear, the other area of pushback I get about negotiating is "I *hate* negotiating! I am *so* bad at it!" To these people, I say humans tend to hate things they think they are bad at, so the best way not to hate negotiating so much is to build confidence by doing it anyway. The more you do it the easier it will become. It is absolutely a skill that you can learn and improve upon. Don't allow the fact that you don't intuitively know how to do it be an excuse not to develop your skills.

There is a lot of emotion wrapped up in negotiating, especially for a job. Some say it feels egotistical to ask for more money, or that people will see them as money-grubbing and not serious about the job. Some are afraid of being told "no" and feeling they are worthless and a failure. Remember, though, you have been offered a job! Of all the people they could offer that job to, they picked you. You are a winner. Now let's get you more money!

Once you've been offered the job, you and the employer have the same goal: figure out the right combination that will get you to say "yes." That being said, they are never going to offer you their maximum as their first volley. Whatever they are offering, they can do better—and you deserve it! A student once told me they felt really weird negotiating contract details for an internship because they imagined it would cause the employer to think "Whiny young human thinks they know better than me."[18] Look at it this way. Internships are supposed to be part of your education and training. You need to practice negotiating as part of your professional development. What better time to start than with an internship? If you are well past the internship phase of your career, don't worry! It is never too late to start negotiating. Whether your next opportunity is your first job or your three

---

[18]Jeana Caporelli, personal communication to the author, March 5, 2015.

hundredth, make a commitment to negotiate for something with every job offer. Negotiations are not personal, they are business. Negotiations are also not, or at least shouldn't be, sneaky. It isn't about tricking someone into giving you what you want. It is in everyone's best interest to approach negotiations in good faith.

The biggest mistake people make when negotiating is going into it without a clear idea of what they want, and allowing their emotional mind to control their actions. Having a written plan will help keep the balance between your emotional mind and your wise mind. Begin with knowing your walk-away point, so you don't take a job that you cannot afford. Your walk-away point is the line below which you cannot go. If they cannot meet at least this level, you must say no. Period. Never reveal your walk-away point to the employer.

Next, figure out what your ideal package would be. I say package because it isn't just about the money. The money is important because you can't pay your phone bill with a job title, but there may be things of value they can provide in addition to salary that will make the deal possible. Approach negotiating as a creative process. *Everything* about a job is negotiable. If they can't give you the salary you want, what else can they offer you that has value to you and may be easier for them to provide? For example:

ability to shadow leadership	equipment or tools	paid time off/vacations
ability to observe meetings	flexible scheduling	parking permit
adjusted work hours	future royalties	project selection
assigned mentor	gym membership	right of first refusal
childcare	health benefits	salary
commute subsidy	housing/private housing	signing bonus
comp time	incremental pay raises	start date[19]
company car	internet or phone subsidy	startup costs
company phone	job title	technology upgrades
education expenses	moving expenses	travel
		work from home

---

[19]Professional courtesy requires you to give at least two weeks' notice before quitting your current job. It will not make a a good impression on your new employer if you do not give that two weeks, because they know you are likely to turn around and do the same thing to them.

Anything that holds value to you can be negotiated. I have a colleague who once negotiated for a juicer to be provided in her housing on an out-of-town contract.

The first offer mentioned is called the anchor, and there are strategic ways to use the anchor no matter who drops it. If you are going to drop the anchor you need to be sure it is a high enough number that you aren't undercutting yourself.[20] There is a saying: you should ask for the highest amount you can while keeping a straight face. If they drop the anchor and it is drastically lower than you were expecting, don't let that derail you or make you think your goal is unreachable. This is just a negotiation tactic. Instead, reply with an open-ended question like "It sounds as if we are pretty far apart. What is the thinking behind that number?"

If dropping an anchor sounds too stressful, consider mentioning what similar jobs are paying. "The other jobs I'm looking at are offering X, so I'm looking to get at least that, and I think with my skills I am actually worth more." Be sure that whatever X is, you would be OK if they agree to it. If you are a union member you will have a minimum set for you, but those minimums are pretty low so don't automatically use these figures as an anchor. They aren't your goal, they are your required walk-away position.

Another anchoring option is to list a range. This is commonly seen as less aggressive, and tends to invoke concerns about counteroffer politeness in the other person.[21] Let's say that you are negotiating a contract and want to get $3,000 for the gig. You know that is reasonable. Start with a range that is above the amount you actually want: "I need the contract to be between $4,000 and $5,000 and include per diem and travel expenses." Or combine this with the above technique and say, "The other regional theatres I'm looking at are paying between $4,000 and $5,000 with per diem and travel expenses." Chances are you won't get that amount, but they are more likely to counter closer to the $4,000 number. If they offer something below $4,000 but at or above your $3,000 goal, use your notepad to do some quick "figuring" and either decide you can "just barely make that work" or make a counter-offer. Either way, by anchoring the conversation higher than what you really want and suggesting a range, you increase your chances of getting your actual number, or even a little higher.

---

[20] "Negotiation Academy," Episode 1.
[21] Daniel R. Ames and Malia F. Mason, "Tandem Anchoring: Informational and Politeness Effects of Range Offers in Social Exchange," *Journal of Personality and Social Psychology* 108(2) (2015): 254–74, https://doi.org/10.1037/pspi0000016, accessed August 9, 2020.

It is unlikely that you will get everything you ask for, so asking for more than you need gives you room to make concessions. There is one school of thought that says you should ask for little things first to get them in the habit of saying "yes." By contrast, Chris Voss and Tahl Raz in *Never Split the Difference* contend that getting people to start with "yes" just makes them suspicious and by the time you get to the things you *really* want, they will have yes fatigue and be more likely to say no.[22] Voss and Raz suggest trying to draw out a "no" early on because it will actually help you get more information. Keep in mind that no can mean other things, like I'm not ready to agree, I don't understand, I don't think I can afford it, I need more information. Try to figure out what the no actually means by asking an open-ended question, like "What about this doesn't work for you?" This keeps the dialogue going and helps you figure out exactly what the problem is, so you can offer solutions.[23]

Here are some additional tips to consider as you are entering into negotiations.

- You do not have to conduct a negotiation in one sitting. You are allowed to take time to think.
- One of the most important things is just to be nice. H. Rodgin Cohen, senior chair at the law firm Sullivan & Cromwell and world-renowned corporate negotiator, guides, "If you are more likeable your partner might be more willing to make concessions."[24]
- Tone of voice is extremely important. It's not just what you say, but how you say it. People will likely respond at or above the level you speak, so always use a calm, deferential tone. Practice giving the ends of your sentences a downward inflection, which implies certainty, and not upward inflection, which will imply aggression and accusation.[25]
- While negotiations can take place through email, you miss out on tone of voice and/or non-verbal cues if you do this.
- Round numbers can come across as arbitrary; consider using odd numbers instead. If you tell an employer you need $763 a week, you give the impression you have done the math and really do know exactly what you need. Consider how this sounds compared to $750 a week.

---

[22]Voss and Raz, *Never Split the Difference*, 94.
[23]Ibid., 79.
[24]"Negotiation Academy," Episode 3, time stamp 2:45, accessed August 9, 2020.
[25]Voss and Raz, *Never Split the Difference*, 32–3.

The difference is only $13, but $763 seems like an actual calculation and will be taken more seriously.

- You must go into a negotiation clearly knowing what you are asking for *and* why they should give it to you. Be prepared to back up your numbers to help them see the value you bring to the position. Don't get defensive if they challenge your numbers. Remember, this is not personal, it is business.

- Ask as many open-ended questions that start with "what" and "how" as you can.[26] Asking questions that can be answered with a yes or a no stops the conversation. Open-ended questions don't have fixed answers, give you more information, and allow you more time to think. "What is your thought process on that?", "How did you come up with that number?", "How can we solve this problem?", "How can I make that work?", "What are you hoping to get out of this?" Ask them with a tone of voice that indicates you need their help in solving this problem. It will put them in the frame of mind to continue making counter-offers.

- When faced with an offer that doesn't meet your needs, respond with a question rather than a statement. Don't say "no" or "That's not enough." Ask "How would I be able to pay my bills with that?" Make them think about the realities of their offer and then wait for an answer. It is very likely that they will come back with a higher offer.

- Endure the silence. Do not feel compelled to fill silences after you speak. Make a statement or ask a question, and then bite your tongue. Silences can invoke panic and cause you to blurt out a lower offer and negotiate against yourself![27] Wait for their answer.

- Learn to say "no" without actually using the word "no."[28] "Thank you for that offer but I don't see how it works." "I'm sorry. I just can't do that." "That would be too much of a stretch for me." "Yeah. That's closer. Thank you! But I still can't meet my needs with that."

- If the money just isn't there in their offer, get them to think about other means of compensation.[29] "If we put money aside and approach this like a package, what else could you offer to make this work for me?"

[26]Ibid., 3.
[27]"Negotiation Academy," Episode 10, timestamp 7:00, accessed August 9, 2020.
[28]Voss and Raz, *Never Split the Difference*, 190, 240.
[29]Ibid., 199.

- If you are unable to negotiate a higher salary or project fee and anticipate this will be a long-term business relationship, perhaps you can negotiate a guaranteed higher fee on your next project with them or get a review clause in your contract. James Moody, author of *The Business of Theatrical Design*, advocates this, and even tells a story about having a review clause in one of his contracts that said they *had* to fire him if they did not give him a raise before each new season. That clause worked for him for fourteen years.[30]

- Write down your plan and notes, and have these with you when you are negotiating. You should include your ideal compensation package, walk-away position, goal, the range and package you plan to offer, and a specific anchor in case you are asked for a single number (and remember to use odd numbers). Include "what" and "how" questions as prompts to remind you of ways to respond. List a few different ways to say no without saying no. Make a list of ideas of other forms of compensation beyond salary. Include research information. Include reminders about why you are worth what you are asking for.

- If you have tried all your tactics and feel you have come to the final offer, but you aren't sure what you should do, then tell them how much you appreciate their offer and say you will let them know tomorrow if you can make it work for you or not. And then make your decision. A student asked me once, "When do you stop negotiating?" I told them, "When you are done."

Bottom line: negotiate. Then show up and be amazing, and they will realize that juicer was worth every penny.

Accepting the Job Offer ... or Not

There isn't any feeling quite like receiving a job offer, especially if you are just starting out in your career or making a career pivot. It is validating that someone sees enough value in what you do to be willing to pay you for it. After receiving your offer and negotiating the terms, you then have to decide whether to take the job. This decision should be based on facts; do not let your emotions drive it. If you know your negotiation didn't result in a

---

[30]James L. Moody, *The Business of Theatrical Design* (New York: Allworth Press, 2013), 207.

compensation package that you can accept, if it didn't meet your walk-away point, you need to turn down the offer. You don't owe them anything and you don't need to feel guilty. Be gracious and professional when letting them know; you don't want to burn any bridges.

That doesn't mean you can't be honest—in fact, you should be honest. Employers need to know if they are losing the best people because they aren't paying enough; hopefully they will begin to reconsider their low wages. The group Costume Professionals for Wage Equity was formed to shine a light on low wages in the industry, and the lack of pay parity and staffing numbers between production areas. On its website it offers these suggestions when turning down a job due to low pay: "Thank you for your offer … "

> " … I think this company is a good fit for me and I would love to come on board pending a further conversation about compensation."
> " … While I am very interested in the position, financially it is not workable for me."
> " … I have decided to take another position because the compensation for hours worked is more financially viable for my needs."[31]

I would personally take an even more direct approach and delete phrases like "financially viable for my needs." In most cases it is probably not financially viable for anyone. "Thank you for your offer. I think this position is a great fit for me. However, when I do the math the stipend works out to about $3 an hour. I'm not sure how anyone could support themselves on that. If you are ever able to pay a living wage I would love to be considered again." Or "Thank you for your offer and for considering my counter-offers. I am going to have to find a position that pays more for fewer hours. I wouldn't be able to pay my bills if I took the job at the price you are offering. I hope we get the chance to work with each other in the future."

There may be other factors that mean the job just isn't right for you. Valerie Webster, costume director at Pittsburgh Public Theatre and a freelance costume designer, recalls turning down a major regional theatre in New York City. "It was a good decision for my family," she says. "We have a much better quality of life than we could have afforded in NYC."[32] So while money played a role in her decision, there were other factors she took into consideration. Meredith Tomkovitch has worked in wardrobe for Feld Entertainment,

---

[31]Costume Professionals for Wage Equity, "Questions to Ask at a Job Interview," February 21, 2020, http://cpfwe.org/wp-content/uploads/2020/02/Interview-Questions-Printable-1.pdf   accessed August 9, 2020.
[32]Valerie Webster, personal communication with the author, October 31, 2019.

Cirque du Soleil, and Ferrari World in Abu Dhabi, and is currently director of costuming at Resorts World Genting in Malaysia. She has turned down positions from companies that she thought were struggling financially, and is confident these were very good decisions.[33] Other reasons given by those I interviewed for turning down jobs include:

- wanting to go on tour
- wanting to stop touring
- unreasonable expectations
- not wanting to work out of town
- not enough time
- conflicts with current contracts
- maintaining mental health
- desire for time off
- better work/life balance
- lack of opportunity for their partner in the new location
- the job would interfere with finishing their degree
- not wanting to work with someone who was also working on the project
- not wanting to work on that show or project
- company has bad reputation
- partner unwilling to relocate
- not a long-term job
- to spend more time with their family
- and because they just had a gut feeling that it wasn't the right job for them.

Whatever your reason is, turning down a job is totally fine. If it isn't about money and is for another personal reason, the easiest way to turn a job down is to say you can't fit it into your schedule. Or tell them it isn't a good fit, or it just isn't going to work out. You don't owe them an explanation.

Accepting a job is a lot more straightforward than turning it down. Once you can accept the negotiated terms, let them know that you are excited to start the job, can't wait to work with them, and look forward to receiving the contract.

There are also going to be jobs that you don't get. Don't let that discourage you. I encourage people to trust that the employer, who is aware of exactly

---

[33]Meredith Tomkovitch, personal communication with the author, October 31, 2019.

what the job entails, knows what kinds of people have succeeded at it in the past and what kinds didn't fare as well. They probably just saved you from a job that would have been a bad fit for you. Sometimes you will find the reason has nothing to do with you. That was the case for Grace Trimble, a costume designer, technician, and dresser based in New York City, when she applied for a position supervising interns. "I had three interviews with a company last year. I was really disappointed not to get it but I found out that they went with someone who was a graduate of their program. There was no amount of resume tweaking or cover letter rewriting that would have changed the fact that they hired someone who already had experience with them."[34] Anthony Narciso, a freelance sound designer, says he doesn't always get scheduled for cruise-ship gigs he is expecting because they make a decision based on the cost of getting him to the ship and "sometimes I'm not the most convenient option."[35] David M. Upton is a lighting designer and production manager based in New York City. He says, "Rejection is definitely part of the game. I try not to dwell on it and just keep going after the next job."[36]

Contracts, Riders, Letters of Agreement, and NDAs

Once you come to an agreement with the client or employer, you need to formalize your deal. Whether in a legal contract or by less formal means, always get employment details in writing and never rely on verbal agreements. If the employer is providing the contract, be sure to read every line to confirm it matches what you agreed to. Discuss any details you don't understand or don't agree to prior to signing the contract. Many freelancers have their own contracts that they offer to clients, outlining the details of the agreement beyond compensation. Depending on the size and complexity of the contract, you may want to have an entertainment attorney review it for you. Gordon Firemark of Firemark Entertainment Law in Los Angeles says, "My view is that nobody should ever sign a contract they haven't read and understood completely, *and*, nobody should ever work on a theatrical project without a contract." He goes on to say that designers, technicians,

---

[34]Grace Trimble, personal communication with the author, November 6, 2019.
[35]Anthony Narciso, personal communication with the author, November 6, 2019.
[36]David M. Upton, personal communication with the author, November 8, 2019.

and stage managers "bring tremendous value to the productions they work on, and they need to take their work seriously as a business. This means investing in getting good advice and getting professional help negotiating their deals."[37]

Listed below are items included in some of my contracts that you may want to consider.

- *Schedule and due dates.* Depending on the job, these may include the complete rehearsal and performance schedule and any specific dates that apply to your position, such as design due dates (prelims and finals), tech schedule, required dates you must be in residence, planned meeting schedule, etc.
- *Compensation.* The amount you will be paid and when that payment will occur, including any allowance for reimbursement of out-of-pocket expenses, travel, housing, or per diem. It should also address what happens with your compensation if the project is postponed, canceled, extended, or transferred. The postponement and cancellation details were particularly important for those in the middle of production when Covid-19 shut down the industry.
- *Responsibilities.* An outline of the responsibilities of both parties signing the contract.
- *Ownership.* Can the designs and/or paperwork be used for subsequent productions, revivals, tours, etc., and are you owed additional compensation if they are? The drawings, models, etc. are the property of the designer and should be returned to them upon opening of the show. Are you allowed the right of first refusal?
- *Recordings and broadcast.* What are your rights if the production is recorded and broadcast or streamed as part of the initial plan or subsequent to a live production?

You can find the agreements between LORT and the various unions on the League of Resident Theatres website, and on each union's website you can read in detail how these items, and many more, have been addressed on behalf of union members. It is also a good idea to familiarize yourself with the contracts of the unions representing people you will be working with, as there are details in their contracts that will relate to the work you do.

---

[37]Gordon Firemark, entertainment attorney, personal communication with the author, February 27, 2020.

In some cases the contract might be kept quite simple and the smaller details are included in a rider. A rider is an attachment to a contract that adds details to the agreement. It could also outline changes to the contract or update details if the agreement changed after the initial signing, for example to document schedule alterations or change in scope.

An even less formal way to document your terms is by a letter of agreement. Letters of agreement are typically formatted like a letter, state the details of the agreement, and clearly indicate that both parties agree and accept.

Some contracts will include a non-disclosure agreement (NDA) preventing you from revealing protected information to which you had access as part of your work. These are most common when working on large corporate projects like films and theme parks, but can be used by any company. It is important that you read and understand the limitations you are agreeing to by signing the NDA so you are sure to never violate it. The NDA may limit what you can discuss about the project (if anything) and what you can include in your portfolio. If you are ever unsure about what your NDA covers, follow up with your employer for clarification.

Unions

Unions have an important and powerful history in our country and our industry, and will play a role in your professional life whether you join one or not. The modern labor movement began around the turn of the twentieth century when factories made productivity skyrocket and business owners very rich. Part of the reason they were able to make so much money is because they exploited their workers as far as possible and kept the money for themselves. Workers endured long hours from sunup to sundown, no breaks, no days off, unsanitary and unsafe conditions, and locked doors that prevented them from leaving or escaping from fires—which led to the deaths of hundreds of factory workers.

Unions improve working conditions through a process called "collective bargaining," whereby the workers agree to allow the union to negotiate a single contract for all its members. As a group, employees have more power to demand the compensation and working conditions needed to support themselves, their families, and their communities. The union not only negotiates the contract but also provides support in enforcing the contract and has a grievance process. In his 2020 Labor Day message, Kent Collins, AEA stage manager and host of the Half Hour Call YouTube channel, recommends that you read the union contracts and "consider that every single item … in there … whether it's providing furniture in actor housing, transportation home at the end of a national tour, or even clean water in rehearsal and performance venues … had to be included because someone somewhere at some point did not provide it."[38] He goes on to point out, "legislation has been passed in many states that significantly weakens the power of unions to defend fair working conditions. These are often passed under the guise of being 'pro-worker,' hence the chipper title of 'right to work state.' But the only people that union busting laws like 'right to work' help are the already wealthy business owners." Unions lobby for worker protections at both state and national levels, trying to have laws passed that will extend positive working conditions to all workers, not just union members.

Because of that lobbying, unions are a topic of political opinion and debate. While they are lobbying for workers' rights and protections, there are also lobbyists on the side of business and industry fighting against changes the unions want: from their perspective, implementing the unions' demands will cost employers money and could drive them out of business, which would be bad for workers. An additional argument against unions is that you give up your individual ability to negotiate pay and benefits. In some unions that is true, but in United Scenic Artists and Actors' Equity the unions set minimum compensation levels while allowing the individual to negotiate for additional pay and benefits above those minimums. Those opposed to unions believe that unions artificially inflate wages and cause people to be paid more than they are worth.

All the work unions do costs money, and union membership is not free. You are typically required to pay an application fee, an initiation fee upon joining, annual dues, and a percentage of your union contract income—all told, it can cost anywhere from several hundred to several thousand dollars to join. Also, as a union member you are bound by the decisions of the union even if you don't agree with them. You are required to follow all the rules set forth in the agreement. Claudia Lynch, Broadway stage manager and coordinator of the BFA Stage Management program at the University of Central Florida, points out, "there is language in the agreements that states that a union member may *not* waive any rules that the union has agreed to.

---

[38]Kent Collins, "Why Unions Are Important," Half Hour Call, September 7, 2020, https:// youtube/0UsnYEshDa4, accessed September 7, 2020.

So, as an AEA member, you can't say 'it's OK—I will work overtime and you don't have to pay me.' But how is that a negative?"[39]

The unions you will most likely encounter are AEA (Actors' Equity Association), representing stage managers and actors; USA (United Scenic Artists Local 829), with categories for scenic artist, scenic designer, costume designer, lighting designer, sound designer, projection designer, computer artist, art department coordinator, and costumer department coordinator; and IATSE (International Alliance of Theatrical Stage Employees, Moving Picture Technicians, Artists and Allied Crafts of the United States, Its Territories and Canada), which is the broadest union and the umbrella organization for USA, and covers stagehands, front-of-house workers, wardrobe attendants, makeup artists, hair stylists, motion picture and television production technicians, broadcast technicians, scenic artists, designers, animators, audio visual technicians, and more.

Unions typically have rather strenuous requirements for membership. Because they are guaranteeing employers that their members are highly skilled and qualified, individuals must demonstrate they meet a certain threshold of professional knowledge and experience prior to being accepted. For example, USA, depending on the category in which you wish to join, requires an exam, portfolio review, and/or interview. AEA changed their admission requirements in 2021. The new policy is called Open Access. Under the previous system, equity membership was limited to those hired by an Equity employer either on an Equity contract or as part of their candidacy program. This made employers the de facto gatekeepers for membership. The Open Access membership policy allows any person who can demonstrate that they have worked as a professional actor or stage manager to join the union. Each IATSE local, of which there are nearly 400, has its own membership requirements, so it is best to visit the IATSE website, find the information for the local in your area that covers the work you do, and contact them directly. All unions have their own benefits and limitations; for example, AEA members are not allowed to accept any non-Equity contracts, while USA members are strongly encouraged always to file union contracts when working for non-union theatres. Every union, and in the case of IATSE every local, is different. For the most up-to-date information you should read all you can on their websites and call to get answers to any additional questions.

Don't confuse labor unions with professional organizations. Professional organizations are primarily networking and educational bodies that

[39]Claudia Lynch, personal interview with the author, September 6, 2020.

provide opportunities for segments of our industry to connect and stay up to date with current technology, products, and techniques. Many have an annual conference or convention you can attend. Some of the best-known professional organizations in our industry are the United States Institute for Theatre Technology (USITT), International Association of Amusement Parks and Attractions (IAAPA), Stage Managers' Association (SMA), Themed Entertainment Association (TEA), Black Theatre Network (BTN), International Organization of Scenographers, Theatre Architects and Technicians (OISTAT), Entertainment Services and Technology Association (ESTA), Alliance of Special Effects & Pyrotechnic Operators (ASEPO), Costume Society of America (CSA), and dozens more. Whatever your niche or specialty, I guarantee that there is a professional organization waiting for you to discover them on the web.

Taxes and Business Deductions

The subject of taxes causes a great deal of anxiety for most people, but simply reading the instructions on the tax forms can provide enough information to calm that anxiety. The IRS gives all the information if you're willing to take the time to read it. This section might inspire you to read the instructions and do your own taxes, but even if you don't you will at least better understand what information you need to collect to pass on to a tax preparer.

The most important thing to remember is taxes are not something to be afraid of. They also aren't going away, so rather than spending your life being apprehensive you will do yourself a big favor, and probably save yourself a lot of money, by educating yourself about your tax responsibilities.

Important Terms

Before we go any further, it is important to define several terms that will make discussing the tax process a little less confusing.

Pay-as-you-go tax. Despite April 15 being known as "tax day" in the US system, you actually have to pay taxes throughout the year as you earn money, not just once a year. This happens through either withholding or estimated quarterly tax payments, or a combination of both. If you don't pay enough throughout the year, you may be subject to an underpayment penalty of up to several hundred dollars—extra money you have to pay for not having paid enough in the first place.

Withholding. Money that your employer deducts from your pay and submits to the IRS on your behalf on a quarterly basis. This money is put towards your income, Social Security, and Medicare taxes. You can keep track of these amounts by looking at the withholding amounts on your paycheck stubs. At the end of the year you will receive an IRS Form W-2 Wage and Tax Statement from your employer with the total amounts of withholding for the year. Income you do not earn as an employee will not have taxes withheld, including (but not limited to) independent contractor income, but that doesn't mean the income is not subject to taxation; rather, it means that you are responsible for submitting the taxes yourself throughout the year through estimated quarterly payments. The IRS recommends that you review your withholding amount annually, but especially when tax laws change or you have a major life change like marriage, divorce, home purchase, children, significant income shift, capital gains, etc.[40]

Estimated quarterly tax payments. If you have income that is not subject to withholding (meaning taxes are not taken out and sent to the IRS on your behalf, including self-employment/independent contractor work or through the sharing economy), and you anticipate you will owe $1,000 or more when you file your taxes, you must estimate what your tax liability is for that income and submit it to the IRS on a quarterly basis. Quarterly tax payments are due on April 15, June 15, September 15, and January 15 (although for organizational purposes making the final quarterly payment for the year in December rather than January could make tracking easier, with all payments taking place in the same tax year). You can avoid making estimated tax payments if you also have a job for which taxes are withheld from your pay by amending that job's W-4 and having an additional amount withheld from each check. The IRS website has very clear information on who needs to pay estimated taxes and how to calculate them.

Underpayment penalty. If you didn't pay enough through withholding or estimated tax payments and, after calculating your taxes, you think you owe an additional $1,000 or more, you may have to pay a penalty for not paying this tax sooner. There are a few circumstances in which the penalty can be waived, and you can avoid it if you have paid at least 90 percent of your total tax owed for the current year or 100 percent of the tax you owed the previous year.

---

[40]Internal Revenue Service, "Tax Withholding," https://www.irs.gov/individuals/employees/tax-withholding, accessed September 22, 2020.

Taxable income. There are two ways this term is used. Firstly, it describes money or goods you received that are considered income and must be reported as such on your tax return. As you might expect, this includes money from your paychecks, all tip income (even tip income you did not report to your employer), and bonuses. Many people don't realize that it goes beyond these more obvious sources to include unemployment compensation, jury duty compensation, cancelled debts, awards, contest winnings, prizes, interest, etc. If it is of value and you received it, you should check to see if you need to include it in your income. Second, taxable income is used to describe the portion of your income that is left after you have taken out all your deductions and adjustments. This is the amount used to determine how much tax you owe.

Gig work/gig economy. Also known as the sharing economy,[41] this covers income from work that is full-time, part-time, temporary, or "side hustles" for which you do not have a traditional employer/employee relationship. Often gig workers provide on-demand work services or goods. According to the IRS's Gig Economy Tax Center, all income received through this type of work must be declared even if the amount was below $600 and you did not receive an information return such as a 1099. It includes anything for which you are paid in cash (including through apps or electronic transfers), property, goods, or virtual currency. Examples of gig work include providing ride-sharing or delivery services, renting property (including a portion of your home for more than fifteen days), selling goods online, providing creative or professional services, or any other on-demand, short-term, project-based, or freelance work, even if temporary.

Sole proprietor/independent contractor/freelancer. While there is a slight distinction between these identities, the differences are mostly just semantics. All these titles describe people who work for themselves and are considered self-employed business owners with no commitment to a single employer. The only thing you must do to be considered a self-employed business owner is receive income as a non-employee, even if it isn't your main source of income. It is important to understand your rights and responsibilities, particularly when it comes to income taxes. This income and any related expenses are reported on Schedule C, Profit or Loss from Business.

---

[41]Internal Revenue Service, "Gig Economy Tax Center," https://www.irs.gov/businesses/gig-economy-tax-center, accessed September 12, 2020.

Employee. There are many definitions of an employee, depending on the legal context. The IRS does not have a straightforward definition, but it can generally be summarized as someone who works for another person and that person controls what they do and how they do it. This is often referred to as the employer's right to "direct and control."[42]

Gross income. The total of all your earnings before any deductions, taxes, or adjustments.

Net income. The money you have left to spend after all deductions, taxes, and adjustments.

Adjusted gross income. AGI is the amount of total gross income minus adjustments to income, not deductions. AGI is considered "above the line," while taxable income is "below the line." Common adjustments include subtractions for investment retirement accounts, student loan interest, half of self-employment tax, educator expenses, and self-employed health insurance. AGI is also used in reference to the net profit or loss from self-employment.

Personal deductions. You may be surprised to learn that you are not taxed on 100 percent of the money you earn. This is where deductions come in. You can either itemize personal deductions or elect to take the standard deduction, which is an amount the IRS has decided is reasonable to let you keep without taxing it. If you plan to itemize your non-business deductions, you should read the instructions on the IRS website for the 1040 Schedule A for the most up-to-date information on allowable deductions, which will include things like some of your medical and dental expenses, gifts to qualified charities, some taxes and interest, and mortgage insurance, among other things. If the total of all these things is less than the standard deduction which you can take without any documentation, you should not itemize. As the IRS says, "In most cases, your federal income tax will be less if you take the larger of your itemized deductions or your standard deduction." Personal deductions are not the same as business expenses/deductions.

Filing status. Options include single, married filing jointly, married filing separately, head of household, and qualifying widow or widower. Check the IRS website if you are unsure which status applies to you.

[42]Internal Revenue Service, "Behavioral Control," https://www.irs.gov/businesses/small-businesses-self-employed/behavioral-control, accessed September 13, 2020.

Pass-through taxation. This is when the taxes of a business are accounted for or "passed through" on the owner's individual tax return rather than on a separate corporate tax return, thus allowing the money to be taxed only once. This is commonly the case for partnerships, LLCs, and S-corporations. Some classify sole proprietorships this way as well.

Limited liability company (LLC). This is a business structure protecting a business owner's personal assets in regard to the business's debts and liabilities. This means that creditors cannot go after the owner's personal assets to settle debts of the business. LLCs use pass-through taxation, and income/loss is reported on the owner's personal tax returns. There are advantages and disadvantages to forming an LLC. Do you need to be an LLC? Todd Thurston, a New York-based actor and tax preparer who specializes in the entertainment industry, reflects:

> Every situation is different, but the answer is generally no unless you're in a business that really needs the liability protection so if somebody sues you, they're going after business assets and not going after your personal assets. But it's very fuzzy with a single member LLC or sole proprietor. I have yet, after all these years, to find a really strong tax or financial argument for doing an LLC if you are a sole proprietor. Forming an LLC can be expensive depending on the state. LLCs are a state entity that aren't recognized by the IRS. Even in my business, I'm not an LLC.[43]

As Jeanette Smith, an editor and writing coach from Dallas, wrote in a blog post on the Freelancer's Union website, "Legally and financially, talking to a CPA and attorney are the only sure ways to know if an LLC is right for you."[44]

Taxpayer identification numbers. When filing your personal taxes your Social Security number is your taxpayer identification number. This is also typically the case for many independent contractors. There are some circumstances, like paying employees, which require you to apply for an employer identification number or EIN. Check the IRS website to determine if you need an EIN and how to apply.

---

[43]Ibid.
[44]Jeanette Smith, "How Forming an LLC Boosts Your Investment in Your Business," Freelancers Union blog, December 6, 2018, https://blog.freelancersunion.org/2018/12/06/how-forming-an-llc-boosts-your-investment-in-your-business/, accessed August 15, 2020.

Personal exemptions. In the past a fixed amount per person was subtracted from a taxpayer's adjusted gross income, thus reducing their taxable income. The Tax Cuts and Jobs Act 2017 eliminated personal exemptions and doubled the standard deduction through to 2025. It is unclear whether personal exemptions will return after 2025.

Tax deductions. These are subtracted from your income before the amount of tax you owe is calculated.

Business deductions. When you operate a business (including as a sole proprietor/freelancer/independent contractor), you spend money to run the business. You can deduct these expenses from the money your business earned to determine if the business had a profit or loss. These deductions get listed on Schedule C. If, after deducting your expenses, you made a profit, you will add that amount to your personal income. You pay additional self-employment taxes on that amount if it is over $400. If your business lost money, you will deduct the amount lost from your personal income.

Tax credit. Any tax credits you are entitled to are taken off the amount of tax you owe. Think of it like a tax coupon that gets taken off right at the end before you pay your bill. Tax credits can be either refundable or non-refundable. If the credit is non-refundable and is larger than the amount of tax you owe, you will not pay any tax and the overage amount just disappears. If the tax credit is refundable and is larger than the amount of tax you owe, the IRS will send you the difference as a tax refund.

Tax refund. If, having done your taxes, you find that you paid more to the IRS through withholding or estimated quarterly payments than you actually owe in taxes, you will be due a tax refund. If you discover that you did not pay in enough throughout the year, you have to pay the difference. So if you calculate that your taxes for the year are $5,000 and through withholding/estimated quarterly payments you paid $6,000, you will get a $1,000 tax refund for overpayment of taxes. If you have only paid $4,500, you must write a check for the $500 difference that you haven't paid, not the full $5,000.

Self-employment taxes (SE tax). As an employee, in addition to your salary your employer is required to pay half of your Social Security and Medicare taxes. They contribute on your behalf an amount equal to what is shown for those areas on your W-2. If you are self-employed (sole proprietor/independent contractor/freelancer) then you are both the employee and the employer. That means you must pay both shares of Social Security and Medicare taxes. You do not pay this tax on the gross income for your business; only after you have deducted all your business expenses and determined your profit do you calculate SE tax (as of 2020, 15.3 percent of your profit over $400). Fifty percent of SE tax is also deductible as an adjustment on your personal tax return.

Standard mileage rate. If you have to drive your car as part of running your business you can either calculate the actual expenses of driving the car for business (gas, oil changes, tires, etc.), or elect to take the standard mileage rate which folds in all business-related car expenses except business tolls and parking. The rate does change from year to year, so you always need to check the rate before you do your calculations—over the last ten years it has fluctuated between 55 and 58 cents per mile. To use this deduction you must track the mileage you drive related to your business. Calculate the total number of miles and multiply it by the standard mileage rate to get the dollar amount that you can deduct on your Schedule C for business use of your car. Any tolls or parking fees you pay while on these business trips are also deductible. It is important to note this is specifically for miles you drive in connection with your work as a sole proprietor/independent contractor, not for commuting to a regular job as an employee. Commuting expenses are not tax deductible.

IRS Form W-4 employee's withholding certificate. Redesigned for tax year 2020, this form tells your employer what amount of federal income tax they should withhold from your paychecks. The IRS recommends that you complete the online tax withholding estimator on its website prior to filling out the form. Previous W-4 forms didn't acknowledge other income streams beyond the job at hand. The new form guides those with regular employee compensation as well as non-employee income to consider increasing their withholding to help cover any non-employee tax liability in lieu of quarterly tax payments.

IRS Form W-2 Wage and Tax Statement. This is called an informational return. Employees should receive a copy of their W-2 by January 31 for the previous tax year, listing the total income for that job and all deductions the employer made on your behalf. At a minimum it will show your gross wages, tips, and other compensation for the year; the total federal income tax withheld from your pay; total wages and tips taxed for Social Security and total Social Security taxes withheld from your pay; wages and tips taxed for Medicare and total Medicare tax withheld from your pay; and withholding for local, city, and state taxes if applicable. There are many more boxes and codes for information related to retirement, insurance, dependant care, etc., and these will be customized to your situation. In addition to the copy sent to each employee, a copy is also sent to the IRS so it has the information on file, hence the term *informational return.* You will receive a W-2 from each employer you work for.

IRS Form W-9 Request for Taxpayer ID Number. If you are being paid as an independent contractor, the party hiring you will ask you to fill out this form so they have your correct contact and taxpayer information on file when they submit your 1099-NEC information to the IRS.

IRS Form 1099-NEC.[45] NEC stands for non-employee compensation. This, like the W-2, is an informational return. Any entity that has paid you $600 or more in non-employee compensation, for example as an independent contractor, is required to submit this information to the IRS using this form. You will also receive a copy of the form for your tax purposes. It is important to note that if you were paid less than $600 the payer is not required to issue you with a 1099-NEC, but you are still required to report that money as self-employment income.

IRS Form 1040 US Individual income Tax Return. Typically called the "1040," this is the standard personal federal income tax form used to file your tax return with the IRS. Depending on your financial situation, you will likely need to attach additional schedules and forms (*schedule* is another word for form that the US adopted from the British tax system). Think of the schedules and forms as worksheets that help you to calculate the numbers you need to enter on the 1040.

Schedule C Profit or Loss from Business. You report your income and business expenses on this form, and determine whether your business made a profit or lost money. This number is entered on Schedule 1. Once you have calculated any other entries that apply to you on Schedule 1, you transfer that number to your 1040. This is indicated on the forms and in the instructions.

Schedule SE Self-Employment Tax. If you have a profit of $400 or more from self-employment you need to pay self-employment tax, which you calculate using the instructions for this form.

Form 4868 Application for Automatic Extension of Time to File US Individual Income Tax Return. If you are unable to file your tax return on time, you can use this form to get an automatic six-month extension. However, it is very important to note that this is just an extension to file your tax return, not an extension to pay any taxes you owe. If you believe you will owe taxes you should submit the amount you expect to owe along with this form. When you eventually file your tax return, if you end up owing additional money you may be liable for interest

---

[45]Prior to tax year 2020, non-employee compensation was reported on form 1099-MISC.

and penalties for not paying that amount by the original tax deadline. If it turns out that you overpaid, you will receive the difference back as a tax refund.

Research or entertainment? Gone are the days when you could write off all your movie and theatre tickets, cable, Netflix, etc. as a business expense. The IRS has made this clearer in recent years. Todd Thurston says:

> You need to be able to prove connection in order for it to be deductible now. If you buy a ticket to a show and you can prove that you either have an interview coming up at that theatre, with someone that worked on the show, for that show at a different theatre, or some kind of connection, then it is easier to justify and defend that expense.[46]

Home office deduction. The IRS has guidelines you must follow to use the home office deduction. "A lot of people think the home office deduction is a big red flag for an audit, but if you're a 1099 worker they anticipate you are probably working from home. As long as it's reasonable and can be substantiated if ever questioned then you should be OK," says Thurston.[47]

Business Income and Deductions

When you run your own business you are responsible for additional taxes based on how you are compensated. Running your own business also impacts how you keep financial records, what records you need to keep, and which tax forms you must fill out. The distinction is a really important one, and also not really up to you. Ultimately, the IRS determines whether you are or are not a business based on how you've earned your income. Thurston says, "the minute you get paid and no tax has been taken out, you are automatically a business whether you intended to be or not."[48] Any time you attend a job interview be sure you are aware of their plan for your classification. If you need further confirmation, pay attention to the form your employer gives you when you start work. If they ask you to fill out an IRS Form W-4 then you are being hired and paid as an employee. Taxes will be withheld from your check and you will receive an IRS Form W-2 at the end of the year listing your total income and withheld taxes. If, on the other hand, the company has you fill out an IRS Form W-9 then you are being paid as an independent contractor. No taxes will

---

[46]Todd Thurston, interview with the author, August 21, 2020. This does not constitute tax advice, and you should consult a tax professional.
[47]Ibid.
[48]Ibid.

be withheld from your checks, and if you are paid more than $600 you will receive an IRS Form 1099-NEC at the end of the year listing the total amount you have been paid. Remember, even if you do not receive a 1099-NEC at the end of the year, you are still obliged to report and pay taxes on all income.

When you run your own business, you don't pay taxes on all the money your business brings in, only on your profit. To determine your profit, subtract your expenses from your income. Whatever money is left over is your profit, and that is the part you are taxed on. Todd Thurston explains, "If you spent money to make money, then it's probably deductible."[49] The IRS says you can deduct any "ordinary and necessary expenses directly related to operating your business."[50] Listed below are some of the common things likely deductible on your Schedule C if the expense was related to your work as an independent contractor. For the complete list and any exclusions or updates you should read the instructions for the Schedule C form or consult a tax professional.

- Advertising and/or promotional materials, including resumes, cover letters, portfolios, business cards, website design, headshots, etc.
- Vehicle use: track mileage driven for business use if taking the standard deduction, or track actual expenses related to your business mileage.
- Money paid to employees or contractors you have hired.
- Business insurance costs like liability insurance.
- Office supplies like printer ink, paper, pens, stationery, and post-it notes, and postage and shipping expenses.
- Accountant, attorney, and tax preparation fees directly related to your business.
- Equipment repairs and maintenance.
- Business use of your home.
- Subscriptions to industry publications and employment job boards.
- Tools and supplies, which may include hand tools, rendering supplies, and kit supplies.
- Research, training, and continuing education including books, seminars, conferences, movies, or shows connected to a specific job.
- Union dues[51] and professional memberships (USA, USITT, SMA, etc.).

---

[49]Ibid.

[50]Internal Revenue Service, "2019 Instructions for Schedule C (2019)," updated 2019, https://www.irs.gov/instructions/i1040sc, accessed October 18, 2020.

[51]Union dues that are related to W2 income should not be included on your Schedule C. For most stage managers and stagehands, union dues are almost always related to W2 work because the union requires they be paid as employees. United Scenic Artists does not have this same requirement and its union contracts are typically for independent contractors.

- A portion of business meal expenses.
- Business use of cellphone and internet.
- Business travel.

It is not unusual to have expenses that are part for business and part for personal use. In those cases, just separate the expenses and deduct the business portion. So if you bought a ream of printer paper and used half of it for personal reasons and half for business, you can deduct half of the cost on your Schedule C as a business expense.

Thurston says the biggest mistake he sees people making on their taxes doesn't have anything to do with understanding taxes at all. It's not tracking their income accurately. "Everybody tends to focus on deductions, deductions, deductions, but what's really important for freelancers is to keep a ledger of all of your income. You need to know the date of the payment, how much they paid you, how they paid you. Did you get a check? Venmo?" He goes on to say, "Anyone who has paid you $600 or more is required to send you and the IRS a 1099-NEC. If you leave off income that was reported to the IRS, you will get a letter from them with a bill for the missing owed tax and several different late fees and penalties." Overlooked income can cost you even more than overlooked deductions.

There is no one right way to keep track of your income and expenses. You can save receipts and sort them at the end of the year, scan them into an app that helps organize them for you, or log your financial information into a software program that will spit out a report with all your categories already totaled for you. No matter what system you choose, make sure it is one you will actually use. Thurston says: "it takes discipline. It just takes getting in the habit of keeping good records."

In addition to not keeping track of income carefully enough, Thurston says another mistake he sees people make is not paying estimated quarterly taxes, or, if they pay them, not keeping track of when and how much they paid. You "really need to know how much you paid and when you paid it. It's critically important because it determines if you have to pay a penalty."

Everything covered in this chapter relates to federal income taxes, but don't overlook the fact that a majority of states and even some major cities have a separate income tax system in addition to the federal tax system. It is impossible to go into detail about state and local taxes due to the sheer number of differences, but you can find information about state taxes through your state's Department of Revenue. Remember that if you work in multiple states you may need to file a state return in each of them.

Planning and Protecting Your Financial Future

Too many people wait until they have "enough" money even to begin saving for retirement. Others want to wait until they have time to understand the complicated world of finance and investments. The reality is you will probably never have enough money or enough time, and the longer you wait to begin saving for retirement, the harder it will be to secure your financial future. In preparing this section I spoke with Bailie Slevin, financial advisor and owner of Entertaining Finance. She has a strong personal drive not just to help her clients place their money for maximum growth and efficiency, but to educate them, and as many other people as possible, about how their money works. She says, "I don't want my clients to be successful because I did it for them, I want to empower them to make really good choices because they understand them. They should be able to make great choices whether I'm there or not." When she is working with someone's money she doesn't want to put it somewhere they don't understand—that seems to her like malpractice.

> I won't ever do that. I've never done that. I had a potential client tell me to just put his money where I thought it would work. I said that is not what I do and he said, well, that's what I want. And I said, well, that's not what I do, which maybe makes me foolish because he had a lot of money, but that's what I believe.

Slevin primarily works with people in the arts and entertainment industry, having begun her career as a stage manager in New York City. She has strong opinions about the notion of the starving artist: "People in the arts have been told, point blank, that they're supposed to be stupid about money, you're supposed to starve. Well, that means you're supposed to be poor. That's dumb. Quote me on that. It's the dumbest thing I've ever heard." Her hope in educating her clients is that they will help spread their knowledge and start a movement of financially literate artists. I'm sharing with you the key factors that Slevin, through Entertaining Finance, uses to educate her clients in her quest to create her own financial literacy movement.

Types of Money

As you begin to learn the language of money, Slevin explains the importance of understanding the three ways your money can be treated with taxes as it grows: taxable, tax deferred (which she refers to as tax procrastinated), and tax free.

Taxable money is liquid. That means you have access to it within 24 hours or less. Taxable money can be held in bank or investment accounts. The value in a bank account can't go down unless you take the money out, whereas investment account values can rise or fall. Investment accounts can be made up of stocks (ownership of a piece of a company, the value of which goes up or down depending on the success of the company), bonds (a type of loan to a company which pays interest), or mutual funds (a package of selected stocks and bonds overseen by a fund manager). You pay ordinary income tax or capital gains tax on this money as it grows.

Tax-deferred money is considered illiquid, meaning you don't have immediate access to it; if you decide to take money out of a tax-deferred account prior to turning 59.5 years old, you will have to pay financial penalties. At age 59.5 years you can withdraw the money but you will pay taxes on your withdrawals. Your money goes into an account and you don't pay income tax on it when you put it in, so this can reduce your tax burden for now. Examples of these types of accounts are 401(k)/403(b), investment retirement accounts (IRAs), and annuities. You place your money into one of these accounts, and hope that over time it will grow. But because you did not pay income tax on the money when you put it into the account, you are required to pay income tax on the money and any earnings once you take it out. According to Slevin:

> This is an area where having a financial advisor can really help and decisions become very individualized because tax deferred accounts may result in a kind of negative tax planning if, when you reach the age when you are allowed to take disbursements, you are paying higher taxes on the money than you would have when you earned the money in the first place.

Tax-free money is semi-liquid. You can access all of it, but only after a significant amount of time. You pay income taxes on the money as you put it into a tax free investment, hope it grows significantly, and when you take the money out you don't have to pay taxes on any of it, even the earnings, because you paid the taxes prior to the investment. Examples of tax-free options include Roth IRAs, Municipal Bonds, and the cash value of permanent life insurance.

Basic Budget

Slevin offers her clients a basic outline of what their budget should look like, starting with saving the ideal 20 percent of gross income. Next, she recommends that no one spends more than 15 percent of their income on rent or mortgage costs. A good estimate is that 30 percent of your income will go toward taxes, so you are left with only 35 percent of your income to put toward living expenses—which include insurance, debts, and loans in addition to your needs and wants. That equals 100 percent. If you spend more than 100 percent of your money, you are going into debt. And there are additional budget factors you should consider, especially if you are looking for places to trim your expenses.

Debt expenses allow you the least control, and include things like mortgage and credit card payments. These are debt commitments you have made and have very little ability to change.

Fixed expenses are costs you had control over at some point, but now you are stuck with them. They include anything for which you have signed a contract and typically pay a fixed amount each month. Examples include phone bills, gym membership, insurance premiums, childcare, etc.

Variable recurring expenses are semi-permanent financial commitments, things that we can choose to spend more or less money on or that fluctuate depending on your usage. Examples are streaming services, cellphone data plans, gas and car maintenance, haircuts, pet supplies, groceries, and utilities. If you are looking to trim your budget, you can likely cut some expenses from this category.

Discretionary expenses are money spent on things we enjoy, where we have the choice to make the purchase or not and the ability to choose a higher- or lower-priced option—things like fancy coffee, movie tickets, hair dye, fast food, vacations, and video games. This category is the easiest to trim in your budget, and in some ways also the hardest because of the enjoyment these items bring. However, if you look at the bigger picture it is easier to make good choices about where you spend your money when you see how it directly affects reaching your long-term goals.

Once you understand the different types of spending, you can form your budget. Start by gathering all your financial information. Tabulate your income. Categorize and total your monthly expenditures so you know how much you are spending in each of the areas: debt, fixed, variable recurring, and discretionary. Include the amount you intend for savings as well. Compare your total spending with your income. If your spending/savings goal is more than your income, then you need to find a way to earn more money or you must decide what expenses you are going to cut. Creating a budget is the easy part: following through in making choices every day that fit within your budget is the hard bit, but necessary if you are going to reach your financial goals.

Protection: Insurance and Legal Documents

Now you have a budget, the next step in making a financial plan is to anticipate the worst possible scenarios to be sure you are protected. That means understanding how your insurance policies work, making sure you have the right amount of insurance coverage, and ensuring you have legal documents in place.

If you don't understand how your car insurance policy works and what all the numbers mean, call the insurance agent and ask them to explain the details and options. The *deductible* is the amount you pay out of pocket before the insurance kicks in. Many people don't realize that they can choose their deductible amount: the higher the deductible amount, the lower your premium will be, and vice versa. You also need to understand terms like *collision* and *comprehensive insurance*, because basic car insurance covers damage you do to other people's vehicles but not your own. If you want to have your own vehicle covered, you must specify that in your policy.

Liability is another important point to understand. Car insurance policies include three numbers that represent bodily injury per person/ bodily injury per accident/property damage. Examples are 100/300/50 or 25/50/20. Taking the first example, if you are in a car accident where people suffer injuries, the policy will pay up to $100,000 in medical bills per person with a maximum cap of $300,000. So if four people each need $100,000 worth of care, you will be left responsible for $100,000. The last number is the amount of property damage that will be covered, $50,000 in this example. The second example only provides $25,000 medical coverage per person with a maximum of $50,000, and $20,000 in property damage. Slevin says that the insurance agent should "really work with you so you can say, 'how high can I make my coverage? What does that look like with this deductible?' Make them do their job to design a policy that gives you maximum protection with a minimum premium. You have to make an informed decision."[52]

If you own a home, homeowner's insurance is a given; but if you rent your home you may not realize you can get renter's insurance to prevent financial disaster if you are ever faced with theft, natural disaster, or fire. Renter's insurance typically has a very small premium (averaging between $10 and $20 a month) and, like car insurance, the amount will depend on

---

[52]Bailie Slevin, personal interview with the author, August 17, 2020.

your location as well as the coverage levels and deductible you choose. A key detail to look for in your policy is replacement cost, not the value of your belongings when purchased or at the time of the damage or loss.

Life insurance is another item not to be overlooked. Slevin says:

> Nobody wants to think about it, but it's so, so crucial. I'm seeing far too many situations with one parent dying and clearly there was no planning because the online fundraiser pops up immediately. If that person had been paying a hundred dollars a month for a term policy, there could be $500,000 or a million dollars showing up for that family, depending on when they got the policy, so the one thing they wouldn't have to worry about is money.

The younger and healthier you are when you start a life insurance policy, the lower your monthly premium will be.

Slevin also emphasizes the importance of having proper legal documents. "Make sure you have a will, power of attorney, living will, health care proxy, all of that. It is tough because the insurance and the legal documents are there for the worst-case scenario and nobody wants to think about it." She explains, "This is where a financial advisor comes along, because my job is really to sit as 'future you' and see all the options you have now and make sure you are prepared for all of the things that could happen, so when you get to be 'future you' you don't look back and realize you really messed up."

Eliminating Debt

All too often people think the first step to financial planning and retirement savings is to put money into an IRA, 401(k), or other retirement account. However, the elimination of bad debt, debt with a high interest rate, likely needs to take precedence over asset-building investments. This especially refers to credit card debt. You will spend more in credit card interest than you will make through your investment growth, so paying them off and not continuing to spend beyond your means must be your priority. Just as small daily purchases can lead you into debt, small daily savings can lead you out of it.

Student loans are different, Slevin says: "We do want to pay them off, obviously, but the first thing people need to do is get comfortable with the fact that they're there. If they have interest rates that are low enough, you might not want to pay them off early. Depending on your individual circumstances, it just might not make sense mathematically, financially." That's where an advisor really becomes important because, "we get to have all of your information with none of your baggage and we can help remove the emotion from your decision making."

Disciplined Saving

Even while eliminating your bad debt, you need to work on building a solid base in your savings account. It's not enough just to *have* a savings account, you also need to be diligent in growing your savings. Your initial goal is to have three to six months of income saved, depending on your personal situation. Normally people say that you need three months of expenses, but Slevin emphasizes, "If there is one thing the pandemic has taught us it is that three months of expenses isn't enough and you need to calculate based on your income." Your goal should be to work up to saving 20 percent of your income every month toward this emergency fund. Once your emergency pot is fully funded, you can start to make decisions about where to put your 20 percent savings every month.

This is another place where a financial advisor can help you evaluate your specific situation and goals, and advise you on where your money can best serve you. Slevin advises that this saving should continue

> until you've got one year's worth of income, and then you can do anything. Maybe now is the time to put money into a 401(k), maybe you want to buy a business, maybe you want to buy a house. There's so many things you can do when you have that much security. And that's really the point when you are getting started, get a secure foundation.
>
> We then start talking about priorities and planning. If you are going to buy a house, you still need to be saving 20 percent every month so you might use some of the money you have already saved as the down payment because you are going to go right back to replenishing it. But if you buy a house and the mortgage payments knock you down to only saving 10 percent, then that's a problem.

Slevin summarizes: "The really big takeaway from all of this is that people need to know that the first step in starting your financial planning life and your retirement savings is to just have a savings account that you contribute to regularly and not do anything more exciting than that." One of the key lessons she teaches her clients is "you can only spend each dollar once. You can save each dollar more than once, but once you spend it, that's it. It becomes a question of priorities. Where is that dollar going to do the most good?"

Hiring a Professional

The things discussed in this chapter are incredibly important, and because they are so important they can also feel overwhelming to handle on your own. There are times when you shouldn't try to do it on your own, and there will likely be situations in your career when you need input from a professional. Begin by asking your network, friends, and family for referrals. In almost all cases you are going to want someone who works frequently with people in the entertainment industry. Once you've found the professional you are looking for, they may also be able to assist you in seeking out other experts to support you in your business.

Tax Preparer

The professional you will likely hire most frequently is a tax preparer. The IRS has several recommendations when it comes to selecting one.[53]

- Check their qualifications.
- Ask about their fees (avoid preparers who charge you based on the size of your refund).
- Make sure they are available (you want to schedule an appointment in advance).
- Your preparer will provide worksheets for you to fill out with all your financial information for the year. (If they don't ask you for your previous year's tax return as well as records of your income and deductions, that could be a red flag.)
- Do not use a preparer who asks you to sign a blank form.
- You should have the opportunity to read and ask questions about your return prior to signing and submitting it.
- Be sure any refund comes to you and not your preparer.
- Be sure the preparer has a preparer tax identification number (and that they include it on your return).

I would add to this, find someone who is industry-specific and familiar with what we do and how our business works. There are tax preparers who

---

[53]Internal Revenue Service, "Things Taxpayers Should Remember When Searching for a Tax Preparer," https://www.irs.gov/newsroom/things-taxpayers-should-remember-when-searching-for-a-tax-preparer, accessed September 26, 2020.

specialize in working with the entertainment industry and, even better, there are tax preparers who themselves work in the entertainment industry as actors, designers, stage managers, etc. Finding someone with this expertise is important, so you don't have to educate them on how the industry works and they understand the kinds of deductions that apply to the work you do.

There are four categories of tax preparers, and it is good to understand the differences as you evaluate your needs and options. The first level is a *non-credentialed tax preparer*. This is someone who has registered for an IRS Preparer Tax Identification Number but does not have any credentials or certifications. That doesn't mean they don't have any skills. There are many ways someone can learn how to do taxes; for example, the IRS offers the Annual Filing Season Program (AFSP), which requires up-to-date continuing education. You can search the IRS website for preparers who meet these requirements. A non-credentialed tax preparer may have limited abilities to represent you before the IRS in the unlikely case of an audit.

The next level of tax preparer is an *enrolled agent*, who is either a former IRS employee or has passed a comprehensive three-part examination. An enrolled agent is IRS licensed and has unlimited representation rights before the IRS.

A certified public accountant (CPA) is licensed by the state in which they practice. Each state has a board of accountancy that determines the minimum educational and experience requirements for individuals to qualify to take the CPA exam. Most states require a bachelor's degree in Accounting, and many also require work experience with a supervising CPA. Once licensed, a CPA will typically have to complete at least forty hours of continuing education per year. CPAs have unlimited representation rights before the IRS. In addition to filing taxes, CPAs may do bookkeeping, oversee payroll, prepare and analyze financial reports, and conduct internal audits. Slevin suggests that "you probably don't need a CPA until your income is at a place where you want to look at more in-depth planning like creating a personal retirement plan."[54]

A *tax attorney* is generally only needed if you are in trouble with the IRS. They advise their clients on tax issues that may require a lawyer, like settling back taxes, unreported income, appealing an audit determination, or defending criminal charges related to tax fraud. Tax attorneys have unlimited rights to represent a client before the IRS.

---

[54]Slevin, personal interview with the author, August 17, 2020.

Financial Advisor

For a financial advisor to be most useful for you, you must have your emergency reserves fully funded and additional money available to invest. That money could come from an unexpected windfall or through diligent and careful saving. But it doesn't mean you should wait until that time to consult with a financial advisor. Early on, a financial advisor can provide feedback and guidance related to insurance and other forms of financial protection, help you set goals and priorities, and educate you about your future financial options. Many financial advisors offer consultations for an hourly or flat fee. Meeting with a financial advisor early in your career and following their advice could help you reach your financial goals more quickly.

Entertainment Lawyer

You can hire an entertainment lawyer proactively or reactively depending on your needs. Proactively an entertainment lawyer can advise you on your intellectual property rights, help you write or review contracts, and assist in negotiations, among other things. Reactively, you would hire an entertainment lawyer if you are being sued for violating a contract or someone's intellectual property rights, or if you need to sue someone for such violations. Gordon Firemark, attorney at law, is an entertainment lawyer in Los Angeles, CA. He explains: "A good entertainment lawyer will help set up your business, develop some standard operating procedures [and] basic contract terms, and protect your intellectual property." While hiring an attorney does come at some expense, Firemark goes on to say, "Many lawyers working with artists have flexible fee schedules, so it needn't cost an arm and a leg to protect yourself."[55] Some entertainment lawyers specialize in certain segments of the industry, like film, music, or theatre, which could help guide your search.

---

[55]Firemark, personal communication with the author, February 27, 2020.

22 Photographer photo credit placement: vertical, inside bottom right

23 Photographer photo credit placement: beneath photo, left

24 Photographer photo credit placement: horizontal, inside bottom right

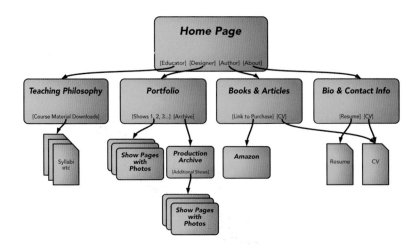

25 Sample website organizational flowchart

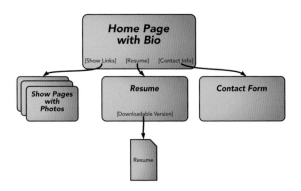

26 Sample website organizational flowchart

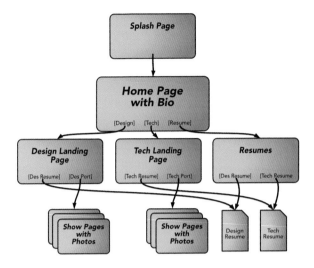

27 Sample website organizational flowchart

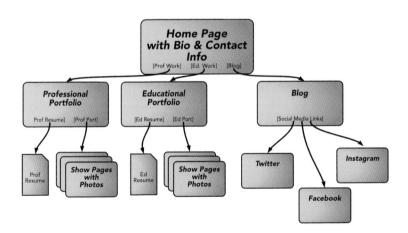

28 Sample website organizational flowchart

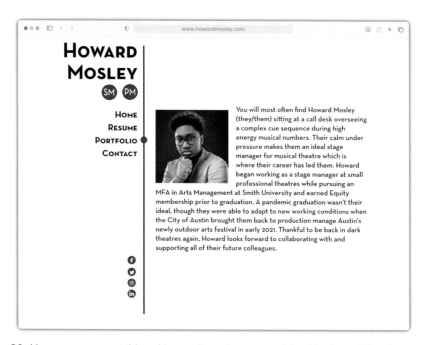

29 Home page matching Howard's other materials (designed by Jason Tollefson)

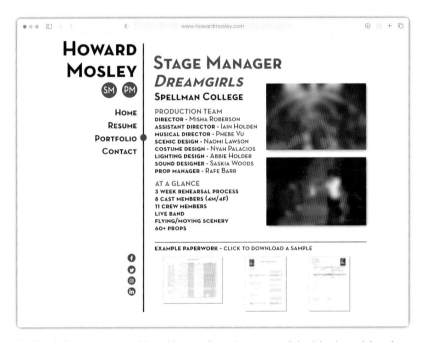

30 Portfolio page matching Howard's other materials (designed by Jason Tollefson)

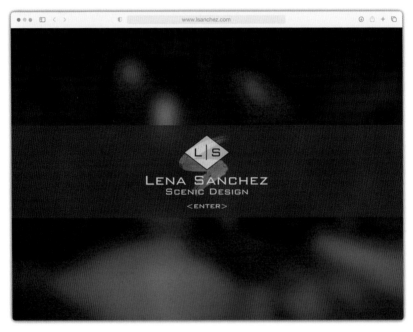

31 Home page matching Lena's other materials (designed by Jason Tollefson)

32 Portfolio page matching Lena's other materials (designed by Jason Tollefson)

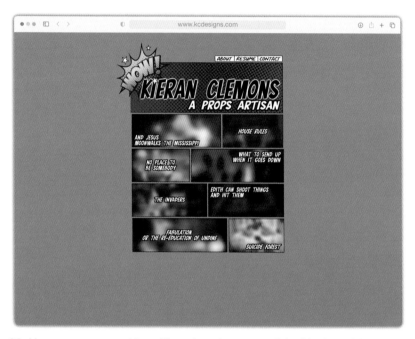

33 Home page matching Kieren's other materials (designed by Jason Tollefson)

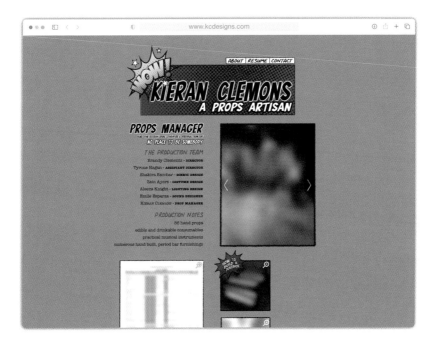

34 Portfolio page matching Kieren's other materials (designed by Jason Tollefson)

STAGE MANAGER

DREAMGIRLS

SPELLMAN COLLEGE

PRODUCTION TEAM
MISHA ROBERSON - DIRECTOR
IAIN HOLDEN - ASST DIRECTOR
PHEBE VU - MUS DIRECTOR
NAOMI LAWSON - SCENIC DESIGN
NYAH PALACIOS - COSTUME DESIGN
ABBIE HOLDER - LIGHTING DESIGN
SASKIA WOODS - SOUND DESIGNER
RAFE BARR - PROP MANAGER

AT A GLANCE
3 WEEK REHEARSAL PROCESS
8 CAST MEMBERS
11 CREW MEMBERS
LIVE BAND
FLYING/MOVING SCENERY
60+ PROPS

FULL CAST

LIVE BAND

35 Presentation portfolio page: Howard (designed by Jason Tollefson)

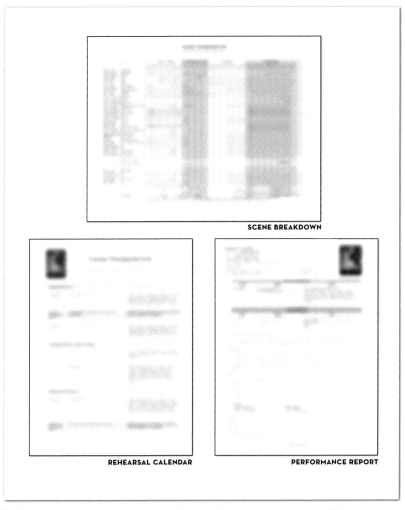

36 Presentation portfolio page: Howard (designed by Jason Tollefson)

37 Presentation portfolio page: Lena (designed by Jason Tollefson)

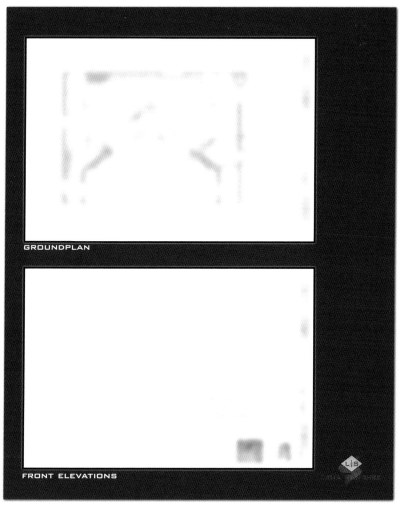

GROUNDPLAN

FRONT ELEVATIONS

38 Presentation portfolio page: Lena (designed by Jason Tollefson)

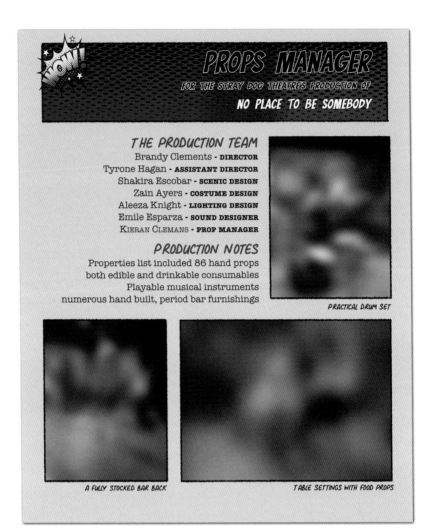

PROPS MANAGER

FOR THE STRAY DOG THEATRES PRODUCTION OF

NO PLACE TO BE SOMEBODY

THE PRODUCTION TEAM

Brandy Clements - **DIRECTOR**
Tyrone Hagan - **ASSISTANT DIRECTOR**
Shakira Escobar - **SCENIC DESIGN**
Zain Ayers - **COSTUME DESIGN**
Aleeza Knight - **LIGHTING DESIGN**
Emile Esparza - **SOUND DESIGNER**
KIERAN CLEMANS - **PROP MANAGER**

PRODUCTION NOTES

Properties list included 86 hand props
both edible and drinkable consumables
Playable musical instruments
numerous hand built, period bar furnishings

PRACTICAL DRUM SET

A FULLY STOCKED BAR BACK

TABLE SETTINGS WITH FOOD PROPS

39 Presentation portfolio page: Kieren (designed by Jason Tollefson)

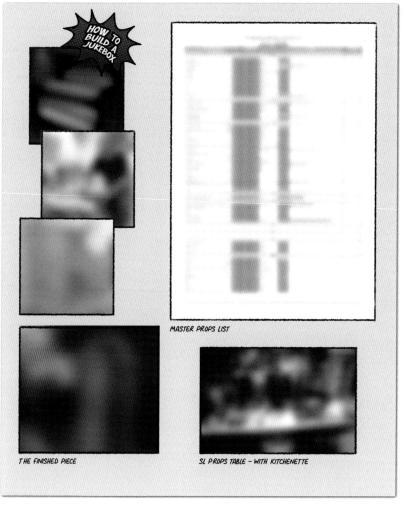

MASTER PROPS LIST

THE FINISHED PIECE

SL PROPS TABLE – WITH KITCHENETTE

40 Presentation portfolio page: Kieren (designed by Jason Tollefson)

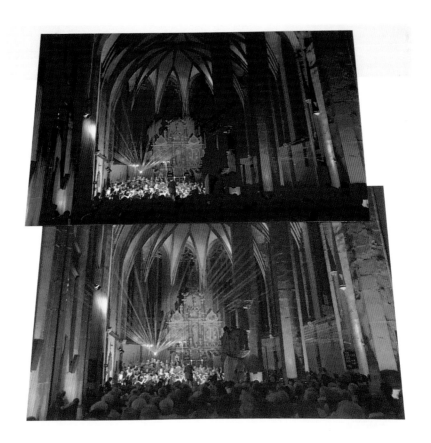

41 Printer versus photo paper. When printing a physical copy of your presentation portfolio, paper choice is critical. Notice the difference in quality and color saturation when printed on plain paper (bottom) versus photo paper (top).

8

Career Profiles

Ryan Gravilla—Principal Lighting Designer for Disney Parks Live Entertainment at Walt Disney World

Ryan grew up in Detroit in a decidedly non-theatrical family. He liked science and math, and planned to become an astronaut. He didn't move into theatre until high school, where he found himself being cast in larger and larger roles and decided that was what he wanted to do with the rest of his life.

Ryan's parents had strong opinions about college. He eventually went against their wishes to follow the voice in his head, attending Wayne State University to study acting. He quickly realized there was a lot more to acting than remembering his lines and waiting for the audience to clap. More importantly, discovering the joy and excitement of technical theatre, he found a way to put his creativity on stage without any personal emotional risk. Moreover, he could take the science and technology part of his brain and apply it artistically, using lighting fixtures as his paint brushes. His eagerness led him to take on as many shows and lighting projects as he could. In his junior year, burnt out and needing a break, he followed his childhood fascination with Walt Disney World and moved to Florida to participate in the Disney College program. For four months he drove a boat transporting guests in the Florida sunshine and didn't think about theatre, though he did dream about being a cast member again some day.

When he returned to school, his brain was spinning with ideas and newfound energy. A classmate who had been working at Cedar Point

Amusement Park in Ohio invited him to go along for the upcoming summer and, once again, the little voice in his head told him to say yes. That summer he worked as a technical supervisor for five or six theatres around the park, opening a show a week, and met a co-worker named Chuck Davis. Ryan didn't know it at the time, but this was the person who would make his Disney dreams come true.

Ryan received his BFA in Theatre Design and Technology and headed back to Cedar Point for another summer, this time as a lighting designer as well as technical supervisor. Chuck Davis was back again for a short time as the sound designer before returning to Florida and his job at Walt Disney World. Chuck called Ryan partway through the summer and told him there was a sudden opening, and to get his resume and cover letter in immediately. Within two weeks Ryan's dream had come true: he was living in Orlando and working for Disney as a technician at Pleasure Island.[1] He considers the four years he spent at Pleasure Island as his grad school experience, as he learned so much about so many different aspects of doing entertainment beyond traditional theatre lighting: how to light a scene on the fly, the impact lighting could have on an actor's comedic timing, how to light bands, and much more. He eventually proved himself and got to work in the largest nightclub venue on the island, with 100 moving lights in the air and a full wall of par cans. He described it as "lighting designer heaven."

After four years he felt he had mastered every lighting position in Pleasure Island and looked for his next step. A production planner position opened at Epcot and Ryan transferred there. He didn't love spending so much time at a desk after being in a nightclub every night, but he was great at his job. Soon he was noticed by one of the resort's lighting designers and invited to join the creative team working on Disney Cruise Line. He remained a production planner at Epcot for about a year while doing temporary assignments on cruise ships, and was officially promoted to being a full-time lighting designer in 2008. He worked his way up to senior designer, and became the principal lighting designer in 2015. In his current post he leads all the lighting designers in the department, typically seven full-time designers (two senior and five staff) plus twelve designers on temporary assignment/associate designers, one intern, and three project-based hourly lighting planners. His team is based at Walt Disney World although they support projects globally,

---

[1]Pleasure Island was a separately ticketed area at what was then called Downtown Disney. It targeted guests aged 21 and over with dance clubs, comedy clubs, bars, restaurants, and live music.

including Disney Cruise Line and the parks in Hong Kong, Shanghai, Paris, and occasionally Tokyo.

Reflecting on how his career evolved pretty much as he planned, he's glad he made the decisions he did but he does think about how differently things could have turned out.

> I'm incredibly fortunate. I got a degree in something I love. Theatre is one of those things that you have to love in order to do it and do it well because it is a sacrifice. It is long, weird hours. It is not always great pay and you've got to get something else out of it. If you're not getting something out of it there's a lot easier ways to make money.

Ryan has been living his Disney dream for more than two decades. His work has taken him to Germany and Hong Kong. He has crossed the Atlantic by sea four times, gone through the Panama Canal, sailed to Alaska, and been in every nook and cranny in the Caribbean, all aboard a Disney cruise ship. Domestically he has done shows in Ohio, California, Miami, and New York, and his work has taken him to Oregon, Pennsylvania, and Texas. He's lit an ice castle in the middle of Times Square, designed a fundraising event starring Bernadette Peters, designed the Disney Fantasy Christening Celebration in New York starring Neil Patrick Harris, and if you have ever sailed on a Disney cruise ship you undoubtedly saw his work in the Walt Disney Theatre.

Looking back, he recognizes two things that were part of every new opportunity that came his way. Firstly, he kept his head down, contributed to an overall positive work environment, worked hard, and was the kind of person that colleagues wanted to work with. When supervisors found out what his career goals were, they helped bring those opportunities to him. The second thing to which he owes his career success is listening to the little voice in his head that told him to take the risk and say yes.

Ryan recently realized that he's at a point in his life and career where people are looking to him as a role model. When juniors come to him and ask "How do I become you?", he tells them to find someone with more experience and learn everything they can from that person. When you have learned all you can from that person, identify another person who is at the next level and learn everything you can from them. He describes his first mentor, Laura "Rikki" Haynes, as incredibly approachable and kind, giving of her time and expertise. He kept his mouth shut and his eyes and ears open, soaking up everything he could learn from her. He advises finding the things that interest and excite you, and getting really good at them. Oh, and listen when that little voice in your head whispers, "Hey, you really should do this."

Meredith Tomkovitch—Director of Costuming, Resorts World Genting, Malaysia

When Meredith finished her BFA in Theatre with a concentration in costume design at the University of Illinois Urbana-Champaign, she knew how to do theatre but had very little knowledge of how to make a living doing theatre. Grad school wasn't right for her, and she didn't think the investment would pay off in the end. She opted instead for practical experience—a choice she says she does not regret.

After graduation, Meredith landed a position at a regional opera company as a second assistant wig/makeup artist, followed soon thereafter by an eighteen-month contract on a cruise ship. Next she worked for two years for Feld Entertainment as head of wardrobe on shows like *Monsters Inc.*, *Incredibles*, and others. Thinking she was tired of touring she took a job as a dresser on Cirque du Soleil's *LOVE* in Las Vegas, but soon missed being on the road, so after a year in Vegas she went back on tour as head of wardrobe with a Cirque du Soleil show that traveled both domestically and internationally.

As her tour was ending, a friend passed on an opportunity for a wardrobe manager at Ferrari World in Abu Dhabi. The timing was perfect: they wanted someone immediately, and she was available. She had traveled internationally on tour, and the casual six-month contract seemed more like an adventure than a major life change. It quickly turned into an open-ended contract and shifted to something more permanent.

Three years later she was contacted by a recruiter for a new theme park opening outside Kuala Lumpur. Meredith had never been to Malaysia but she knew the cost of living was much lower and was excited by the challenge, so she took the opportunity. She has now been in Malaysia for several years and has settled down. While she prefers living internationally at the moment, she expects to return to the US one day, if only for retirement. She says the quality of life in Malaysia for the price she pays is second to none: she enjoys a great apartment in the city center, easily accessible childcare, and a varied social life. But it is difficult being separated from family back in the US, and missing special occasions is hard. There is also a lot of red tape involved in living overseas—from setting up a bank account to signing apartment leases to getting a car. It was easier once she had done it once or twice, but the process requires patience.

Her advice is to be willing to do the crew work and the small tasks. You never know where sewing on hundreds of buttons might lead you and what connection you might make with your co-workers. When hiring people, she wants applicants to know as much as possible about the company, area, and position beforehand, and ask engaging questions throughout the interview. And keep in mind that when you are interviewing with a company overseas, the same legalities regarding interview questions don't apply and some things like family status are critical information for international relocation.

Meredith says she wouldn't be in her job today if it were not for the jobs in her past. Each one helped prepare her for her current role. To her surprise, she has been able to support herself and her family fully by working in costuming. Be open to the opportunities that present themselves. You never know where in the world you may end up.

Yuri Cataldo—Co-Founder and General Partner at Athenian Venture Capital, Innovation Engagement Manager

Yuri didn't have what he would call a traditional college theatre experience. He began undergraduate school as a mechanical engineering major, but wasn't convinced it was the right path for him. In his second year, recognizing that Yuri was struggling and bored, a professor asked him why he was there if this wasn't what he wanted to do. Having no good answer, Yuri dropped out of the program and began a period of exploration, switching universities three times and taking a smorgasbord of classes to match his wide variety of interests before landing as a theatre major studying costume design at Indiana University. This allowed him to explore many areas of interest. He received permission to take graduate-level classes in costume design, drawing classes in the art department, literature classes in the English department, etc. He loved how theatre encompassed so many of his interests: psychology, sociology, art, design, analysis, and even a little engineering.

From the moment Yuri started studying theatre he knew he wanted to be a Broadway designer. When looking at the Broadway designers he idolized, he realized all but one of them had a grad school degree and almost all of them at one of two schools: Yale or NYU. While working on his BA he started contacting grad schools to find out what they were looking for in students, and then tailored his studies to meet these criteria.

After finishing his BA in Theatre, he did a year-long residency at Juilliard and spent summers working in the costume shop at the Santa Fe Opera. He, like so many others, found the Santa Fe Opera is where he met the most people who helped him along in his career. He ended up going to Yale, where his experience was equal parts amazing and awful. "They throw you in the deep end and your goal is not to drown."

When he finished grad school, Yuri moved to New York City and managed to find work with several Broadway costume designers, including David Woollard, Carrie Robins, and Linda Cho. He developed a niche as a skilled fabric swatcher and shopper. He worked hard and consistently until the collapse of the economy in 2008, which saw many people in the entertainment industry out of work and struggling. That, combined with a divorce, changed everything instantly. He moved home with his parents and landed a job as an adjunct professor teaching five classes at the local university. At the same time he was cleaning offices at night and working as a server in an attempt to pay off the huge debt from his divorce. Even with all that, he ended up filing for bankruptcy.

Needing better paying and steadier work, he talked his way into an advertising sales job at a local TV station. He knew he wanted to start a company, so he did business research at night and sold advertising during the day. He indulged his fascination with bottled water, and in 2013 launched a water called Indigo H2O, which between 2013 and 2016 won three international awards for taste, including Best Tasting Water in the World. In 2015 it was featured at the Oscars, the Golden Globes, and the Grammys. He started to make connections between what he had learned in theatre and what made him a successful business owner, and began doing lectures about the connection between arts and entrepreneurship at places like Stanford, Princeton, and Notre Dame. The sales of his bottled water shot up 4,000 percent, but it all came crashing down when he got a cease-and-desist notification from the state government. He wasn't doing anything wrong, but didn't have enough money to fight and was forced to shut the company down.

After that major disappointment, his attention turned even more toward arts entrepreneurship. He was hired into his dream position at Emerson College to design a creative entrepreneurship program from the ground up, with the goal of teaching students how they could make money from their art. After a difficult year discovering he was not very good at academic politics, his contract was not renewed.

His next big move was to a large and well-known technology company. He says he got the job because an actor friend introduced him to his current boss. There he helped create, and continues to work in, their open innovation space, bringing in academic teams, startups, and resident industry teams and giving them access to workshops and support for their projects. Yuri also co-founded Athenian Venture Capital, a firm that backs early-stage technology companies led by diverse teams. While his career did not develop as he had envisioned, he credits his theatre training for his current success. "Creating a show from scratch is a similar process to creating a company from scratch. Now they call that 'design thinking' but it's the exact same process." And, just like theatre, there is never enough money, there's never enough time, and there's never enough resources. He says his experience in the fitting room taught him how to talk to people—calm their fears and insecurities—which has led to his success as a speaker and a negotiator. Never underestimate the value of your soft skills and theatre training.

Jeramy Boik—Scenic Designer, Technical Director, Landscape Architect, Builder of Tiny Houses

Jeramy started his undergraduate career at the University of Idaho intending to study architecture, but the offer of a scholarship if he changed his major to theatre was too strong. He appreciated how the theatre program was geared toward professionalism, but was disappointed how few hands-on opportunities he got. Familiar with the program at South Dakota State University and having friends there, he made the choice to transfer to SDSU to finish his degree in Communication Studies and Theatre with an emphasis on scenery. After graduation he was immediately hired as the technical director at the Civic Theatre of Allentown in Pennsylvania, where he worked for six years. In 2004, needing a change of scenery and more financial security, he moved across the country to Colorado, taking a job as the technical director for Pikes Peak Center for the Performing Arts, a roadhouse for national tours. While he was initially excited about the position, it was the one job in his career he knew right away was not for him.

After only a couple of months he decided to switch paths and go to grad school to study architecture.

He quickly discovered that landscape architecture spoke to him, so he switched his major again. At the end of his three-and-a-half-year Master of Landscape Architecture program he took an internship at the Denver Zoo, which turned into a full-time job. This he described as "really cool," with a lot of necessary regulation and red tape. There were moments of creativity, like designing a shipwreck for the polar bear exhibit, but also lots of mundane work. He freelanced around Denver as a scenic and lighting designer all through grad school and a little during his time at the zoo, getting gigs through word of mouth. After four years at the zoo he spent about a year on a large freelance landscape architecture project.

Missing the energy and creativity of theatre, Jeramy applied for and got his next job as tour technician with Up With People, a non-profit performing arts group touring internationally. He was only on the road for six months before being promoted to technical production manager, based in the organization's headquarters in Denver. In that position he would go on the road to supervise as they switched continents or kicked off new tours. After three-and-a-half years of this, he found himself back in the same pattern he had left in Allentown: working non-stop, sacrificing all his free time to the show, and ultimately burning out. Having recently started a new relationship, he wanted a life outside work. He realized he was unable to find any sort of balance working in the entertainment industry, and the pay was so low he couldn't do the things he wanted even if he did have the time.

His next adventure took him to Rocky Mountain Tiny Houses, where he applied to be a crew leader. He knew he was clearly qualified, but the person doing the hiring was skeptical that theatre carpentry and technical direction would translate into tiny house construction. Jeramy convinced him that his qualifications went way beyond carpentry: his theatre experience made him an expert at budgeting, time management, and crew supervision. One of his biggest selling points was his commitment to meeting deadlines— he pointed out that theatre is the only industry that sells tickets to their deadlines! He got the job and worked as a crew lead, design assistant, and carpenter. Again, after four years he and his now husband Nate were ready for another adventure. They moved to Hawaii and bought a piece of rural land. While Nate works outside the home, Jeramy designed and built an off-the-grid tiny house for them and has started his own company designing and building similar homes for individual clients. He is also back to doing theatre. The shows he is involved in now are mostly volunteer productions with and for young people on the island, teaching them what goes into a theatrical show and passing on skills that they can apply to their lives and possibly their careers.

When Jeramy reflects on his circuitous career path he says it is definitely all connected. Every skill he learned along the way applies to every job he has had, and there is no way he would be where he is now without his theatre training. What you learn working on a show stays with you for the rest of your life.

Shawn Boyle—Projection and Lighting Designer, Instructor, Yale School of Drama

Projection designers come from many different backgrounds: Shawn's entry point was lighting. Six months after graduating from Rutgers with his Theatre degree he asked a contact if she would serve as a reference for him as he applied for several jobs. She instead asked him if he'd be OK doing something other than lighting. She was the associate for a projection designer, and thought that he might also be a really great fit with this designer. Knowing that much of his lighting skillset could transfer into projections, he accepted the introduction.

The designer turned out to be Elaine McCarthy, the projection designer for *Wicked* and *Spamalot* among many other shows. During the interview Elaine noticed that Shawn had "model making" listed under his skills. She happened to be designing scenery at the time and needed a model box. He agreed to make it for her, figuring it would be like the many other model boxes he'd made. When the drawings arrived, he learned he had agreed to model the Mark Taper Forum in Los Angeles, which does not have a straight line in the building. The audience is curved. The proscenium wall is curved. The back wall is curved. The deck is circular.

Fortunately, his skills were up to the task and Elaine was impressed that a lighting designer could make a presentable model box. He went on to do her research for the project. He didn't really know what he was looking for in terms of projection design, but he set to work on the list of images she asked him to find. He was obsessed with getting it right, not realizing at the time that there really isn't a right. Elaine was impressed with the scope and quality of images he brought her, and asked him to work on research for other projects.

One day he happened to be in the studio when the Broadway production of *Wicked* called to tell Elaine the producers wanted to put changes made in the London production into the New York production. The company manager had identified just four days for the projection upgrade. Elaine called her associate (the person who had introduced her to Shawn), but she wasn't available. So Elaine turned to Shawn and asked if he wanted to come. He warned that he had no idea what he was doing and she said it was OK, just bring a laser pointer.

He showed up at the Gershwin Theater very nervous. Shawn recalls that Elaine was very gracious and gentle. He tracked paperwork changes, worked with the programmer, and directed the projector focus—all things that felt familiar because of his lighting experience. His success prompted an invitation to assist on the Los Angeles production. When another job came up and neither Elaine nor her associate was available, she asked Shawn what he was doing between September and December.

He made himself available, and was sent to Germany to work on *Wicked* for two months and then on to Australia to tech *Spamalot*, a show he had never even seen. He was terrified, but his lighting and general theatre experience got him through. He continued to work with Elaine for about six years.

Finally, Shawn decided it was time to go to grad school. He had always been interested in teaching and knew he needed a terminal degree to do so. He got into the program at Yale School of Drama and studied with Wendell Harrington. A few years after receiving his MFA he accepted Wendell's offer to come back to Yale and be her co-teacher.

While his career ambitions used to be designing on Broadway, Shawn is now at a point in his career where he just wants to work on shows that inspire him with people he enjoys. There are personal choices he wishes he had made differently when he was prioritizing work over relationships. He traveled for at least forty weeks a year, missing weddings and funerals. His friends stopped calling because he could never accept their invitations. He admits that he fed into these unhealthy practices in his early career, and says now that he knows better he is doing better. "You shouldn't have to sign your humanity away to be a functioning professional."

He offers this additional advice: stay open to possibilities and unattached to outcomes, so when you get that interview that can shift the entire direction of your career you don't miss the opportunity.

Charles "Chip" Perry—Director, Lighting and Television Production, World Wrestling Entertainment

Chip's first paid jobs were working in theme parks while still an undergraduate. During a summer at Santa Claus, Indiana's Holiday World, he had the title of technical director but was essentially a light board op who could make up his own cues as long as no one complained. No one ever did, so he took it as an opportunity to experiment and learn. From there he moved on to Opryland, first as a spotlight operator for the summer concert series and later as an audio engineer for a daytime park show.

A few summers later he was working as master electrician in the venue where the country band Alabama performed regularly. He found himself mesmerized by the technology. After everyone left and before he closed the theatre down at night, he taught himself how to program moving lights and scrollers on the Whole Hog by trying to recreate lighting he had seen at concerts. "I took the opportunity to teach myself by putting in lots of hours on really expensive lighting equipment."

At the end of the summer Alabama was preparing to head out on tour, and their lighting designer hired 24-year-old Chip to come along as master electrician. Chip felt like he might be in way over his head, but took every opportunity to learn and grow in a hands-on way. Before this he had never even packed a full truck, let alone been in a position to have to yell at Chicago Teamsters during load out, but he was lucky to have people around him who were willing to help him learn. Just eighteen months later, when the lighting designer moved on to other projects, Chip stepped up into the position and even took on some production management responsibilities. After a few years Alabama was ready to take a break from the road, but Chip wasn't. He joined Kenny Chesney on his first headliner tour as both lighting designer and production manager. It wasn't long before he realized he had gotten himself in over his head again, which made him even more committed to rise to the challenge. He also came to the realization, on his thirtieth birthday, that while this was a great job for somebody, it wasn't for him. It was the first time he left a job without any idea what he would be doing next.

Chip spent a few years working on large but shorter-term shows like Bonnaroo, Hall and Oates/Kenny Loggins tour, and WWE (World Wrestling Entertainment) WrestleManias. Twelve years out of college he decided it was time to take things in a different direction. He attended the URTA grad school interviews, with the usual uncomfortable feeling that he had no idea what he was doing and that including every project he had ever done and hundreds of photos of varying quality in his portfolio was wrong. Despite his concern, someone saw something in him and he was invited to attend the University of Florida's MFA program, where he says he became a much better designer.

MFA in hand, he found a visiting assistant professor position at a university, which he really enjoyed, though he couldn't shake the idea that if his colleagues really knew how much he was winging it they would quickly show him the door. Chip was again more successful than he imagined: the position was temporary but he applied for and was hired into the permanent job. This position came with the expectation that he continue to work professionally, so he reached out to his network to see who had a spot for him. The first to answer the call was the production designer for WWE, who hired him as lighting director for WrestleMania 29 in New Jersey's MetLife Stadium, a position he held again the following year at the Superdome in New Orleans. The next summer he was lighting director on the televised shows *Raw* and *Smackdown* and monthly pay-per-views. About halfway through the summer the production designer decided he liked having Chip around and made him an offer he couldn't refuse, financially or artistically, so Chip accepted the new post and submitted his resignation to the university.

Chip's current position is lighting director for WWE televised productions, with direct responsibility for in-arena lighting for *WrestleMania*, *Raw* (USA Network), *Smackdown* (Fox Network), *Main Event*, and *WWE Superstars*. He loves that his job changes from week to week, and sometimes even halfway through a live televised show. When asked why he thinks he was never fired despite his constant fears, he thinks maybe it was because even if he wasn't quite ready for the job, he was always willing to work hard. Even under stress Chip tackles every job with a good attitude and avoids causing strife. "And my phone keeps ringing so, at some level, I guess I've done well. And I haven't missed a mortgage payment."

Jenny Sargent—Opera Stage Manager Turned Banquet Director

Jenny Sargent loved every minute of her time earning her BFA in Stage Management and Technical Theatre at Rutgers. Her undergraduate experience was so great that she didn't see any reason to go to graduate school. The thought of working in opera had never really crossed her mind, but after an internship at New York City Opera she was hooked and so were they; she was hired full time as a stage manager. "I loved every second of opera. I loved the repertory structure, all of it." It was her life for ten seasons, only filling in with freelance work in the summers. And then, suddenly, the company went bankrupt and she found herself with no job and not much hope or desire to keep working in the city. There were suddenly ten opera stage managers looking for work, competing for what few jobs there were. Some were able to transition to traditional theatre, but without Equity membership she found she was branded as an "opera stage manager," which made it difficult to find opportunities in other genres. Not having cultivated a network outside the opera scene, she had no contacts to help her make connections.

Forced to reevaluate her life, Jenny realized she needed to find something that fit her lifestyle and family better. After a lot of soul-searching about how her skills could translate into another industry, she realized that her strengths were managing time and people, and that she could apply those strengths to parties, banquets, and small events. Having no experience in food service, she knew she was going to have to start with the basics and work her way back up to management. She got a serving job and began putting her resume out there asking for any opportunity to learn. She had to get new references and build an entirely new network. She says she lucked out when she learned that a golf course five minutes from her house was looking for a banquet manager. The person doing the hiring recognized the potential of her management background and decided they could teach her the banquet skills.

A banquet event is basically a theatre show with less rehearsal, so Jenny adapted very quickly. After six years with the golf course she was able to transition to a new location where she is the banquet manager and training to become the assistant general manager. Her position gives her the flexibility to be home with her family while still working in an environment with live events. She equates working with a bride on their wedding day to supporting an opera diva on opening night.

Jenny tells her staff all the time that it doesn't matter where you learned the skills, because managing people is managing people no matter what the job. As a stage manager she dealt with blocking, notes, and communication between different departments. Her current job is basically the same thing: her banquet hall floor plans are another version of a ground plan, and planning seating charts and traffic flow is basic blocking. Instead of rehearsal reports she is making sure the kitchen gets the client's information in the format they need. She even has to plan scene changes, accommodating multiple small events in the afternoon, then choreographing a one-hour changeover to a lavish wedding that same evening. She still even gets a few opening night jitters before larger events.

Jenny's best advice is to prepare for the unexpected and save as much money as you can when you can, because you just don't know what might happen down the road. You think you are secure in your job and then your company goes bankrupt or there is a pandemic, and suddenly you and everyone you know are looking for work. Having money to fall back on in those situations while you figure out your next step makes everything much easier. "Even if it's just as simple as an automatic withdrawal of $20 a week. I still do that: $20 just automatically goes into my savings account. I don't ever see it." Every little bit helps.

Claudia Lynch—Broadway Stage Manager, College Professor

Claudia planned to study comparative literature and French, but when she got to college she stopped by the theatre department to see if she could volunteer; by October she was a theatre major. A director, Alan Case, bought her the Lawrence Stern book about stage managing and told her, "I think you probably need to do this for a living, so let's figure out what a real stage manager does."

Between her junior and senior years she got a job at Porthouse Theatre in Ohio, where she was mentored by Joshua Friedman. He helped her get her first job after graduation doing props for the National Playwright's Conference at the O'Neill Center. It was five weeks, and she got room and board and $125 … total. There she met Carmelita Becnel, who is now the production stage manager at Princeton University. Carmelita connected Claudia with her next gig, working for Arena Stage in New York on a new Anna Deveare Smith workshop production called *House Arrest: First Edition*. She was asked to come back to Washington, DC with them as an intern production assistant (PA) for the full run of the show. They gave her an apartment and $100 per week.

After that she returned to New York, where she learned of a last-minute opening for a PA with the Directors Lab at Lincoln Center. Claudia had listed her mentor, Josh Friedman, as a reference on her resume, and as luck would have it the production coordinator doing the hiring had also worked with Josh. She called Claudia and said, "I need somebody tomorrow. Josh says you're good. Can you do it?" Her connection to Josh also helped her land her next job with the Contemporary American Theatre Festival in West Virginia, and then a year-long job as a PA at the Cleveland Playhouse.

Next she returned to another Directors Lab at Lincoln Center, then got an interview with the production stage manager, Thom Widmann, for a new show coming to the Mitzi E. Newhouse Theatre at Lincoln Center. To her surprise, she got the job as a PA on the creation of *Contact* developed by Susan Stroman and John Weidman. Her seven-week contract was extended through the run. When they found they were going to Broadway, which in this case meant moving upstairs in Lincoln Center to the Vivian Beaumont, Claudia was rehired as a PA for the run. The gig ended up lasting three years, and in that time she was able to negotiate a higher salary and health benefits, and become a member of Actors' Equity.

She stayed at Lincoln Center as second assistant stage manager (ASM) on *Dinner at Eight*, where she met and worked with Adam John Hunter; she followed him to her next gig, *Little Shop of Horrors* on Broadway, which lasted a year and a half. Then it was back to Lincoln Center to work with a new stage management team on *The Rivals*. When Thom Widmann asked her to work with him again on a new musical coming to Lincoln Center called *The Light in the Piazza*, she was happy to accept the first ASM position. After that she moved on to the second assistant ASM on *Company*.

Claudia considers herself to be a career ASM who dabbles in PSMing. She prefers the collaboration on the deck with the actors and crew during the rehearsal and tech process. By her early thirties she felt she was capable of taking on any role in the stage management team. She noticed she was passed over more than once for PSM positions for "someone older" (and male), though she happily accepted ASM positions on the shows.

She finally got her first PSM position for an out-of-town tryout of *A Catered Affair* in San Diego, but gladly returned to her usual ASM role when the show moved to Broadway and Adam stepped in as PSM. Thanks to Adam's recommendation she got her next PSM job for the off-Broadway debut of *Rock of Ages* at New World Stages, a position she retained when the show transferred to Broadway. Adam joined her team and they swapped their usual roles. As the show ended its run at the Brooks Atkinson Theatre in 2011 to move to the Helen Hayes, Claudia decided she needed a break. She left the show and lived off her savings for a year while she decided what her next step would be.

Josh, with whom she had worked on her very first professional gig, called her next and she went to the Alley Theatre in Houston to stage manage *Death of a Salesman*. Returning to New York, she joined Adam at Classic Stage Company for John Doyle's 2013 off-Broadway revival of *Passion*, but she was still feeling unenthusiastic. At sitzprobe for *Passion* she had a revelation. She thought, "I am sitting here next to Stephen Sondheim and this isn't even the first time I've sat next to Stephen Sondheim working on a show, and I'm feeling jaded about this whole thing. What would 21-year-old Claudia say about what I'm doing right now?" And she decided in that moment that as long as she was going to be doing this, she had to be happy doing it.

She did a string of shows at New York City Center as part of the Encores! series. In the middle of rehearsals for *tick, tick ... BOOM!* with Leslie Odom Jr., Lin Manuel Miranda, and Karen Olivio, Manuel Miranda's character was contemplating his future in the arts and Claudia was doing the same. Her beloved mentor from college, Alan Case, passed away and she couldn't leave the show to go to the funeral. She firmly decided that she didn't want to do this all the time any more.

When she saw a social media post for the University of Central Florida looking to hire a one-year-replacement stage management professor, Claudia immediately applied, got the job, and moved to Orlando, with the full intention of teaching for nine months and heading back to New York. Much to her surprise, she loved teaching. She applied for and got the permanent position. She returned to City Center for the next few summers to work on the Encores! series, and then one summer they didn't call. "In theatre, and in New York especially, the minute you are out of the game, you are *out* of the game." She couldn't stage manage a Broadway show from Orlando, so they moved on without her. And that was OK.

When someone says this business is all about who you know, Claudia can show you exactly what that meant in her career. You still need the interview skills, the resume, all of it, because you never know when you'll have to use them. Even when she was unofficially offered jobs without applying, she still had to attend meetings with producers, general managers, and directors to secure her position on the team. And now, as her students graduate and go out into the industry, she is using the very same network of people who used to help her find her next job to help her students find their way as well. "Working on Broadway was wonderful, and now there's a reason I'm here doing this."

Aaron Jackson—Lead Set Designer, Art Directors Guild, IATSE Local 800

Aaron started college at Baylor University as an acting major, but within a year he switched to scene design, eventually earning his BFA. He became a high school theatre teacher but realized quickly this wasn't what he wanted to do long term, so he left that to try his luck freelancing. Unfortunately, even doing five or six productions at a time he still needed to supplement his income working as a barista and later a custom picture framer. He says he did a lot of cool stuff, but never made any money. After three years of this, Aaron realized if he ever wanted to make a career out of design he needed to find a better way. He decided grad school made the most sense.

Choosing the right grad school can be an exhausting process, but in Aaron's case fate had a role as well. Rather than him choosing the University of Washington in Seattle, he feels it chose him. He was in New York to interview for several graduate school programs, and met with Tom Lynch in the lobby of the hotel for an interview for the University of Washington School of Drama. By the end of that interview he knew he was going to be studying at the University of Washington.

Aaron really enjoyed the laboratory that grad school provided. They designed a different play every week, complete with ground plan, model, elevations, color choices, and fabric swatches. The relative safety of school let him take big risks and fail often, but with the overall effect of success through experience. It taught him that his ideas were good and valuable, but if an idea wasn't what the director wanted he would toss it and come up with something better.

At the end of his second year Aaron had to arrange his internship, and decided that his best chances of paying off his student loans were in Los Angeles. He crafted a letter that he sent to a huge list of art directors and production designers in Hollywood, describing everything he could about himself and his artistic journey and asking for the opportunity to come and watch them work or for a chance as an intern. And some really big names said yes.

Christopher Brown was the art director for *Mad Men* at the time and an alum of the University of Washington; he offered Aaron a six-week internship on the show. Aaron's other big yes came from Alex McDowell: this took a bit more persistence on Aaron's part but he landed a position as a production assistant in the art department, a job he held for the next three years. It was a bit like grad school part two, where he learned how the television and movie industry worked and was able to see which jobs fit best with his background and skill set. He laughs: "I got my master's degree and then became a lunch boy. And I loved every minute of it."

His big break came when an art director he had worked for needed a six-week fill-in lead set designer on a Disney movie. The producers had to file for a union waiver so Aaron could take the job. These six weeks changed his life. At the time it required six weeks' work as a set designer to qualify for union membership, so when the job wrapped he paid his union dues and has never been unemployed since.

Aaron is now a lead set designer working on between two and six TV shows and movies a year. His work for the production designer is similar to the work an assistant designer would do for the scenic designer in theatre. He drafts, creates models, determines finish selections, and makes sure all the departments that need drawings get what they want, including every revision and update. He works twelve-hour days, five days a week, most of the year. Because the hours are long, he turns down out-of-town jobs to be able to focus on his family and personal goals at home.

Aaron's advice is to not feel rushed to succeed. Take your time and learn as much as you can about theatre and art history around the world. Take time to wonder and read, and let those things fuel your creativity and imagination. "A lot of set designers in my position have their eye set on being a production designer. I probably will become a production designer one day but I'm not in a hurry; I'm a really perfect fit for the job I have now."

Jerrilyn Lanier-Duckworth—Costume Designer, Educator on African American Hair and Makeup for Theatre

When Jerrilyn's literature class at the University of Southern Mississippi required her to see the theatre department's production of *Medea*, she was smitten. "There was a beautiful actress of color who played Medea and I was so fascinated by her … I talked to her after the show and asked her how I could get started in theatre." The next semester Jerrilyn registered for a costume practicum course. She knew that in the two years she had left before graduation she couldn't learn all she needed, so she decided to go on to graduate school. While there she met Martha Ruskai, who came to campus to teach a workshop on hair and makeup, and Jerrilyn was hooked. She bought Martha's book, *Wig Making and Styling: A Complete Guide for Theatre and Film*, and worked tirelessly to learn all she could. After graduating with her MFA in 2012 she began freelancing in theatre, dance, and film at places like Pennsylvania Shakespeare Festival, Millbrook Playhouse, Oklahoma Shakespeare Festival, and multiple colleges and universities, going back and forth between costuming, hair, and makeup.

In 2018 she was hired to do a workshop at the University of Alabama on African American hair and makeup for their production of *Seven Guitars*. After the workshop many students stayed behind, continuing to ask questions. Jerrilyn realized she had identified a gap that she could fill. Her first step was the creation of a Facebook page, "Bridging the Gap: A Look into African American Hair & Makeup for Theatre." She quietly launched the page January 2, 2019, and by February 1 it had been shared hundreds of times. "I knew there was a need, but I didn't realize how big the need was." When the Covid-19 pandemic hit and her summer design gigs were all cancelled, she decided to offer a few online workshops to work toward creating more inclusive hair and makeup experiences for Black performers by educating designers about African American hair and makeup. The response was phenomenal. By the end of 2020 she had given about thirty university workshops and presented to at least 500 online attendees. But while she has been overwhelmed by the positive response, she also, appallingly, gets plenty of hate mail from people in the industry who think things are just fine the way they are and don't appreciate the conversations she is starting about race. These negative responses only prove the need for her work. Her attendees have not only been appreciative of the conversations and open forum to ask questions, but are putting what they have learned into practice. Jerrilyn also gets messages from performers, often in tears, saying they are working with someone who took her workshop and the difference is dramatic.

She will be creating a non-profit component to help provide Black film and theatre students with art supplies, travel for auditions, character shoes in the right colors, scholarships, etc. She sees a system designed to keep people of color out. As a freelance artist she was able to find enough work to sustain her, but, even with an MFA, when she applied for jobs she was often told she would be better suited for an unpaid internship. She spent eight years applying to at least 200 university jobs and nobody called; meanwhile, her white classmates had teaching jobs right out of grad school. She wants to share what she has learned about navigating the racist segments of the industry with students of color, and support them to reach their goals. Her greatest joy would be to get put out of business because her services are no longer needed. Until then, she will keep trying to bridge the gap.

Ted Ozimek—Senior Project Manager II, Electronic Theatre Controls

Unlike many of us, Ted fell into theatre having never been in a show. He had no desire to be in one, nor was he interested in being a designer. What he did enjoy was theatre technology. He spent summers working in a rental shop supplying gear to local ice shows, industrials, fashion shows, etc. and, while earning his BA in Theatre from the University of Iowa, he had lucrative opportunities doing IATSE calls and other over-hire stagehand work. He worked one summer between his junior and senior years at the Santa Fe Opera as an electrician. When he graduated, he took a position at Bucknell University for eighteen months as assistant technical director.

Ted loved his job at Bucknell, but it was only part-time and would never be a permanent position. He decided to go to grad school to get an MFA in Technical Direction so he could teach full-time at a university. During grad school at Purdue University Ted experienced a watershed moment. He realized he didn't want to work on theatre productions: it wasn't the lifestyle he wanted and he wasn't passionate about the art. He didn't want to work nights and weekends and holidays. What he wanted was health insurance, a steady paycheck, and not to live out of a suitcase. Those became his priorities.

Around this time he attended LDI (Live Design International) and met Bill McGivern of ETC (Electronic Theatre Controls). He told Bill he was interested in an internship, and followed up with a letter the next week. After spending the summer of 2000 as a paid project management intern at ETC, he knew he had found the company he wanted to work for. He went back to Purdue for his final year, and immediately upon graduating joined ETC as a full-time project manager, the position he is still in today.

As a project manager for ETC, Ted's work begins when he receives the purchase order for a project. He evaluates the bid documents to be sure the equipment indicated will meet the intended use. He uses his deep knowledge of ETC products to design a functional lighting system, then liaises between everyone working on construction and installation to provide outstanding customer service to those involved in the project. He says one of the reasons he is good at what he does is because in graduate school he learned how to communicate with people at different skill levels. With over twenty years' experience with the company, he also trains new project managers, dealers, and reps. His work has taken him around the country and world, including to Singapore, Saudi Arabia, and India. His projects have included work at the Smithsonian National Museum of African American History and Culture, the Marina Bay Sands theatres in Singapore, *The Late Show*'s Ed Sullivan Theatre renovation, Jazz at Lincoln Center, the Smithsonian National Air and Space Museum, CNN's 30 Hudson Yards studio, and the American Academy of Motion Pictures Museum.

When asked about his five- or ten-year plans, Ted says he already has the perfect job and would be very happy to remain in his current position until retirement. It isn't what he thought he was going to be doing, but it perfectly dovetails with the priorities he set for himself. "My advice is to really think about what your long-term goals are for your career and personal life. Production work wasn't the right path for me, but that doesn't mean it's not right for someone else." And he wants people to know that "whatever you think your path is going to be going forward, it doesn't have to remain the same." If you achieve your dream and realize it wasn't as good as you were expecting, do something different. "Your job after graduation is not the end, it's the beginning; maybe the beginning of a lifetime career or just the beginning of your journey as you find the work you are passionate about."

Bailie Slevin—Stage Manager Turned Financial Advisor for Theatre Artists

In high school, offered the choice between a spot in the chorus in *West Side Story* or being the stage manager, Bailie decided to learn what a stage manager was even though she really wanted to be a performer. She quit after two weeks, but begrudgingly returned when they said they couldn't manage without her. And that's when she started to fall in love. She went to college at Emerson, studied theatre management and production, and did an internship with and worked at Northshore Music Theatre. After a short, unpleasant stint as a receptionist at a talent agency, she decided to go to massage therapy school to make her an even more valuable asset as a stage manager, not thinking of it as an alternative to stage managing but as an enhancement to her stage managing business plan. When she was nearly at the end of her eighteen-month program, she was in a terrible auto accident that shattered her right arm and required multiple surgeries.

While she was able to finish her program, she was not able to pursue massage as part of her career; she wasn't even able to return to stage managing right away. When her parents, who graciously supported her through recovery, hinted that she needed to find work, she pointed out that she could no longer do the things she was trained for and couldn't even manage temp jobs with her physical limitations, frequent physical therapy appointments, and inability to drive. She challenged them that if they could find someone who would hire her with these limitations, she would be happy to work. The next day her parents told her that she was going to work for the only person they could find who would agree to all that: her dad.

Bailie's dad is a financial advisor, so with a new office wardrobe she began processing paperwork at his office. Realizing she didn't understand what she was helping with, she attended some training classes and found out how much she didn't know about how money worked. She started asking her friends if they knew about the things she was learning, and discovered they didn't know either.

When her arm healed enough to enable her to get around, she had to decide whether to go back to stage managing or to continue down this new path. After doing an internship in general management with Laura Green, she decided she would make more of an impact on the industry by educating theatre people about money and helping them create financial success. She committed to developing and growing her business as a financial advisor specializing in clients in the entertainment industry. Fifteen years later she focuses on working with the Broadway and touring communities to get people on savings plans as soon as they book their first big job and before they have a chance to make poor financial decisions.

Bailie's company, Entertaining Finance,[2] is committed to educating as many people as possible, at all income levels, about how money works and grows; she is convinced that when everyone is more knowledgeable about money, it benefits us all. Because of her education and experience in theatre combined with her work as a financial advisor, Bailie is often hired by theatres and arts organizations to run educational workshops for their company members.[3]

Brad Berridge—Director of Sound Operations, Feld Entertainment

Brad's love of sound and music grew from a very young age. His father was a folk gospel musician in the 1980s, and Brad's spot backstage was next to the sound console. He was fascinated by the knobs and buttons, which he swears he never touched, and while watching the VU meters he developed an inherent understanding of how sound worked. When he got to college he was the only one in the theatre program who knew how to use sound equipment, which meant he was given many opportunities. He credits the direct training in storytelling he received while getting his bachelor of

---

[2]See www.entertainingfinance.com.
[3]Potential Conflict Disclosure: Registered Representative and Financial Advisor of Park Avenue Securities LLC (PAS). Securities products and advisory services offered through PAS, member FINRA, SIPC. Financial Representative of The Guardian Life Insurance Company of America®(Guardian), New York, NY. PAS is a wholly-owned subsidiary of Guardian. Entertaining Finance is not an affiliate or subsidiary of PAS or Guardian. OSJ:52 Forest Ave., Paramus, NJ 07652, 201-843-7700.California license OJ17279.

science in Theatre from the University of Southern Indiana, along with his summer stock experiences, in launching his career.

His first job out of college was a US tour as A1 with a small professional production of *The Wizard of Oz*. Joining a tour already in process and having to jump right in to learn the track was helpful experience when he eventually moved to New York.

After a detour into concert production he finally made it to New York City. He papered the town with his resume, and was hired by Lincoln Center Institute (now Lincoln Center Education) to work in their studio theatre. That led to over-hire work doing load-ins and shop prep at Jazz at Lincoln Center, where he networked for his next gig. Because he followed the advice he received in undergrad and kept his resume up to date and circulating, his papers were on the top of the pile when there was a last-minute opening for an A1 on the out-of-town tryout for *Showtune*. The show transferred to off-Broadway and Brad went with it. He was finally making a steady income doing something he loved; but he also got an inside understanding of the life of a New York sound designer, and he and his wife agreed that it wasn't the life they were looking for long term.

They spent a couple of years in Nashville, then moved to Massachusetts when his wife was offered a full-time position at Jacob's Pillow dance festival. They had both worked short contracts there in previous summers, and loved the atmosphere and mission of the company. Brad landed a position as the full-time staff sound engineer at Williams College; he loved the job, and stayed for seven years. Throughout those years and beyond, Brad freelanced with companies including Williamstown Theatre Festival, Berkshire Theatre Festival, Barrington Stage, Utah Shakespeare Festival, New York Theatre Ballet, and the Eugene O'Neill Theatre Center. Eventually he was freelancing so much that he left his university job; he had more than enough work to sustain himself as a sound consultant, engineer, designer, and composer, including several shows off-Broadway and multiple world-premiere productions. He took a couple of semester-long visiting professor teaching gigs at Indiana University and the University of Cincinnati.

At USITT in 2016 Brad mentioned to a group of trusted sound colleagues that he didn't want to continue freelancing, because it meant being on the road 250 days of the year. He said, "I wasn't an active parent or an active husband. I was part-timing my life for my career."

One of those friends then recommended him for his current position as director of sound operations for Feld Entertainment. He now works for the largest themed family entertainment company in the world on shows like

Disney on Ice, Disney Live, Sesame Street Live, Jurassic World Live, Marvel Universe Live, Trolls: The Experience, Nickelodeon: Slime City, Monster Jam, and *Super Motocross.* He designs and implements sound systems for touring and permanent/semi-permanent productions, trains production crews on the operation and maintenance of show systems, manages a team of five full-time sound professionals, and collaborates in the development of new productions.

Though early on, like many, Brad thought he wanted to be a Broadway designer, he learned after working regionally and off-Broadway that most Broadway jobs go to a very small circle of people. He wasn't willing to sacrifice his marriage and family for the chance to claw his way into that circle. At Feld he found the balance of financial success, artistic satisfaction, and the family life he was looking for.

Index